M000296678

The Complete Guide to
BUILT-INS

Second Edition

Complete Plans for Custom Cabinets, Shelving, Seating & More

Creative Publishing international

MINNEAPOLIS, MINNESOTA
www.creativepub.com

Creative Publishing international

Copyright © 2011
Creative Publishing international, Inc.
400 First Avenue North, Suite 300
Minneapolis, Minnesota 55401
1-800-328-0590
www.creativepub.com
All rights reserved

Printed in China

10 9 8 7 6 5 4 3 2 1

Library of Congress Cataloging-in-Publication Data on file

President/CEO: Ken Fund
Group Publisher: Bryan Trandem

Home Improvement Group

Associate Publisher: Mark Johanson
Managing Editor: Tracy Stanley

Creative Director: Michele Lanci-Altomare
Art Direction/Design: Brad Springer, James Kegley, Kim Winscher

Lead Photographer: Corean Komarec
Set Builder: James Parmeter
Production Managers: Laura Hokkanen, Linda Halls

Edition Editor: Dan Cary
Page Layout Artist: Danielle Smith
Technical Editor: Eric Smith
Shop Help: Charles Boldt
Contributing Designer: Theresa Coleman

The Complete Guide to Built-Ins
Created by: The Editors of Creative Publishing international, Inc., in cooperation with Black & Decker.
Black & Decker® is a trademark of The Black & Decker Corporation and is used under license.

Contents

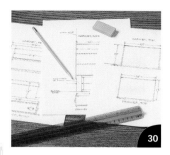

The Complete Guide to Built-Ins

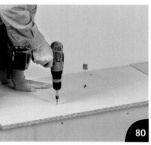

Contents (Cont.)

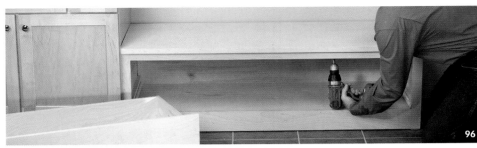

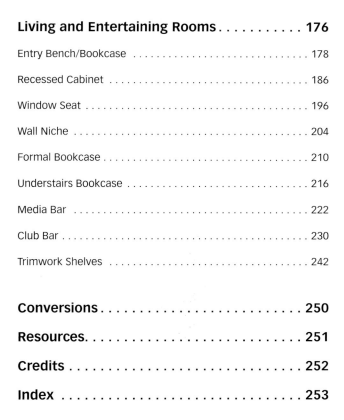

Living and Entertaining Rooms **176**

Conversions **250**

Resources **251**

Credits **252**

Index **253**

Introduction

Built-in is a fairly open term, so it can be difficult to say with absolute conviction what counts as a built-in and what doesn't. One possible definition is that a built-in is a furnishing that you'd leave behind if you moved to a new home. A full-height-floor-to-ceiling bookcase that's anchored to the wall or a kitchen island are a couple of examples. But that definition is narrower than it needs to be. What about a storage bench that's attached to the wall and trimmed with base molding but is intended as seating at your very portable kitchen table? Or a kitchen island that isn't permanently attached to the floor? Are these built-ins? And does it matter?

Well, here's what we do know. *The Complete Guide to Built-Ins* is a practical, step-by-step guide for home carpenters of all skill levels. It contains complete plans for 27 different projects you can build to make your house more livable, more functional and more attractive. You'll find plan drawings, cutting lists, and how-to photos for things you can build in the kitchen, bathroom, living room, bedroom, basement, or practically any other room in your home. You'll find basic design and planning information and a primer on some of the more useful techniques you'll need, like making doors and drawers.

Many of the projects featured in the book are constructed using stock cabinetry. This strategy saves time and ensures that your results have a finished appeal. But if using stock cabinets ramps up the cost or limits your design options, there are plenty of projects built from sheet goods and lumber sold at any building center. One project even shows you how to recycle an old metal cabinet and some salvaged granite and turn them into an attractive kitchen island.

Because the size and scale of most built-ins is dictated by the spot where it is installed, you may need to do some refiguring of part sizes to get any of these built-ins to fit into your home. In most cases, we've included exact dimensions for the overall size as shown, and then included a few hints as to which part or parts you may need to alter. In other cases, we've listed one key dimension as a variable and shown you how much to subtract from that value to find each part size that would be affected by a change in width or height. In all cases, pay attention to the part sizes and double-check your work if you're making adjustments. To minimize recutting, we strongly recommend that you cut each part as needed instead of precutting them all.

So congratulations on your decision to add a unique built-in to your home. Whatever the term may mean to you, we hope your project turns out just as beautifully as you'd dreamed. And if you decide to rip it out of the house and take it with you to your next home, just patch in with a little trim along the base of the wall and no one will be the wiser.

Gallery of Kitchen Built-Ins

This kitchen built-in has just about everything you could ask for: a breakfast nook with storage-bench seating; floor-to-ceiling cupboards; and a countertop with appliance cubby below and glass-door cabinets above. It's practically a room unto itself.

Breakfast nooks and banquettes are very popular in and near the kitchen. Try to locate yours next to a window so it doesn't feel claustrophobic. Storage benches are practical, but they can be a little clunky in some designs. Adding legs and drawers makes them feel more open.

A kitchen with a view is a perfect spot to integrate an eating area without interrupting the floorplan or flow of the space. Often, a dining area is created by adding a small bumpout addition.

Built-in storage benches can be added along a wall and used as seating for your kitchen table. The great advantage to this approach over a built-in nook is that the table can be removed easily if you have a big cooking event or party planned where open kitchen floor space is important.

A modest kitchen island (technically, this one is a peninsula) can be a perfect spot for a desk and homework area. The bookshelves and cupboard are excellent spots to house cookbooks, too.

A traditional kitchen island meets every definition of a built-in. They can be created mostly to supply countertop workspace and casual dining. You can also plumb them for a supplementary prep sink or even add a cooktop and a downdraft or overhead vent fan. In most cases, you should try to match or complement the kitchen cabinetry, but in less traditional kitchens a highly contrasting island is very dramatic and effective.

Gallery of Bathroom and Laundry Built-Ins

A wall niche with shelving is a useful storage feature anywhere in the house. In a bathroom the approach succeeds especially well because it creates storage without consuming floor space and because you can use materials and finishes that resist moisture better than an off-the-shelf shelf. The niche shelving seen here is made with a back panel of tileboard with beaded grooves and sturdy plywood shelving that's filled and painted with easy-to-wash enamel paint.

Nonwood materials can be important parts of a built-in design. Here, the ceramic tile bathroom wall plays host to a series of vertically stacked display cubbies. Carefully crafted from solid beech, the cubby boxes fit perfectly into the wall openings. A low-voltage cabinet light illuminates each display unit with soft, warm light.

Stock cabinetry and even large furnishings can look and function exactly like custom-made built-ins. All it takes is a little trim around the bottom and some matching trimwork elsewhere in the room and it will look as if the new built-ins have always been there.

Mini laundry centers are becoming highly desirable bonus features in modern bathrooms. And with a well-designed and executed built-in cabinet, the presence of a washer and dryer won't make your lovely bathroom look like a utility room.

A window seat is normally built in a sunroom or library, but a comfortable bench with a nice view is a welcome addition to a bathroom as well. Here it is combined with a vanity in the same way that window seats are often combined with bookcases.

Kitchen cabinetry can be adapted quite effectively for use in a bathroom. With the exception of the bank of drawers, which is a custom feature, the storage elements in this bathroom suite are all created with high-end stock cabinetry.

Gallery of Bedroom & Spare Room Built-Ins

A writing desk and a wall of assorted cubbies add highly useful features to this bedroom, but not at the expense of sleeping convenience and comfort. The bank of custom floor-to-ceiling doors and drawers is a classic design element that brings real warmth into the room.

A sleeping alcove with underbed storage drawers is as cozy as it is efficient. And if you've shopped for bedframes lately, you'll understand how economical this simple built-in project is. A couple of sheets of decent plywood, some hardware and you're practically done: a custom built-in for less than the cost of comparable furniture.

Who needs a dresser when you have underbed drawers? The eight dresser drawers tucked into this bed frame can easily handle the foldable clothes storage needs for two people (provided you keep your off-season clothing elsewhere, of course).

A room divider is a welcome addition to any room where you want to create some separation between functional areas. With its roots in Scandinavian design, this all-wood divider frames a flat panel television in the seating area of a master bedroom, while at the same time creating a screen that separates the sleeping space.

This sleeping alcove is not just for kids. Its sophisticated styling has an Eastern design influence that suggests peacefulness. Adjoining a private bathroom, it is a perfect solution for a homeowner who has occasional need for a guest bedroom. But because the built-in contains plenty of permanent storage and can also function as a daybed, the room can be used for other activities when it is not in use as a guest bedroom.

Gallery of Living and Entertaining Room Built-Ins

A floor-to-ceiling built-in bookcase gives any room the gravitas of a formal library. Wider hallways are prime locations for open bookcases, since doors and drawers will cause hazardous obstructions, Try to maintain at least a 3-ft.-wide clear passage area. For natural wood tones, use quality hardwood or hardwood plywood with solid wood edging and finish it with stain and a clear topcoat. Or, you can use less costly building materials and paint the bookcase your wall or trim color.

An open bookcase with an integral cabinet below pairs nicely with a window seat in this built-in grouping. The presence of the cabinet/bookcase and the window seat create the illusion of a luxurious bay window. The effect is enhanced by the fact that the crown molding motif on the ceiling of the room is carried over on top of the cabinet. The overall feeling of freshness and space is partly a result of the paint choice: white semi-gloss is a can't-miss selection for built-ins and trimwork.

Understairs areas are just coming into their own as designers and homeowners are putting these once-overlooked spaces to hard work. On the built-in front, bookcases and cabinetry are probably the most common uses. The angles can get a bit tricky if you're not a skilled trim carpenter, however. A more foolproof project is one like this wine rack: all of the parts are joined at 90° angles. You simply build the wine rack with its squares in a diamond orientation and slide it into place as a single unit.

Built-ins offer a fine opportunity to show off fine design and craftsmanship. The retro-modern entertainment center is not a project for beginners. It involves some fairly advanced veneering work, some tricky curves, and the use of custom powder-coated metal doors. But if you have the skills and patience you'll be thrilled with the result. Note that the fire seen on the large screen is only a looping video image.

Built-in storage also can act as a visual room divider in larger spaces, creating the opportunity to display keepsakes that can be viewed from both rooms, and giving homeowners additional nooks to stow other items away.

A built-in bookcase that follows a staircase is a design feature that succeeds for many reasons: it makes good use of space, it has a sense of movement that adds fun to the room, and it is an eye-catching element that is sure to be noticed. Just make sure all of the shelves are easily reached from the step without the need for a ladder or stool.

Sports equipment, shoes, and coats are typically among the top clutter culprits in most houses. By creating a coat cubby or locker-room-styled organization near the most-used entryway, you'll create a greater chance that those items might be put away. When designing built-ins for kids, take advantage of the whimsy of color and style when decorating custom built-ins, and take the opportunity to maximize the storage possibilities.

A uniquely shaped room can benefit from a custom built-in couch that maximizes the space inside the frame. Drawers keep throw blankets handy for colder days, and games ready for guests. Custom upholstered cushions like the ones seen above can be made for you at most upholstery shops, but they do tend to be fairly expensive. A cheaper option is often to find off-the-rack cushions that you like and design a built-in to fit them.

This entryway built-in addresses several problem areas with one clever solution. The boot cubbies at top keep overshoes and shoes in their place (you'll want to line them with cut-up pieces of an entry mat). The drawers below ensure that hats and gloves are always at the ready. And the custom dog bed will be much appreciated by the family pet, who will enjoy nothing more than snoozing beneath his leash and near his favorite door.

A wall-hung breakfront is an invaluable built-in furnishing in any dining room. Designed to store tableware and tablesettings, a breakfront also has a buffet-style surface for serving food and beverages. By making the built-in yourself, you can design it to blend with your home's architecture.

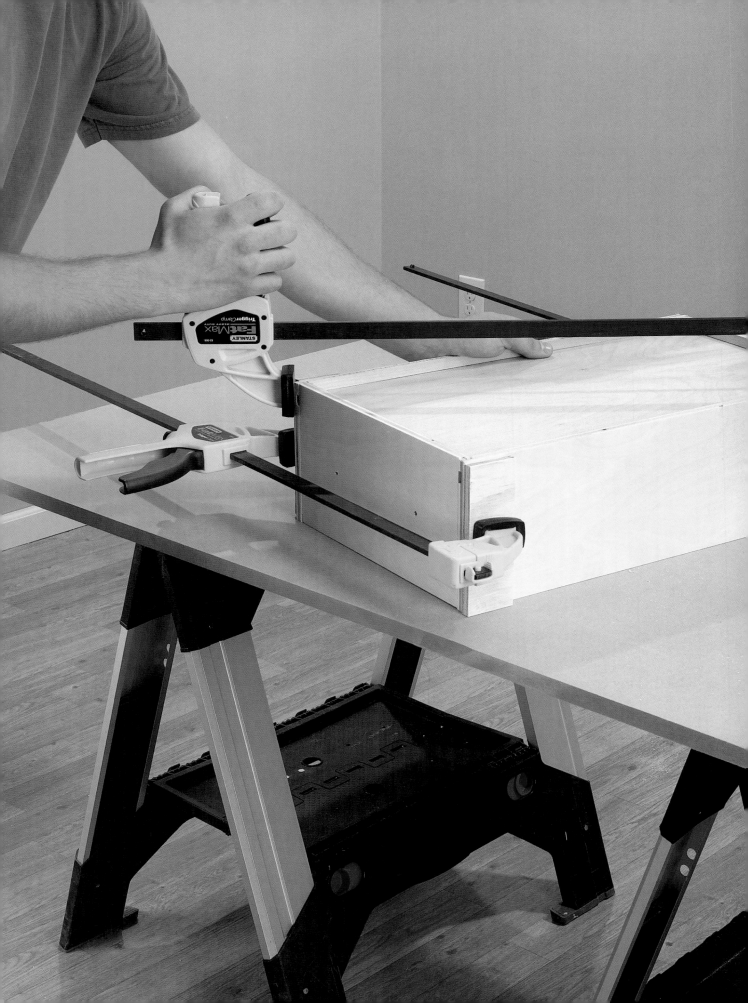

Built-In Basics

J ust as no two houses are exactly alike, no two built-ins will look exactly the same in two different houses. Thus, designing and building a built-in requires a little more thought and planning than simply leafing through a furniture catalog and phoning in a credit card number. You'll need to consider size and scale, traffic patterns and views, egress and access, color and texture, form and function, and a whole host of other variables. There are helpful tools you'll need to know about and building materials that lend themselves especially well to making built-ins. And regardless of the project or projects you ultimately choose, there are common techniques you should have under your belt: things like measuring and marking, finding level, locating studs, and building cabinet doors and drawers.

The purpose of this section is to introduce you to the background knowledge and skills that will help give you the greatest possible chance for success with your built-in project. Read and understand it before you start—you'll be glad you did.

In this chapter:

- Tools and Materials
- Planning a Project
- Jobsite Preparation
- Project Safety
- Establishing Level, Plumb & Square

- Building Drawers
- Building Doors
- Hanging Cabinet Doors

Tools and Materials

Building shelves and built-ins is a challenging job that requires patience, attention to detail, and the right tool for each task. Without these basic requirements, the work will be more difficult and the results will suffer.

Start off right by using high-quality tools. Good tools last longer and are generally more accurate than less expensive versions.

Many people buy tools only as they are needed to avoid purchases they will not use. This rationale should only apply to power tools and higher-priced specialty items. A high-quality basic tool set is important for every do-it-yourselfer to have on hand. Doing so avoids improper tool usage and makes your job easier, with improved results.

The hand tools you will need for most finish carpentry jobs can be broken down into two types: layout tools and construction tools. It is common for most people to own construction tools, but to lack necessary layout tools for basic carpentry jobs. Purchase the highest-quality layout tools you can afford. They are crucial for helping you avoid costly measuring and marking mistakes.

LAYOUT TOOLS

Layout tools help you measure, mark, and set up perfect cuts with accuracy. Many layout tools are inexpensive and simply provide a means of measuring for level, square, and plumb lines. However, recent technologies have incorporated lasers into levels, stud finders, and tape measures, making them more accurate than ever before, though at a slightly higher price. Although these new tools are handy in specific applications, their higher price is not always warranted for the do-it-yourselfer.

- **A tape measure** is one of the most common tools around. The odds are good that you already own at least one. (If you are making frequent trips for building supplies, invest in a second tape that stays in your car.) Carpentry projects require a sturdy tape measure with a length greater than your longest stock. A 25-ft. tape measure has a wider and thicker reading surface than a 16-ft. variety, but either is adequate for most carpentry jobs. If you can't tell the difference between the smaller lines on a standard tape, consider

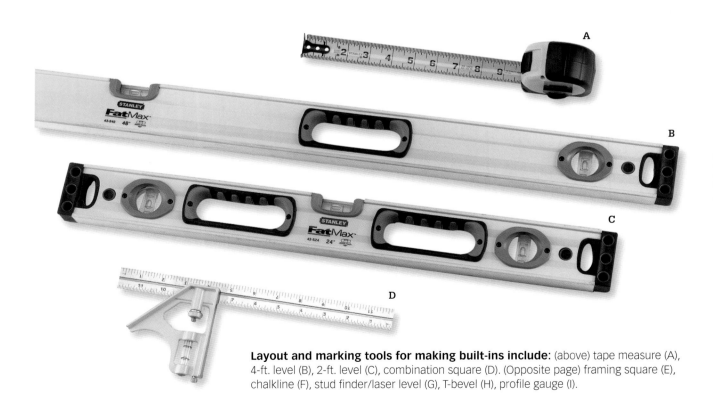

Layout and marking tools for making built-ins include: (above) tape measure (A), 4-ft. level (B), 2-ft. level (C), combination square (D). (Opposite page) framing square (E), chalkline (F), stud finder/laser level (G), T-bevel (H), profile gauge (I).

purchasing an "Easy Read" variety. It is important to read the tape accurately.

- **A framing square,** also known as a carpenter's square, is commonly used to mark wood for cutting and to check for square. Framing squares are also used for laying out stairs and rafters.

- **Chalk lines** are used to make temporary straight lines anywhere one is needed. The case of a chalk line, or the "box," is teardrop-shaped so that the tool can double as a plumb bob. Use a chalk line to mark sheet goods for cutting or to establish a level line in a room. Keep in mind that chalk can be difficult to remove from porous surfaces.

- **A stud finder** is used to locate the framing members in a wall or ceiling. Higher-priced versions also locate plumbing, electrical, or other mechanicals in the wall. Although stud finders are not completely necessary, they are convenient for larger jobs.

- **Levels** are available in a variety of lengths and price ranges. The longer and more accurate the level, the higher the price. The two most commonly used sizes are 2-ft. and 4-ft. lengths. A 2-ft. level is handy for tight spaces, while the 4-ft. variety serves as a better all-purpose level. Laser levels are handy for creating a level line around the perimeter of a room or for establishing level lines over longer lengths. They provide a wide range of line or spot placement, depending on the model.

- **A T-bevel** is a specialized tool for finding and transferring angles precisely. T-bevels are generally used in conjunction with a power miter saw to find the angle of non-square corners. This tool is especially handy in older homes where the original states of square, plumb, and level may no longer apply.

- **A profile gauge** uses a series of pins to recreate the profile of any object so that you may transfer it to a work piece. Profile gauges are especially useful when scribing to an irregular wall.

- **A combination square** is a multifunction square that provides an easy reference for 45- and 90-degree angles, as well as marking reveal lines or a constant specific distance from the edge of a work piece.

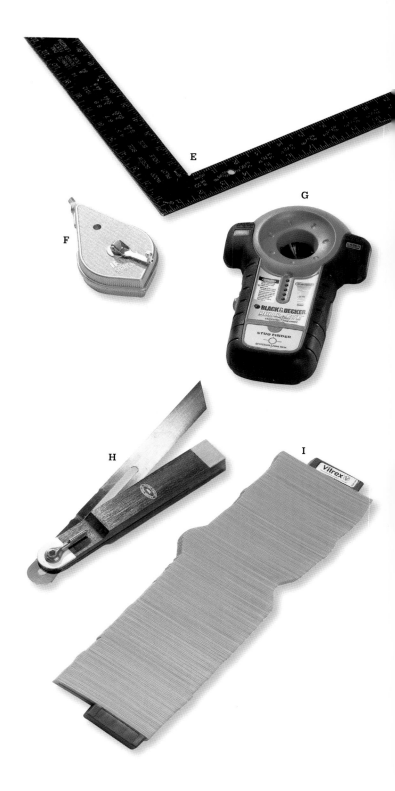

E

F

G

H

I

CONSTRUCTION TOOLS

- **A good quality hammer** is a must for every carpentry project. A 16-oz. curved claw hammer, otherwise known as a finish hammer, is a good all-purpose choice. Some people prefer a larger straight claw hammer for heavy tear-down projects and rough framing, but these hammers are too clumsy and heavy for driving smaller casing and finish nails, and tend to mar the surface of trim.

- **Utility knives** are available with fixed, folding, or retractable blades. This tool is used for a wide variety of cutting tasks from cutting drywall to back-beveling miter joints. Always have additional blades readily available. Folding fixed-blade utility knives offer the durability and strength of a fixed blade with the protection of a folding handle.

- **A set of chisels** is necessary for installing door hardware as well as notching trim around obstacles and final fitting of difficult pieces. Keep a set only for use with wood, and do not use them for screwdrivers or demolition.

- **Block planes** are used to fit doors into openings and remove fine amounts of material from trim. A finely tuned block plane can even be used to clean up a sloppy miter joint.

- **A coping saw** has a thin, flexible blade designed to cut curves, and is essential for making professional trim joints on inside corners. Coping saw blades should be fine toothed, between 16 and 24 teeth per inch for most hardwoods, and set to cut on the pull stroke of the saw to offer you more blade control.

- **A sharp handsaw** is convenient for quick cut-offs and in some instances where power saws are difficult to control. Purchase a crosscut saw for general-purpose cutting.

- **Protective wear,** including safety glasses and ear protection, is required any time you are working with tools. Dust masks are necessary when sanding, doing demolition, or when working around fumes.

- **Pry bars** come in a variety of sizes and shapes. A quality forged high-carbon steel flat bar is the most common choice. Wrecking bars make lighter work of trim and door removal due to their added weight. No matter what type of pry bar you use, protect finished surfaces from scratches with a block of wood when removing trim.

- **Side cutters and end nippers** are useful for cutting off and pulling out bent nails. The added handle length and curved head of end nippers makes them ideal for pulling larger casing nails. Pneumatic brad nails and smaller pins will pull out easier with side cutters. Purchase a nail set for countersinking nail heads. Three-piece sets are available for different nail sizes.

- **A rasp and metal file set** is important for fitting coped joints precisely. The variety of shapes, sizes, and mills allow for faster rough removal of material, or smoother slow removal, depending on the file.

- **Use a putty knife** to fill nail holes with wood filler and for light scraping tasks.

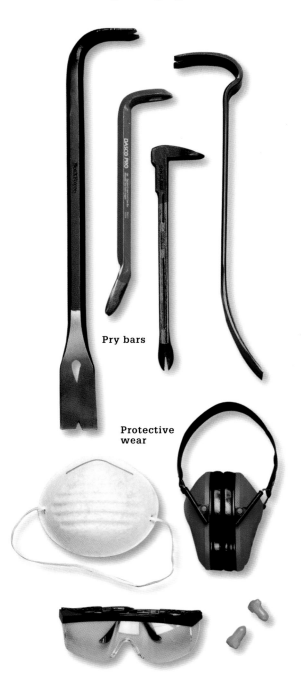

Pry bars

Protective wear

Handsaws

Putty knife

Nail sets

Utility knives

Coping saw

Hammer

Rasp and metal file set

Side cutters and end nippers

Block plane

Chisels

Compound power
miter saw

Circular saw

Jigsaw

Reciprocating saw

Cordless drill

POWER TOOLS

Despite the higher price as compared to hand tools, power tools are a great value. They allow you to work more quickly and accurately than with hand tools and make repetitive tasks like sanding, drilling, and sawing more enjoyable. Basic home carpentry does not require every power tool shown here, but some tools, such as a power miter box, are crucial for professional results. Purchase power tools on an as-needed basis, keeping in mind that while the cheapest tool is not always your best option, the most expensive and powerful is probably not necessary, either. Cheaper tools generally sacrifice precision, while the most expensive tools are made for people who use them every day, not just occasionally.

- **A cordless drill** is one of the handiest tools available. Although drills are not normally used to install trim, they make quick work of installing structural components. Occasionally, trim-head screws are used to install trim, in metal studs, or where extra holding power is needed.
- **A circular saw** is ideal for straight cuts in plywood and quick cut-offs of solid material. Purchase a plywood blade to make smooth cuts in plywood, and a general-purpose blade for other cuts.
- **A jigsaw** is the perfect tool for cutting curves, or notching out trim around obstructions. Jigsaw blades come in an array of designs for different styles of cuts and different types and thicknesses of materials. Always use the right type of blade and do not force the saw during the cut or it may bend or break.

Router

Random orbit sander

Biscuit joiner

Power planer

Finish sander

Belt sander

Table saw

- **A biscuit joiner** (also called a plate joiner) is a specialty tool used with glue and biscuits to make strong joints between two pieces of stock.
- **A reciprocating saw** is used for removal and tear-down applications. This tool is especially handy for removing door jambs.
- **A compound power miter saw** will yield professional results. Most have a 10" or 12" diameter blade. A compound power miter saw has a head that pivots to cut both bevels and miters. Sliding miter saws have more cutting capacity but are less portable. A fine-tooth carbide-tipped blade is best for built-in and shelving projects.
- **A belt sander** is not essential but is a handy tool for quick removal of material.
- **Random-orbit sanders** are a good choice for smoothing flat areas, such as plywood, quickly.

Random-orbit sanders don't leave circular markings as disc sanders do, and can sand in any direction regardless of wood grain.
- **Finish sanders** are available in a variety of sizes and shapes for different light sanding applications.
- **A power planer** is used to trim doors to fit openings and flatten or straighten out materials. Power planers are faster to use than manual hand planes, but the results are more difficult to control.
- **A table saw** is the best tool for ripping stock to width, and larger models can be fitted with a molding head for cutting profiles.
- **A router** (plunge router is shown here) has many uses in trim carpentry, especially for cutting edge profiles to make your own custom woodwork.

PNEUMATIC TOOLS

Pneumatic tools can be a key to timely, professional carpentry results. They save time and energy over traditional hammer-and-nail installation. Not only do they drive fasteners quickly, but they countersink at the same time, avoiding multiple strikes to trim, which could throw joints out of alignment. Predrilled holes are not necessary with pneumatic tools. Splitting is infrequent if the work piece is held firmly in place

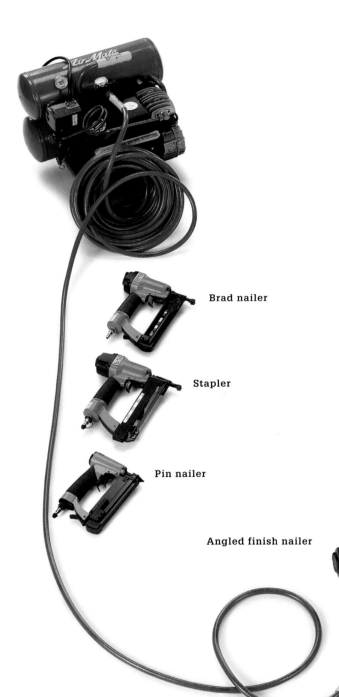

Brad nailer

Stapler

Pin nailer

Angled finish nailer

and the nails are positioned at least 1" from trim ends. Nail guns also allow you to concentrate on the placement of the work piece with one hand and fasten it with the other. You needn't fumble around with single fasteners because they are already loaded in the gun.

The cost of pneumatic tools, compressors, and fasteners has decreased over the years, making them not only the professional's choice, but a great option for the do-it-yourselfer as well. Pneumatic kits are available at home centers with two different guns and a compressor at a value price. For small or infrequent jobs, consider renting pneumatics.

Portable compressors are available in different styles, including pancake and hot-dog styles. Any compressor with air pressure capability of 90 psi or greater will drive a finish or brad nailer. Consider options like tank size, weight of the unit, and noise levels while the compressor is running. Talk to a home center specialist about what your specific compressor needs are and keep in mind any future pneumatic tools you might want.

The two basic pneumatic tools used in trim carpentry are a finish nailer, and a brad nailer. A finish nailer drives 15- and 16-gauge nails ranging from 1" to 2½". These nails work for a variety of moldings, door and window trim, and general-purpose fastening. Angled finish nailers are easier to maneuver in tight corners than straight guns, but either option will work. Brad nailers drive smaller 18-gauge fasteners ranging in length from ½" to 2". Some brad nailers' maximum length is 1¼". Because the fasteners are smaller, it is no surprise that the gun is lighter and smaller than a finish gun. Brad nailers are used to attach thinner stock, and have less tendency to split the wood. Headless pinners drive fasteners similar to brad nails, but without the head. These nails have less holding power, but are normally used to hold small moldings in place until the glue dries. Be sure to load headless pins with the points down, taking note of the label on the magazine. Narrow crown staplers are used to attach thin panels and in situations where maximum holding power is needed, but the fastener head will not be visible. Because staples have two legs and a crown that connects them, their holding power is excellent. However, the hole left by the staple's crown is large and can be difficult to conceal.

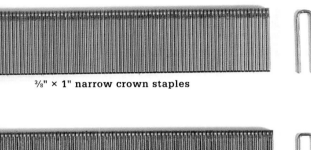

23 ga. × 1¼" pin nails

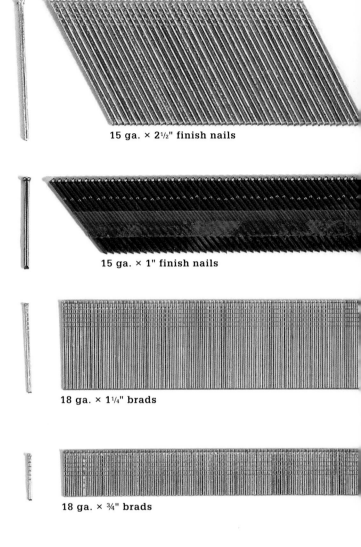

15 ga. × 2½" finish nails

15 ga. × 1" finish nails

18 ga. × 1¼" brads

18 ga. × ¾" brads

⅜" × 1" narrow crown staples

⅜" × 1¼" narrow crown staples

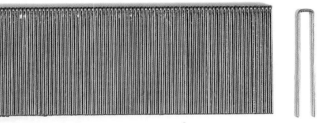

⅜" × 1½" narrow crown staples

PNEUMATIC FASTENERS

Angled finish nails and regular finish nails range in length up to 2½". The angled variety have the same designations as the straight nails, but come in angled clips. These nails are made from galvanized wire, so they are suitable for exterior applications. Use finish nails to attach larger moldings and trim casings. Drive fasteners at regular intervals along the moldings and keep the position of the nails at least 1" from the molding ends. Fastener length is dependent upon the size of workpiece installed. Typical stock moldings and dimensional lumber are ¾" thick. When installing built-ins, the fastener must pass through the molding and drywall and into the stud behind. Generally, half the fastener should be embedded in the backing or stud, so in most applications, 2" fasteners should suffice.

Brad nails range in length up to 2" for some guns and leave smaller holes to fill than finish guns. Brad nails are commonly used for thinner casings that are nailed directly to a solid backer. A specific example of this is along the inner edge of a door or window casing. The outer edge of the trim is nailed with a finish gun through the wallboard, while the inside edge rests against the door jamb, so it can be fastened with a brad nailer. Headless pins leave almost no nail hole to fill but are limited in length to 1". Their holding power is greatly diminished due to the lack of head, but they are generally used in conjunction with wood glue. Crown staples are used when the fastener head will not be visible, or are angled with the grain.

AC fir plywood

Maple plywood

Cherry MDF

Baltic birch

Lumber core plywood

MDO

MDF

Wainscot paneling

Sheet Goods

There are many different types of plywood for a wide array of uses. For built-in and shelf projects, finish-grade or paint-grade plywood is commonly used. Each type is made up of thinly sliced layers called plies. These layers are made of solid hardwood, softwood, or wood products. The more plies a sheet good has, the stronger it will be. This is only true for veneer-based plies. Medium density fiberboard, or MDF, is made of wood fibers that have been glued and pressed together. These panels are extremely stable and rarely shrink or warp, but will expand when wet. Plywood thicknesses range from ⅛" to 1". Many species of wood are available for the outer plywood veneers. The core, or inner plies, give the panel its structural characteristics.

AC plywood has a finish-grade face on one side and a utility grade on the other. Standard AC plywood is made of seven plies of softwood, such as spruce or pine. This plywood is a good choice for paint-grade moldings. Hardwood veneer plywood is available in red oak and maple or birch at most home centers. Its inner core is basically the same as AC plywood, but it has a hardwood outer face. MDF oak veneer plywood is made up of three layers: two outer oak veneers and a solid core made of MDF. This plywood tends to be less expensive than a veneer core product and has a smoother face, but is heavy and does not hold fasteners as well.

MDF is available with or without an outer veneer. Baltic birch plywood is made up of equal size plies, all without voids, so the edges are attractive and can be left exposed. This panel is commonly used in Modern-style furniture and cabinets and with a clear finish. Lumber-core plywood has strips of solid wood edge-glued between outer veneer plies. Medium density overlay, or MDO, plywood has a plywood core with a resin-coated paper face. This panel is moisture resistant, unlike MDF, and has the fastening strength of a solid veneer core. The face is perfect for paint-grade applications. Wainscoting paneling is available in several thicknesses from ³⁄₁₆" to ⅝".

Lumber

Solid hardwood is available at most home centers in varying widths. Species vary, depending on your location. These boards make good solid stock material to combine with or mill into new trim moldings because they are already planed to a uniform thickness. If you can't find the type of lumber you need at a home center, check with a lumberyard or a woodworking store in your area. Most lumberyards will charge a nominal flat fee to plane the boards for you. You can also order almost any type of wood online.

Common Defects ▸

Whenever possible, do a quick inspection of each board before you purchase it. Because hardwood lumber is often stained, carefully take note of cosmetic flaws such as splits, knots, checks, and wanes. These issues can sometimes be cut around, but once the finish is applied, the imperfection will show through. Lumber that is twisted, cupped, or crooked should be avoided. If a board is slightly bowed, you can probably flatten it out as you nail it. In any case, always choose the straightest, flattest lumber you can find.

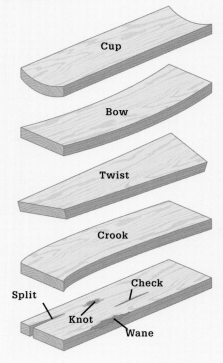

Planning a Project

With any of the built-in and shelf projects found in this book, you can either build the project as shown, or adapt the design to fit your unique space and needs. To build the project as shown, follow the measurements in the parts table that accompanies each project. Small width and height adjustments can be made using the fitting tips on page 32.

When adapting a built-in design, it is very important to make accurate plan drawings on graph paper to show how the project will fit in your space. These drawings let you organize your work and find approximate measurements for parts; they also make it easier to estimate the cost of materials.

To ensure a professional look and functional use, plan your built-ins so they fall within the standard range of sizes used by cabinet makers and furniture manufacturers (page opposite.)

Whether you are adapting a project or following a design as shown, it is safer to measure and cut the pieces as you assemble the built-in in its location, rather than to precut all pieces in advance. Small discrepancies in marking, cutting, and assembly techniques can lead to costly errors if you precut all the pieces.

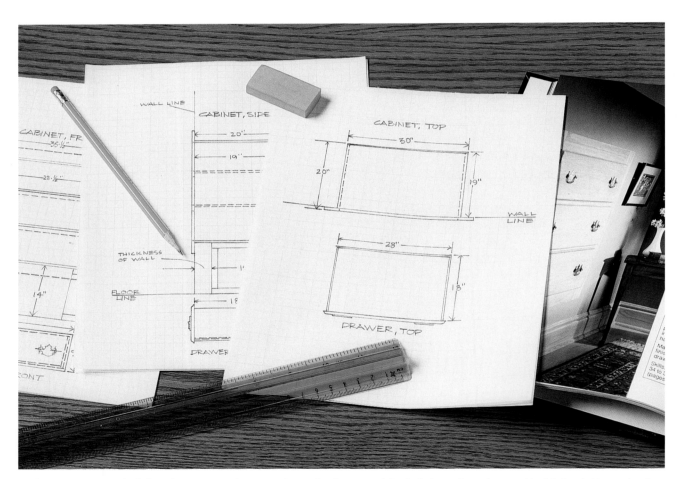

Make accurate scaled drawings on graph paper when adapting one of the built-in projects featured in this book. Use a simple scale, like 1 square (¼") = 1", to draw a side, top, and one or more front views of your project. For a complicated project, draw several front views showing the basic walls (carcase) of the built-in, the face frame construction, and the finished project including drawers and doors. Side views and top views should show all trim pieces and moldings. Make sure to use the actual measurements of sheet goods and dimension lumber when making your drawings.

STANDARD BUILT-IN MEASUREMENTS

Highest shelf should be no more than 72" above the floor to be within easy reach.

Shelves should be at least 10" deep in bookcases, and 12" deep in hanging wall cabinets. Space the shelves so there is at least ½" of open space above the items you are storing.

First shelf in a wall-hung built-in should be at least 18" above a countertop.

Work-surface height varies depending on how the surface is used. Place the surface 28" to 30" above the floor for a typing desk or sewing work center. Place the countertop at 36" for standard kitchen cabinets, at 44" for a dry bar or eating counter, or at 34" for accessible rooms.

Standard seating surfaces, like window seats and desk chairs, are between 16" and 20" high.

Base cabinet depth varies from 15" for a room divider to 30" for cabinets that support a desk surface. Standard kitchen-style floor cabinets usually are 24" or 25" in depth.

Access space in front of a built-in should be at least 36" to provide space for opening drawers and cabinet doors.

Drawer sizes range from a minimum of 3" high, 8" wide, and 8" deep; to a maximum of 10" high, 36" wide, and 30" deep. Large drawers, more than 24" wide, should be equipped with heavy-duty drawer slides for stability.

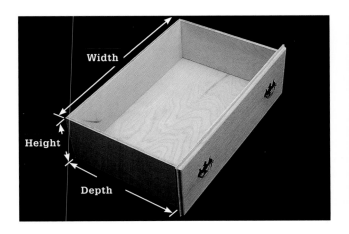

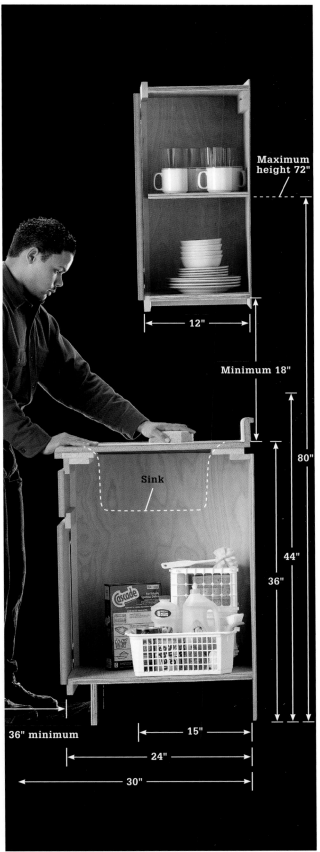

Tips for Planning and Fitting Built-Ins ▶

Filler strip

Face frame

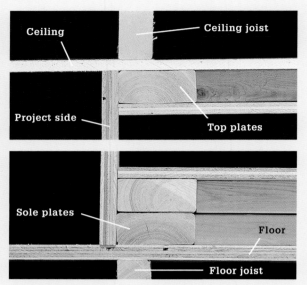

Ceiling

Ceiling joist

Project side

Top plates

Sole plates

Floor

Floor joist

Make small width adjustments (up to 6" on each side) with hardwood strips measured and cut to fill the extra space. Attach the strips to the edges of the face frame with counterbored wood screws. These "filler strips" let you slightly enlarge a project without making changes to the basic design. Filler strips also can be scribed to fit uneven walls.

Make small height adjustments by changing the thickness of the sole plates or top plates that anchor the built-in to the floor and ceiling. The floor-to-ceiling projects in this book are designed to fit rooms with 8-ft. ceilings. If your room height differs slightly, adjusting the sole plates or top plates lets you adapt a project without major design changes.

Nominal size	Actual size
1 × 2	¾" × 1½"
1 × 3	¾" × 2½"
1 × 4	¾" × 3½"
1 × 6	¾" × 5½"
1 × 8	¾" × 7¼"
2 × 4	1½" × 3½"
2 × 6	1½" × 5½"
2 × 8	1½" × 7¼"
2 × 10	1½" × 9¼"

Measure spaces carefully. Floors, walls, and ceilings are not always level or plumb, so measure at several points. If measurements vary, use the shortest one to determine the height or width of your built-in or plan on scribing.

Measure your materials. Actual thickness for plywood can vary from the listed nominal size; ¾" plywood, for example, is usually $^{23}/_{32}$".

Use actual measurements, not nominal measurements, of dimension lumber when planning a built-in. The table above shows the actual dimensions of common lumber.

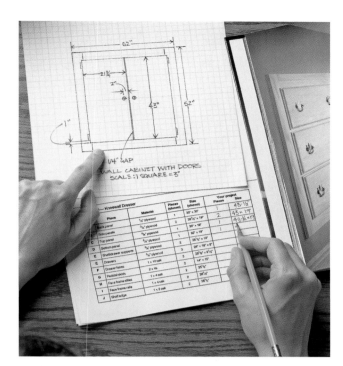

Revise the listed measurements of a featured project, if necessary, and record them. Use your scaled drawings as a guide for estimating the revised measurements. Always double-check measurements before cutting pieces to prevent costly cutting errors.

Make cutting diagrams to help you make efficient use of materials. Make scale drawings of sheet goods on graph paper, and sketch cutting lines for each part of your project. When laying out cutting lines, remember that the cutting path (kerf) of a saw blade usually consumes ⅛" of wood.

Materials	Amount needed	Cost for each	Total cost
Plywood (4 ft. × 8 ft.)			
¼" sheets			
½" sheets			
¾" sheets			
Lumber			
1 × 2 boards			
1 × 3 boards			
1 × 4 boards			
1 × 6 boards			
1 × 8 boards			
2 × 4s			
Moldings			
Door-edge			
Shelf-edge			
Base shoe			
Baseboard			
Crown/cove			
Ornamental			
Hardware			
Finish nails			
Power-drive screws			
Angle brackets			
Countertop brackets			
Drawer slides			
Hinges			
Door latches			
Pulls/knobs			
Other materials			
Wood glue			
Oil/stain			
Sanding sealer			
Paint			
Outlet strips			
Grommets			
Light fixtures			

Total cost:

Make a list of materials, using your plan drawings and cutting diagrams as a guide. Photocopy this materials list, and use it to organize your work and estimate costs.

Jobsite Preparation

Whether you are installing an elaborate, custom built-in or a simple shelf, preparing the jobsite is an important step of your project. Remove furniture and other objects from the rooms you will be working in so that you won't worry about getting sawdust on a nice upholstered chair, or accidentally damaging an antique furnishing. Cover any items you cannot remove with plastic sheeting. You may also want to cover finished floors with cardboard or dropcloths (as in photo below) as well, to protect them from scratches or just to make clean-up easier.

Set up tools such as a power miter saw at a central workstation, to avoid walking long distances between where you are installing and where you are cutting material. This central location is key to professional results because measurements are easier to remember and quick trimming is possible without the added time of exiting and entering the house.

Make sure the work area is well lit. If you don't already own one, purchase a portable light (trouble light) to make viewing the workpieces easier. Keep your tools sharp and clean. Accidents are more likely when blades are dull and tools are covered in dust and dirt.

Keep the work area clean and organized. A dedicated tool table for staging your tools is a great organizational aid. Tool tables also make it possible to conveniently keep tools from disappearing. If you only use the tools that you need and set them on the tool table when you aren't using them, tools stay off the floor and out of other rooms. Add a set of clamps to the table and you have a convenient space for fine-tuning the fit of each piece.

Organize your tools and avoid wearing a bulky work belt by setting up a dedicated tool table where all of your project tools and materials can be staged.

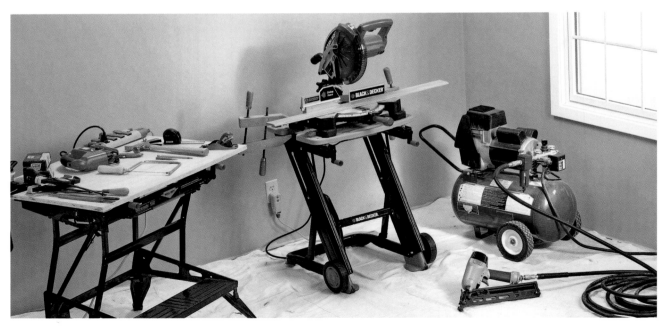

In some built-in or shelving projects, the most efficient way to accomplish the work is to convert the installation room into a temporary workshop.

Project Safety

Personal safety should be a priority when working on any project. Power tools and hand tools can cause serious injuries that require immediate attention. Be prepared for such situations with a properly stocked first aid kit. Equip your kit with a variety of bandage sizes and other necessary items such as antiseptic wipes, cotton swabs, tweezers, sterile gauze, and a first aid handbook.

To help you avoid using the first aid kit, read the owner's manuals of all power tools before operating them, and follow all outlined precautions. Protect yourself with safety glasses, ear protection, and dust masks and respirators when necessary.

Keep your work environment clean and free of clutter. Clean your tools and put them away after each work session, sweep up dust and any leftover fasteners, and collect scraps of cut-off trim in a work bucket. These scraps may come in handy before the end of the project, so keep them around until you are finished.

Maintain safety throughout your project, and remember that being safe is a priority. Everyone needs to use ear protection when operating loud tools. If you don't, you will lose your hearing. People don't just get used to loud noise. They lose their hearing and the noise doesn't seem as loud. The concept that safety applies to everyone but you is foolish. Take the necessary precautions to prevent injury to yourself and those around you.

Safety Tip ▸

Always wear safety glasses and ear protection when operating power tools. Use dust masks when necessary, and protect yourself from chemicals with a respirator. Work gloves save your hands when moving or handling large amounts of material. Knee pads are useful when working on floor-level projects such as baseboard.

Read the owner's manual before operating any power tool. Your tools may differ in many ways from those described in this book, so it's best to familiarize yourself with the features and capabilities of the tools you own. Always wear eye and ear protection when operating a power tool. Wear a dust mask when the project will produce dust.

Establishing Level, Plumb & Square

Good carpenters strive to achieve three basic ideals in their work: plumb, level, and square. Go into any home, however, and you are bound to find walls that bow, floors that slope, and corners that don't form right angles. This doesn't always mean the carpenter did a poor job, but rather reflects the fact that wood and many building materials are natural products that expand, contract, and settle with the seasons. These natural movements do not always occur at the same rate, however, causing fluctuations that sometimes become permanent. That's why it's no surprise that older homes more commonly have larger fluctuations.

These movements can make trimming a built-in project challenging. Level and plumb are hard concepts to apply when the floor slopes heavily and corners float in or out. Compounding the problem further is that power tools sometimes have preset angles that are difficult to fine-tune when the actual angle is 45½ or 44¾ degrees.

In most cases, your installation of built-ins and trim will require compromises. Keep in mind the overall appearance of your project and remember that the concepts of plumb and level can be relative. Strive to achieve them for quality joints, but don't insist on them when they affect the overall appearance of your project negatively. Here are a couple of fine pieces of advice to keep in mind:

- Level to the room is more important than level to the earth.
- Flat is more important than level.

A plumb bob is hung to establish a plumb (exactly vertical) line. Plumb can be difficult to visualize. Most chalk boxes can double as plumb bobs for rough use.

Window and door jambs are normally installed level and plumb, but if they aren't your casing should still follow an even reveal of ³⁄₁₆" to ¼" around the inside edge. Set the blade on a combination square to the depth of the reveal, then use the square as a guide for your pencil when marking. Install the casings flush with the mark.

Use a spacer block as a guide to install moldings near a ceiling. The spacer will allow you to easily follow any ups and downs of an uneven ceiling, making the trim run parallel to it rather than exactly level.

Install baseboard as close to level as possible, paying attention to areas where a floor dips or slopes over a longer length. In these instances, "cheat" the baseboard as close to level as you can, leaving a gap below it. You can only cheat the molding to less than the height of your base shoe, or quarter round. These trim pieces will cover the gap because they are thinner and easier to flex to the contour of your floor. Cheating the molding will also make cutting miters easier because they will require less of a bevel.

Use a T-bevel to measure for miter-cutting trim on out-of-square corners. Use a piece of scrap 1 × 4 to trace lines parallel to the corner walls. Place the T-bevel so the blade runs from the corner of the wall to the point where the lines intersect. Transfer this angle to your miter saw to cut your moldings.

Building Drawers

Drawers, and especially hand-built drawers, used to be limited mostly to storing small items. But the development of very reliable and smooth-operating drawer slide hardware has made it possible for DIYers to build larger, custom drawers that function just as well as smaller drawers. For example, you can now choose to install a set of large drawers instead of doors in a base cabinet, eliminating the need to stoop and reach deep into the back of a base cabinet. This convenience has made it possible for an increasing number of homeowners to opt for drawers instead of doors when designing built-ins.

Modern mechanical drawer slides place less stress on drawer joints. As a result, the joinery required to build a drawer is less critical. It is not difficult to build a functional and durable drawer box.

It's most practical to build drawers that feature a separate drawer box and drawer face because the position of the drawer face can be adjusted to ensure a perfect final appearance. Make drawer fronts that match the rest of the cabinet. Solid-wood slab construction is a common type of drawer front because many drawers are too narrow for frame-and-panel construction. To build a frame-and-panel drawer front you should have a drawer box that is at least 7 inches tall.

Solid wood is most often used for drawer faces because the edge grain is exposed around a drawer face. You can use plywood to make a drawer face, but you must attach solid or veneer edge banding if you want to cover the exposed plywood edges. Plywood is a good material choice for building the drawer boxes. Plywood is very stable, eliminating most of the construction concerns about expanding or contracting wood parts. Use ½"-thick Baltic birch plywood for the sides and ¼"-thick plywood for the bottom. Substitute ½"-thick plywood for the bottom if the drawer is wider than 30" or if you have extra ½" plywood.

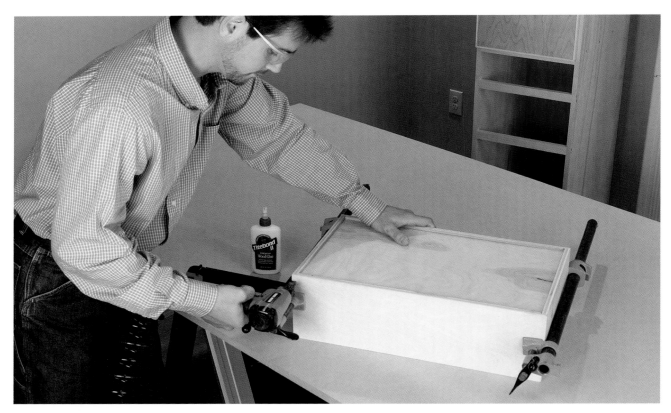

Building drawers from scratch is much easier to do if your shop is equipped with a set of good pipe clamps and a selection of pneumatic nailers.

Drawer Face Styles

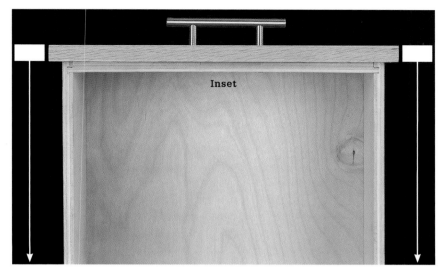

Inset drawer face fits fully inside the face frame or frameless cabinet opening with the front surfaces flush. Inset drawer faces are the trickiest type to install because they must fit perfectly inside the face frame or the uneven gap (called the reveal) around the face will show the error.

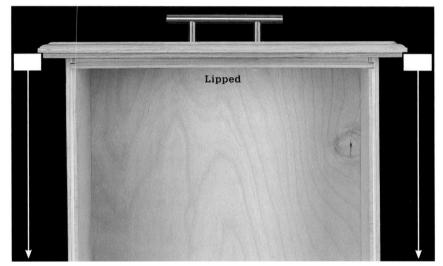

Lipped drawer face has rabbets cut along the back edges to create a recess that fits over the face frame. The net effect is that the front surface of the drawer front will be ⅜" proud of the cabinet. Lipped drawers are not traditionally attached to a separate drawer box, but they can be.

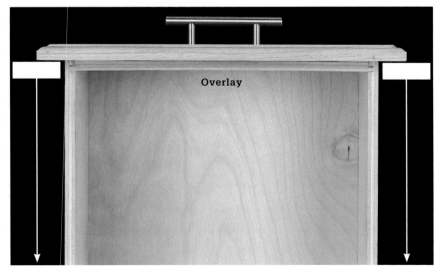

Overlay drawer face closes against the face frame. The front edges of the drawer front normally are profiled. Overlay drawer faces are the most common type used today because they are the easiest to make and install. Overlay faces are almost always used on frameless cabinets.

Determining Drawer Dimensions

Several factors must be considered when you calculate the drawer box dimensions; the type of cabinet, the size of the cabinet, the type of drawer face, and the type of drawer slides you plan to install.

The length of the drawer box is calculated as the distance from the front of the box to the back. Drawer boxes for standard (24"-deep) cabinets are typically 22" long. If the drawer face will be inset (see previous page), then subtract ¾" for the drawer face. If the drawer face is lipped, then subtract the amount of drawer face that will be recessed into the face frame. If the drawer face is overlay, then the drawer box will be flush with the front of the cabinet. You must also leave space (typically 1") behind the drawer to ensure that it will close without hitting the back of the cabinet.

The width of the drawer box is the distance from the left outside edge of the box to the right outside edge. Measure the width of the drawer opening and subtract the required drawer slide clearance (see the manufacturer's installation instructions). Most drawer slides require ½" on each side of the box. For face frame cabinets, measure the distance between the inside edges of the face frame stiles. For frameless cabinets, measure the distance between the inside faces of the cabinet sides. Your width measurement must be precise because most drawer slides have very limited play for adjustment.

The depth or height of the drawer should leave at least ¼" clearance above and below the top and bottom edges of the drawer. For face frame cabinets, measure the distance between the rails above and below the drawer opening. Then subtract at least ½" (¼ + ¼) for clearance above and below the drawer. For frameless cabinets you must lay out the number of drawers that will fill the cabinet and determine each drawer depth, including a ¼" clearance above, below and between each drawer.

Once you have calculated the overall dimensions you can cut the drawer parts to size. The dimensions of each part will depend on the type of joinery you use to construct your drawers.

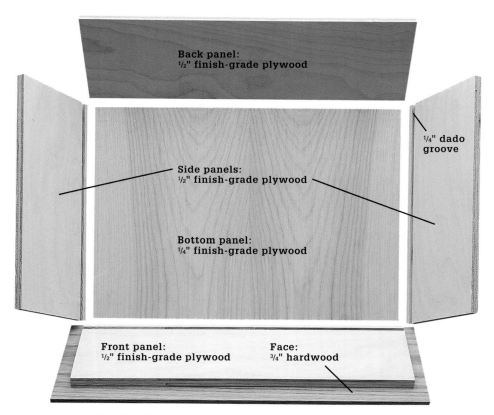

Back panel:
½" finish-grade plywood

¼" dado groove

Side panels:
½" finish-grade plywood

Bottom panel:
¼" finish-grade plywood

Front panel:
½" finish-grade plywood

Face:
¾" hardwood

The basic overlay drawer is made using ½" plywood for the front, back, and side panels, and ¼" plywood for the bottom panel. The bottom panel fits into a ¼" dado near the bottom of the front and side panels, and is nailed to the bottom edge of the back panel. The hardwood drawer face is screwed to the drawer front from inside the drawer box.

Face Frame Cabinets

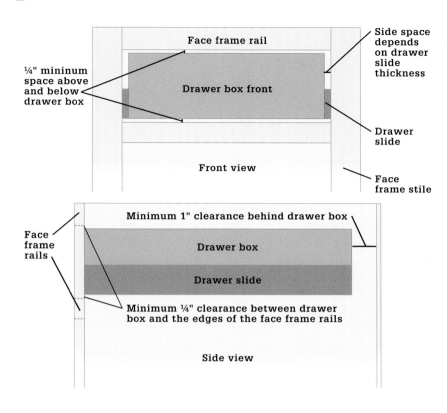

Face frame rail

¼" minimum space above and below drawer box

Drawer box front

Side space depends on drawer slide thickness

Drawer slide

Front view

Face frame stile

Face frame rails

Minimum 1" clearance behind drawer box

Drawer box

Drawer slide

Minimum ¼" clearance between drawer box and the edges of the face frame rails

Side view

Cabinets with face frames.
When determining the required size for custom-built cabinet drawers, use the inside dimension of the face frame opening as your guide. There should be a gap of at least ¼" (and not much more) at the top and bottom of the opening. The side-to-side measurement of the drawer should leave a gap of about ½" to create space for a side-mounted drawer slide. The illustration shown here is for the drawer box and should not affect any false front dimensions if your drawer will have one.

Frameless Cabinets

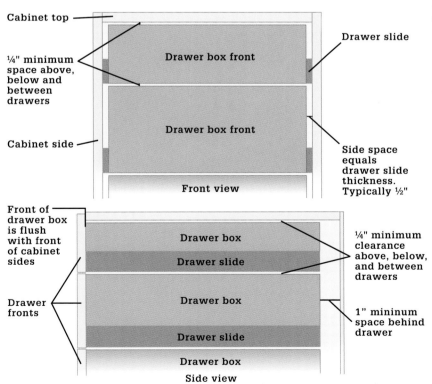

Cabinet top

¼" minimum space above, below and between drawers

Drawer box front

Drawer slide

Drawer box front

Cabinet side

Side space equals drawer slide thickness. Typically ½"

Front view

Front of drawer box is flush with front of cabinet sides

Drawer box

Drawer slide

¼" minimum clearance above, below, and between drawers

Drawer box

Drawer fronts

Drawer slide

1" minimum space behind drawer

Drawer box

Drawer slide

Drawer box

Side view

Cabinets without face frames.
The clearances required for a drawer box in a face-frameless (European style) cabinet are pretty much the same as they are for cabinets with face frames. Laying out drawer slide locations can be a little trickier without face frame rails to frame the top and bottom of each opening. The best way to manage this is to lay your cabinet sides next to each other with the tops and bottoms aligned, and then gang-mark the locations for the slides.

Butt-joint Drawer Box Construction

A very simple, but effective, way to build drawers is to join the corners with butt joints and secure the bottom in grooves that are cut in the sides. You can build this type of drawer using a router table or table saw. Or, you can use a circular saw and miter saw to cut the parts to size and a router to cut the grooves.

First calculate the part dimensions (see illustration, page 41). Then cut the parts to size. Next, cut the groove in the sides that will hold the bottom panel. Use a dado blade set or make multiple passes with a regular table saw blade to cut the groove wide enough to fit the drawer bottom.

Test the fit of the bottom panel. The bottom should fit snug in the groove and the tops should align. If it doesn't fit, then move the fence out slightly and make another pass to make the groove a little wider.

Assemble the drawer box with glue and brad nails. Apply a thin bead of glue to the inside of the grooves. Fit the bottom panel into the grooves. Then apply a bead of glue to the end edges and bottom edges of the front and back pieces. Next, slide the front and back pieces between the sides and attach them (photo 3). Carefully flip the drawer over. Adjust the drawer to be square and attach the bottom to the front and back (photo 4).

DRAWER BOX WITH BUTT JOINTS

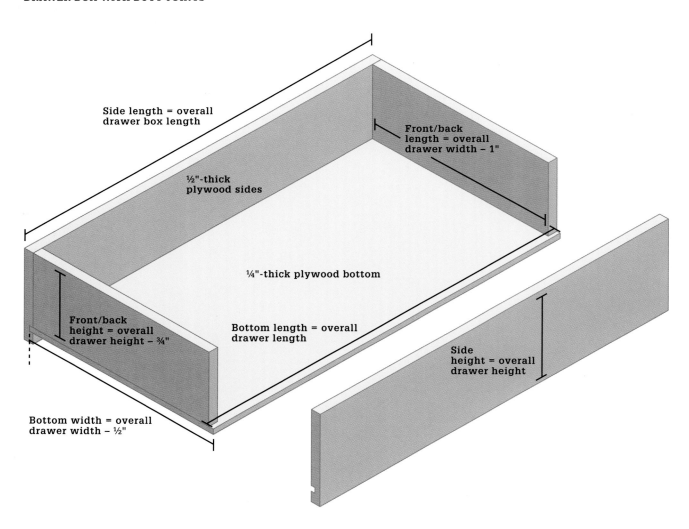

Side length = overall drawer box length

Front/back length = overall drawer width – 1"

½"-thick plywood sides

¼"-thick plywood bottom

Front/back height = overall drawer height – ¾"

Bottom length = overall drawer length

Side height = overall drawer height

Bottom width = overall drawer width – ½"

How to Construct a Drawer Box

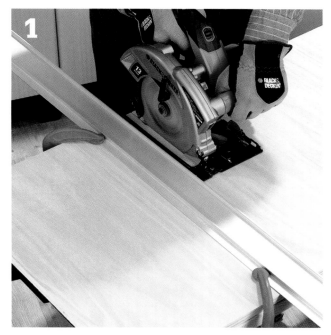

Cut the drawer parts to width on a tablesaw if you have one. Otherwise, use a circular saw and a straightedge cutting guide. Cut the parts to length with a power miter saw.

Cut a slot near the bottom of each drawer box part to create access for the drawer bottom, which usually is made from ¼ or ½"-thick plywood. The slot should be slightly wider than the thickness of the drawer bottom panel. You can cut it with a router or on a tablesaw using multiple cutting passes.

Attach front and back to sides with 18 ga. × 1¼" brad nails. Hold the brad gun in line with the sides to reduce the chance of the nails curving and popping through the front or back pieces.

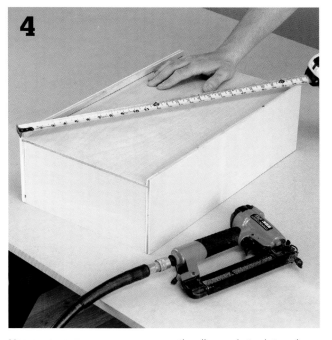

Use a square or measure across the diagonals to determine if the drawer sides are square to the front and back. Adjust the drawer to be square and attach the bottom to front and back with 18 ga. × 1" brad nails.

Rabbet-and-Dado Box Construction

A more advanced and durable joint that is commonly used to build drawer boxes is the rabbet and dado joint. There are several benefits that make the rabbet-and-dado joint a good choice for drawer box corner joints. It features multiple gluing surfaces. The tongue of the rabbet provides structural joint strength against the force of opening or closing the drawer. And, although it's not as intricate as a dovetail joint, it is attractive and more decorative than a simple butt joint.

After the parts are cut to size (see illustration), you can make the joints with a router table and ¼" straight bit. Or, you can follow the same construction process and make these joints with a table saw and ¼"-wide dado blade set.

RABBET-AND-DADO DRAWER BOX

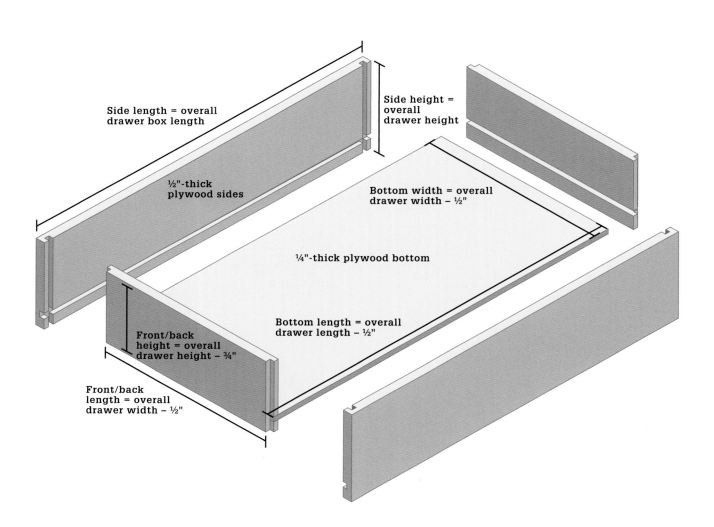

Side length = overall drawer box length

Side height = overall drawer height

½"-thick plywood sides

Bottom width = overall drawer width – ½"

¼"-thick plywood bottom

Bottom length = overall drawer length – ½"

Front/back height = overall drawer height – ¾"

Front/back length = overall drawer width – ½"

How to Make a Rabbet-and-Dado Box

First, cut the dadoes in the ends of the drawer sides. Set the fence ¼" away from the edge of the bit. Set the bit height to ¼" above the table. Cut dadoes across the ends of the inside faces of the drawer sides (photo 1).

Next, cut the ¼"-wide × ¼"-deep grooves that will contain the drawer bottom. Set the fence ½" away from the edge of the bit. Cut a groove along the bottom of the inside face of each drawer side (photo 2). If you are using ½"-thick plywood for the bottom, then make another pass to widen the grooves to ½". Move the fence out ¼", so that it is now ¾" from the edge of the bit. Test the fit of the drawer bottom in the groove. If the groove is too narrow, then move the fence out slightly and make another pass to widen the groove.

The last cut is the ¼ × ¼" rabbet in the ends of the drawer front and back pieces.

Use a miter gauge to guide each piece through the cut. Cut the rabbet in a scrap piece first, to check how well the rabbet fits in the drawer side piece dado.

The front edge of the drawer side should be flush with the front of the drawer front piece. Adjust the bit height to change the width of the rabbet and adjust the fence to change depth of the rabbet. Once you're satisfied with the fit, cut rabbets across the inside face ends of the front and back (photo 3).

Bore pilot holes through the drawer box front (photo 4). These holes must be slightly larger than the diameter of the screws that will attach the drawer face. The oversize holes allow you to make slight adjustments to the alignment of the drawer face in the future.

Dry assemble (no glue) the drawer box to make sure all the parts fit together well. Then assemble the drawer box with glue (photo 5). Assemble the drawer on one of its sides, placing the front, back, and bottom in one side that is flat on the workbench and then place the other side on top. Use parallel clamps or wood cauls to distribute the clamping force evenly across the joints. Make sure the box is square before tightening the clamps and letting the glue set up (photo 6).

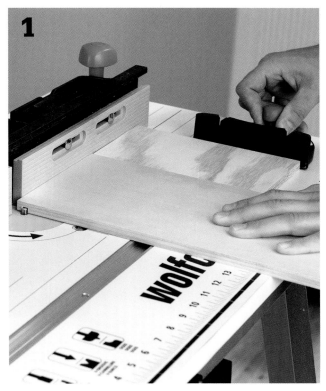

Place the drawer side face down on the router table and use a miter gauge to guide the piece through the cut. Cut a ¼ × ¼" dado located ¼" from each end of the inside face.

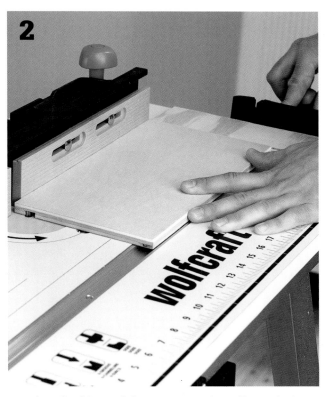

Cut the ¼"-wide × ¼"-deep grooves that will contain the bottom in the front, back, and side pieces.

(continued)

3

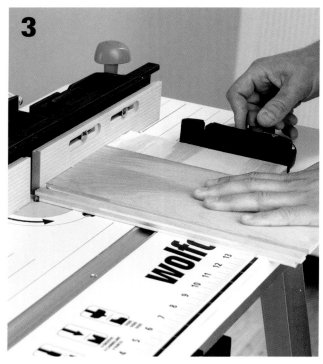

Cut the ¼ × ¼" rabbets in the ends of the front and back pieces. Place each piece face down and use a miter gauge to push it through the cut.

4

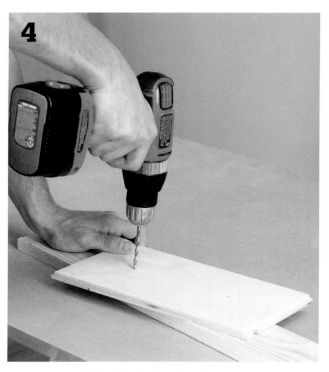

Bore ³⁄₁₆- or ¼"-dia. pilot holes through the drawer box front. Space the holes roughly 6" apart across the middle height of the drawer.

5

Assemble the drawer with glue. Use cauls to apply even pressure across the joints.

6

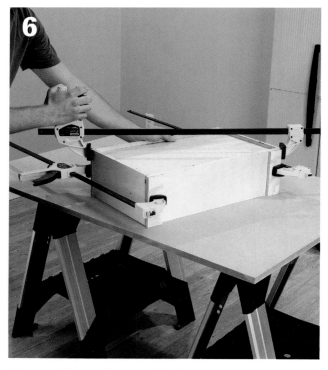

Measure diagonally across the drawer to check for square. If the diagonal measurements are equal, then the drawer is square. If not, then place a clamp across the longer diagonal and tighten the clamp to bring the drawer into square.

Installing Drawers

Drawers are mounted in the cabinet on drawer slides. There are many types of drawer slides, ranging from basic slides that cost only a couple dollars a pair to very advanced motor-driven slides that can cost over one hundred dollars a pair. The two most common and versatile types of slides are roller slides and telescopic ball-bearing slides. Both types feature two basic components; a runner that attaches to the drawer and a guide that attaches to the cabinet.

It doesn't matter how beautifully constructed your drawers are; if the drawer slides aren't installed correctly, then the drawer will not operate properly. The slides must be installed perpendicular to the cabinet face, level to each other and the front edge of each slide must be the same distance from the front of the cabinet.

The slides are mounted directly to the sides of frameless cabinets. Face frame cabinets require a spacer, cleat, or bracket to support the slide and keep it flush with the inside edge of the face frame (see Spacer Options, page 49).

It's easiest to mount the slides flush with the bottom of the drawer box. Place the box on a flat surface and attach the runners (photo 1, page 48). Next, disconnect the guides from the runners. Attach the guides to the cabinet (photo 3). Make a template to position the guides for each drawer at exactly the same height on both sides of the cabinet.

The front of the guide should be flush with the front of the cabinet or face frame when you are installing overlay drawer fronts. The front of the guide should be set back from the front when you are installing inset or lipped drawers. The setback distance equals the thickness of the face that is inset in the face frame. For example, if the drawer face on an inset drawer is ¾" thick, then the guide is installed ¾" back from the front of the face frame.

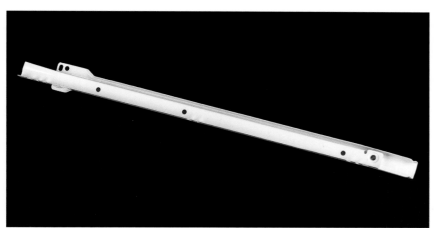

Roller slides are inexpensive and easy to install. The most common versions of these slides open 4" less than the length of the drawer.

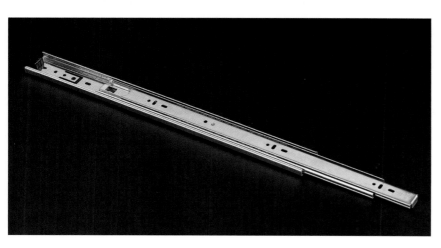

Telescopic ball-bearing slides are available in a wide range of sizes, providing weight-bearing and extension options to suit just about any application.

How to Install Drawer Slides

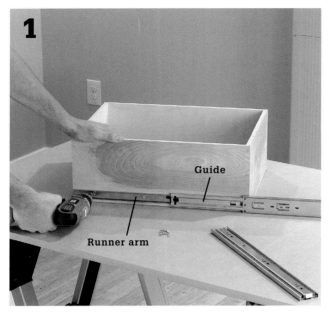

1

Place the drawer slide on a flat surface next to the drawer box. Extend the runner arm from the guide and align the front of the runner with the front of the drawer box. Drive screws into a couple of the slotted screw holes.

2

If your cabinet has face frames, make spacers that are the same thickness as the distance from the cabinet side to the inside edge of the face frame (see previous page) and attach them to the cabinet side. Use a framing square to mark a reference line on the spacers for each slide, level with the face frame rail top.

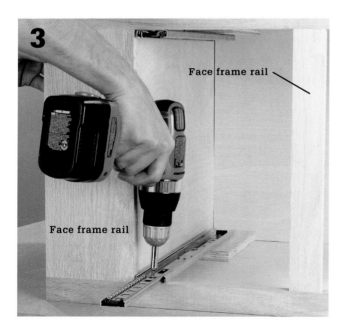

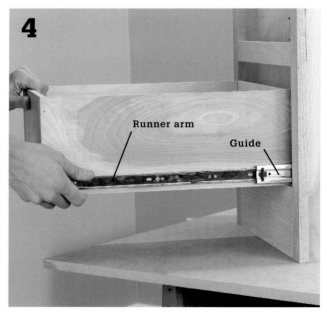

3

Disconnect the drawer slide guides from the runner arms that are mounted to the drawer box. Position the slides inside the cabinet drawer openings so the bottom edges are slightly above the face frame rail and the other ends are flush with the reference lines marked on the spacer. Attach the guides to the cabinet by driving screws into the slotted screw holes.

4

Install the drawer in the cabinet by sliding the runner arms back into the guides and snapping or locking them into place. Test the drawer operation and adjust the position of the runners and guides as necessary. Drive screws into the fixed screw holes once you are assured that the drawer operates properly.

Drawer Slide Spacer Options ▸

The drawer slides in a face-frame cabinet must be flush with the inside edge of the face frame. Mount the drawer slide guide to a spacer or bracket that is attached to the cabinet side or back.

Wood spacer

Back wall bracket

How To Adjust Drawer Slides: Box Is Too Narrow

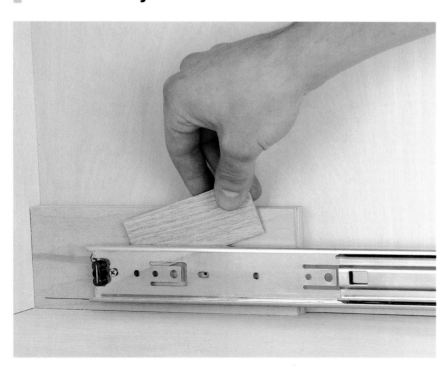

Cut enough shims to match the width that must be added to the drawer. Make the shims out of paper, cardboard, wood or plastic laminate. Install shims between slides and the cabinet side or spacer. Reinstall the drawer and test the fit. Add or remove shims until the drawer fits properly.

How to Adjust Drawer Slides: Box Is Too Wide

Option 1: Attach a sacrificial fence to your table saw fence. Lower the blade below the table. Move the edge of the fence over the blade. Turn on the saw and raise the blade up into the fence to the height of the drawer runner. Adjust the fence so that the width of the amount of blade that extends beyond the fence equals the amount you need to trim off the drawer. Make sure no fasteners are in the drawer in the cut area. Trim the drawer.

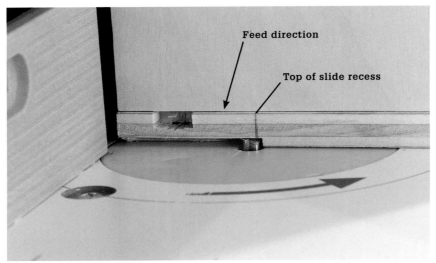

Option 2: Install a straight cutting bit in your router table. Set the fence so that the amount of the bit that extends above the table equals the amount you need to trim off the drawer. Set the fence so your first cut will be at the bottom of the recess for the slide. Move the fence back after each cut and continue cutting until you reach the top of the slide recess.

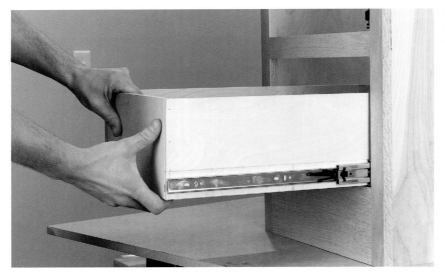

Reattach the runner arm and test the fit of the drawer. If the drawer is still too wide, then move the fence over slightly and trim a little more off the drawer side.

Attaching the Drawer Face

Make and apply finish to the drawer face before you attach it to the drawer box. Carefully position the drawer face before you drive any screws (photo 1). Inset drawer faces are centered in the face frame drawer opening. Overlay drawer faces on frameless cabinets are centered over the cabinet sides. Bore screw starter holes in the back of the drawer face and attach the face with screws that will extend approximately halfway through the face (photo 2). For example, use 1" long screws to attach a ¾"-thick face to a ½"-thick drawer box front.

Finally attach the drawer knobs or pulls. If you are installing several drawers, use a jig to consistently bore the knob or pull pilot holes in the same place on every drawer face (photo 3). The screws that are included with many knobs and pulls are intended for use on ¾"-thick material. You may have to purchase longer hardware screws to attach the knobs to a two-piece drawer face.

A drawer face made of solid hardwood gives the drawer a presentable appearance while maintaining the economy and strength of a plywood drawer box.

How to Attach the Drawer Face

Apply double-sided carpet tape or thin adhesive pads to the drawer front to temporarily attach the drawer face. Press the drawer face against the tape, using paper or cardboard spacers to help center drawer faces in face frame openings as necessary.

Carefully slide out the drawers and attach the faces with No. 8 × 1" washer-head screws or panhead screws and washers. Drive the screws through pilot holes in the drawer box front.

Use a marking jig (See Resources, page 251) to mark drilling points for the drawer hardware pilot holes in the fronts of the drawer faces. Bore a ³⁄₁₆"-dia. pilot hole for each hardware screw. Attach the drawer pulls and install the drawers

Building Doors

If you don't want everything you've got stuffed in your cabinet to be on constant display, then you'll need to build some doors. Doors conceal and help keep dust off the cabinet contents. Doors also act as the face of the cabinet, defining the cabinet style.

There are many types of door construction, but the two most common are slab doors and frame-and-panel doors. These two types of doors can be modified using different wood species, edge profiles and finishes to create a style to fit just about any décor.

In addition to choosing the door style, you must also decide how the doors will be mounted on the cabinet. There are three main types of door mounts; inset, overlay and lipped.

Tools & Materials ▸

Ear and eye protection
Work gloves
Table saw
Router table
Drill/driver
Combination square
Sanders—belt and
    random orbit

36" and 24" pipe
    or bar clamps
Small hand saw—
    Japanese pull saw
    is a good choice
Brad pusher
Standard magnetic
    door catch

Magnetic touch
    door catch (round
    piston style)
Rail and stile router bit set
Piloted rabbeting bit
Concealed hinge
    jig system

Self-centering drill bits
    (for drilling pilot holes
    with jigs)
Wrap-around hinges
Frameless overlay hinges
Soft close hinge and
    cabinet adapters

Building your own cabinet doors lets you customize the design so you can have precisely the door type you want, including these framed doors that will be fitted with glass panel inserts.

Common Cabinet Door Styles

A slab door is a flat panel. These doors can be made from solid stock, but they are most often constructed with a plywood panel that has its edges concealed with wood edging.

Frame-and-panel doors are easily the most popular door style. These doors feature a panel that is framed by two vertical stiles and two horizontal rails.

Door Mount Options

Overlay doors are most often mounted on frameless cabinets with concealed hinges, but these versatile doors can also be installed over a face frame cabinet. They are more forgiving to install than inset doors because there is no exposed gap between the door and cabinet.

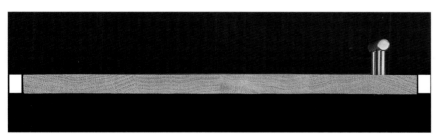

Inset doors are mounted on face frame cabinets. The face of an inset door is flush with the face frame. These are the most challenging doors to install because they must be perfectly centered in the frame opening to maintain an even gap around the door.

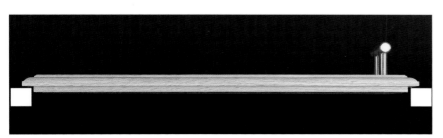

Lipped doors are a hybrid between inset and overlay. They feature a rabbet that is cut in the back edge to fit inside the face frame opening. Lipped mount doors are often used on manufactured face frame cabinets.

Determining Door Sizes

The first step in building doors is to determine the size of the doors. To prevent sagging, the maximum width of each door should be not more than 24". If the cabinet opening is greater than 24" wide, then use two doors.

If you are building large frame-and-panel doors or glass doors, design the doors to have a bottom rail that is wider than the top rail. A wider bottom rail gives the door good proportions by adding a little more visual weight to the bottom of the door. A wider bottom rail also adds more gluing surface, creating a stronger frame to support the weight of the door.

Measuring for Door Dimensions

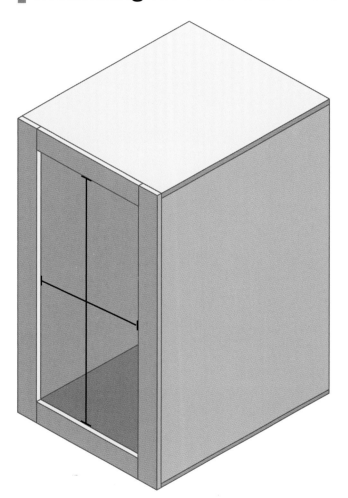

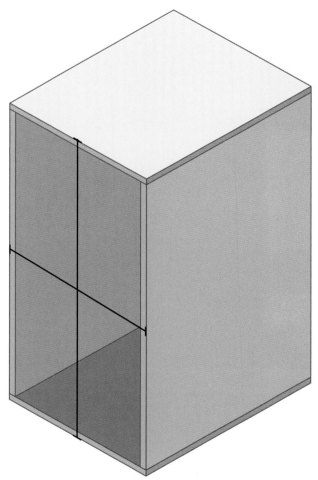

If you're installing inset doors, then measure the height and width of the face frame openings. Determine the door width and height by subtracting the width of the gaps that must be left around the edges of the doors and between doors.

If you are installing overlay doors, then measure the height and width of the cabinet to the outside edges of the cabinet sides, top, and bottom. Then subtract ⅛" from the height and width measurements.

Building Frame-and–Panel Cabinet Doors

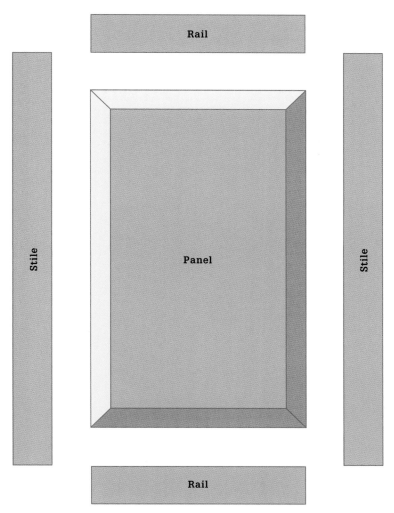

There are several ways to build frame and panel doors. The doors for this cabinet are made using a rail-and-stile, also referred to as a cope-and-stick, router bit set. This set contains two router bits; one bit that cuts the stub tenon in the ends of the rails and another bit that cuts the panel groove and edge profile.

Frame-and-Panel Router Bit Set ▶

One of the most efficient ways to make a frame and panel door is with a router table and bit set often called a cope-and-stick bit set. The two bits in this set cut opposite profiles that fit together to create a tight corner joint. The coping bit (sometimes referred to as the rail cutter) cuts the stub tenons in the ends of the rails. The sticking bit (sometimes referred to as the stile cutter) cuts the groove and top-edge profile in the inside edges of the rails and stiles. There are also single combination router bits that make both the cutting and sticking cuts by adjusting the bit height.

How to Build a Frame-and-Panel Door

Cut the door parts to size. Rout the stub tenon profile on both ends of the rails first. Set the height of the coping bit (the bit that cuts the tenons) (photo 1). Cut test pieces to check the bit height. Then cut the stub tenons in the ends of the rails (photo 2).

Next, rout the groove profile in the inside edges of the stiles and rails. Set the sticking bit height (photo 3). Make test cuts in a scrap piece and adjust the bit height as necessary to create a perfect alignment between the rail and stile pieces. Then cut the grooves in the inside edges of the stiles and rails (photo 4).

Dry assemble the frame and measure the panel opening width and height. Cut the panel to size and sand it smooth. Apply finish to the frame parts and panel. Keep the finish off of the stub tenons and mating joint surfaces on the stile. After the finish is dry, assemble the frame with glue (photo 5).

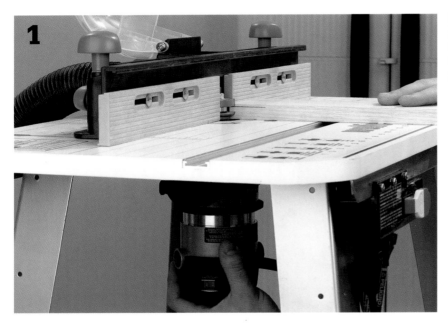

Set the bit height so that the bit will leave an ⅛"-deep rabbet above the stub tenon. Set the fence so that it lines up with the outside edge of the router bit pilot bearing.

Make test cuts in the ends of scrap pieces to check the bit height setting. Then cut the stub tenons in the ends of the actual rails, using a miter gauge to feed the rails face down past the bit.

Set the sticking bit height so that the groove cutting blade is aligned with the stub tenon on the rails. Set the fence so that it lines up with the outside edge of the router bit pilot bearing.

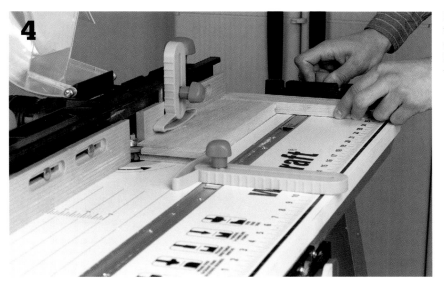

Feed the rails and stile face down past the bit to cut the grooves in the inside edges of the stiles and rails. Use feather boards to help maintain even pressure throughout the cut.

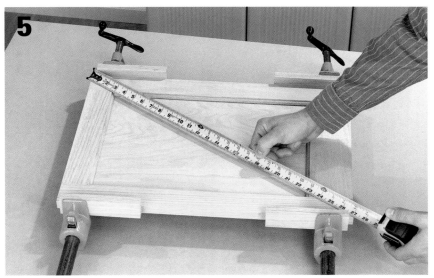

Apply glue to the stub tenon joints, insert the panel in the grooves and assemble the door frame. Clamp the frames. Measure across the diagonals to check the doors for square. If the measurements are equal then the doors are square. If the measurements aren't equal then clamp across the longer diagonal to square the door.

Glass Panel Doors

Glass panel doors are a great way to equip a cabinet to highlight a favorite collection. It's not much more difficult to install glass panels than it is to install solid insert panels made from plywood or another wood product. If you're installing real glass panels, it's always safest to purchase tempered glass for any door application. If you aren't too bothered by it aesthetically, you can also use clear acrylic or polycarbonate panels. These won't shatter, of course, but they tend to get scratched and to start to look a little cloudy over time.

Make and join the door frame rails and stiles the same way you'd do it for a plywood panel door, but assemble the frames without the panel and then install the panels in recesses you cut into the completed frames.

How to Make Glass Panel Cabinet Doors

Assemble the door frame as you would any face frame (see pages 55 to 57). If you have the capability and equipment, use mortise-and-tenon joints for the frame. The back, inside edges of the frame opening must be rabbeted to create a recess for the glass to fit against. Place the door frame face down and secure it to your worksurface. Use a router with a piloted rabbeting bit to cut ⅜- × ⅜" rabbets in the edges of the frame opening (photo 1). Use a wood chisel to carefully square off the corners of the recess (photo 2).

Using the same wood stock you made the frame from, cut ¼- × ¼" retainer strips to hold the glass panels in the door (photo 3). Cut enough retainer strip stock to cover the perimeter of all the glass pieces. Sand and finish the doors and retainer strips to match the cabinet.

Cut the glass pieces (or have them cut for you) so they are ⅛" shorter than the rabbeted frame opening in each direction. Place a sheet of glass in each door. Cut the retainer strips to fit along each side of the glass. Bore ¹⁄₃₂"-dia. pilot holes through the retainer strips, spaced 6 to 8" apart, making sure the pilot holes are positioned so the brads will not contact the glass panel. Place the strips over the glass and attach them to the frame with ¾" brad nails. Use a tack hammer to drive the brads and then set the heads below the wood surface by striking them with a nail set (photo 4).

Glass panel inserts transform a cabinet from a hulking mass to an open, airy furnishing that showcases its contents while providing protection from dust build-up.

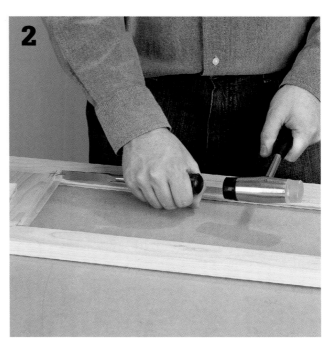

Create the panel recess. First, install a ⅜"-dia. bottom-bearing rabbetting bit in your router. Secure the assembled wood frame to your worksurface. Engage the router and cut a ⅜ × ⅜" recess around the entire back inside edge of the frame opening. Make these rabbet cuts in multiple passes of increasing depth.

Finish the cuts by using a wood chisel to square the corners. Remove the waste wood a little at a time, taking care not to split the wood or damage the corner joints.

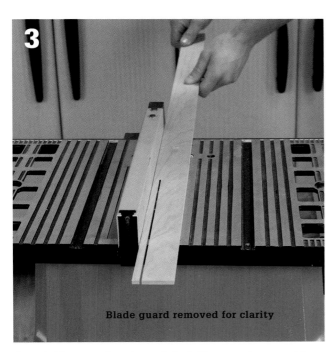

Blade guard removed for clarity

On a table saw, rip-cut wood stock (the same type used for the frame) into ¼ × ¼" lengths and then cut them to fit inside the frame opening, creating retainer strips. Use a push stick to move the narrow pieces across the blade.

Use a brad pusher or small tack hammer to drive ¾"-long brad nails through 1/32" pilot holes in the retainer strips and into the vertical surfaces of the frame recess opening. Then, set the nail heads with a nailset. *Tip: Set a piece of cardboard over the glass surface to protect it.*

Building Slab Doors

Slab doors are flat wood (as opposed to frame-and-panel doors). You can make them from a single piece of wood stock if you can find one wide enough (rather unlikely). Or, they can be made by edge-gluing multiple strips of solid wood, or by attaching edging to a plywood panel. Plywood is used to make most slab doors because it is much more dimensionally stable than solid wood, and thus less likely to cup or warp.

The edges of plywood slab doors should be concealed with solid wood edging. If the doors will be used infrequently, iron-on veneer edge tape may be an acceptable product for treating the plywood edges.

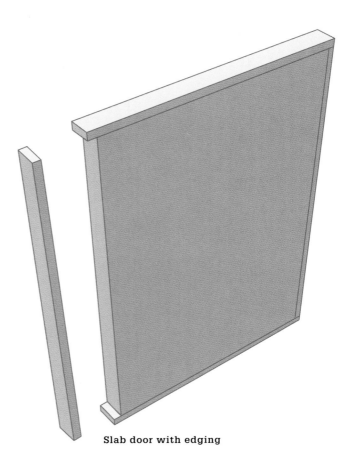

Slab door with edging

Tools & Materials ▶

Tablesaw or circular saw with straightedge
Hand saw
Masking tape
¾" cabinet-grade plywood
¼"-thick edging strips
Glue
Sandpaper
Eye and ear protection
Work gloves

How to Make a Slab Door

To make plywood doors with ¼"-thick solid wood edging, first subtract ½" from the height and width of the finished door size. Cut the plywood to these dimensions (photo 1). Use solid stock that is slightly thicker than the plywood to make the edge strips. This is pretty easy to do, since most of the veneered plywood that we refer to as ¾" thick is actually slightly smaller ($^{23}/_{32}$").

On a tablesaw, rip-cut ¼"-wide strips from ¾"-thick hardwood of the same wood species as the plywood veneer (photo, right). This will create stock for the solid wood edging. Cut the ¼- × ¾" edging strips for both sides of each door, making the strips

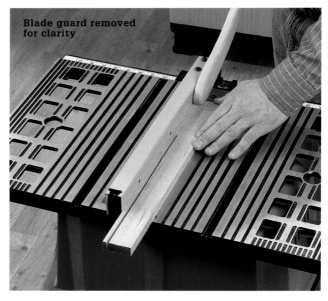

Tip: Make your own edging strips instead of buying premilled molding. Rip-cut ¼"-thick edge strips from ¾" hardwood stock using a table saw. Use a push stick to feed the thin stock past the blade.

slightly longer than necessary so they overhang the top and bottom door edges. Attach the strips to the side edges of the plywood door with wood glue (photo 2). Use clamps or masking tape to pull the strips tightly against the door (some pressure is needed to prevent the glue joint from expanding as the glue dries). Make sure the strips are centered on the door edges so the overhang is equal along both door faces.

After the glue dries, remove the tape or clamps and trim the edge pieces flush with the plywood faces and ends (photo 3). Repeat this process to attach the edge pieces to the top and bottom edges (photo 4). Sand the edging strips so they are perfectly flush with the plywood panel edges. Avoid using a power sander for this—they're too aggressive. Use a sanding block and 150-grit sandpaper.

Use a table saw or circular saw and straightedge guide to cut the plywood panels to size. Remember to allow for the edging strip thickness when determining the required panel size to yield a door that's the final dimensions you need.

Attach the side edging strips with glue. Stretch masking tape across the strips to hold them down tightly while the glue dries. Make sure none of the plywood edge is exposed beyond the edge pieces.

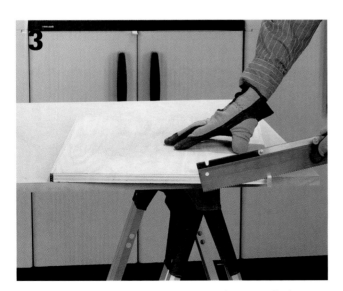

Use a hand saw (a gentleman's saw, back saw, or flush-cutting saw will do) to trim the ends of the edging flush. Touch up the cuts with sandpaper so the strip ends are flush with and square to the panel.

Cut the top and bottom edging strips to length and secure them to the door edges with glue. Trim the ends of the edging strips once the glue has dried. Sand the edges of the edging strips so they are flush with both the back and front plywood faces. Be careful not to sand through the veneer.

Hanging Cabinet Doors

Unlike passage doors for your house, cabinet doors don't come prehung unless you buy stock cabinets. But luckily, mounting a cabinet door is a good deal simpler than hanging a house door directly into existing jambs with butt hinges. This is especially true since newer, easier-to-install hinge hardware has taken over most of the cabinetry market. The two most popular of the newer hinge types are concealed "cup" hinges and wrap-around butt hinges.

Concealed hinges are sometimes referred to as "cup hinges" because of the inset hinge cup component, and also as "European hinges" because, until recently, they were primarily made by European hardware manufacturers. These hinges have been used for many years by professionals and commercial cabinet manufacturers, but they are now available at home centers for woodworking hobbyists and DIYers.

One of the biggest benefits of concealed hinges is their adjustability. Some models can be adjusted on all three planes: up/down, left/right and in/out, making it much easier to achieve a perfect fit.

Concealed hinges feature two components: a hinge cup that recesses into the door, and a mounting plate that attaches to the side of the cabinet or to the face frame. Installing these hinges typically requires a 35mm Forstner drill bit. This type of bit bores the flat bottom hole that the hinge cup fits in. This hole is drilled with a drill press or a special right-angle drill guide. There are also specially designed concealed hinge jig kits that include the bit, right-angle guide, and positioning jig. These kits make installing this type of hinge very easy.

Follow the installation instructions included with most concealed hinges. The basic installation process is to first hold the door in position against the cabinet or face frame. Mark the center location of the hinges on the door and cabinet side or face frame (photo 1). Next, bore the hinge cup mortise (photo 2). Then install the hinge cup component to the door (photo 3). Fasten the mounting bracket to the cabinet side (photo 4). Finally, mount the hinge arms on the mounting plates and adjust the door position.

Concealed cup hinge

Modern cabinet door hinges have two big advantages over simple butt hinges: they are faster to install and they are easier to adjust.

How to Install Concealed Hinges

Mark the center of the hinge location on the back of the door and cabinet side or face frame.

Use a drill guide and jig or a drill press to bore the cup mortise. This mortise dimension is typically 35mm-dia. × 8-mm-deep. Check your hinge installation directions for specific mortise dimensions.

Fasten the hinge cup component to the door with the supplied hinge screws. Use a combination square to make sure the hinge arm is perpendicular to the door edge.

Follow the manufacturer instructions or use a jig to position the mounting plate on the hinge center mark that you made on the cabinet side.

Adjust the door position by loosening or turning the hinge adjustment screws.

How to Install Wrap-around Butt Hinges

Consider using a butt hinge when you are hanging a heavy inset-door on a face frame. Butt hinges are rigid, which prevents the door from sagging the way it might if it were hanging on a concealed hinge with a long hinge arm. Full-wrap butt hinges provide the same appearance and no-sag benefits of butt hinges with the added benefit of being easier to install.

Install wrap-around hinges so that the top and bottom of the hinge barrel is 2 to 4" from the top or bottom (respectively) of the door. Mark the hinge locations on the back of the door (photo 1).

These hinges often feature slotted and non-slotted screw holes. Use the slotted screw holes to initially mount and adjust the door (photo 2). Once the door is fully mounted, centered in the face frame and operating properly, drive screws in the non-slotted holes to lock the door in place. Next, attach the hinges and door to the cabinet (photo 3). It is often helpful to have another person hold the door in position while you fasten the hinges to the face frame. Slightly loosen the hinge screws to adjust the door position. When the door is properly positioned

in the face frame, tighten the slotted screws and drill pilot holes in the non-slotted screws. Drive hinge screws in the non-slotted holes to permanently secure the hinges. Then attach a catch to the door (photo 4).

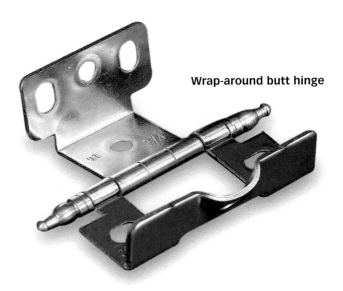

Wrap-around butt hinge

Make hinge location marks on the back face of the door, 2 to 4" up from the bottom and down from the top of the door.

Bore pilot holes through the centers of the slotted hinge holes only. Drive the hinge screws in the slotted holes to attach the hinge to the door.

Get a helper to center the door on the face frame stile, holding the hinge plates against the stile. Bore pilot holes in the slotted hinge holes and then drive the hinge screws in the pilot.

Attach a magnetic catch near the top of the door. Adjust the position of the catch so that the door is flush with the face frame when closed.

Door & Drawer Hardware

KNOBS & PULLS

Despite their small size, knobs and pulls play a major role in defining the style of the cabinets. Simply replacing the knobs is sometimes enough to refresh the appearance of dated or worn-out cabinets.

There is no rule dictating whether to use knobs or pulls on your doors. It's really up to your personal taste. You can use the same knobs or pulls on both drawers and doors or use a combination of knobs and pulls, such as pulls on the drawers and knobs on the doors. Pulls are easier to grab and a better choice if the homeowner has less hand strength.

It's important to install all the knobs or pulls in exactly the same place on every door. The best method is to use a hole-alignment jig to drill the pilot holes (photo 1). You can make a simple jig using scrap wood or clear plastic, or you can purchase a manufactured jig (See Resources, page 251).

How to Install Pulls

Use a jig to consistently mark positions for the pilot holes you'll need to drill in order to install the knobs or pulls.

Position a backer board behind the door frame in the drilling area. A backer board prevents blowout in the wood on the backside of the hole. Drill guide holes for the knobs or pulls at the positions you've marked. Install the pull or knob with the mounting bolt that comes with the hardware.

CATCHES

Most butt hinges do not feature self-closing mechanisms, so they require a catch to keep the door from opening at unwanted times. In most cases, the catch should be installed at the top and near the outside end of the door.

Self-closing hinges do not require a catch, but you can add a high-end touch by installing a soft-close piston. This easy-to-install accessory stops a closing door about ½" before it hits the cabinet and then gently closes it against the cabinet, eliminating banging doors.

Catches & Soft Closers

Hinge-mounted soft-closers fit on a specific matching brand and model hinge.

Cabinet mounted soft-closers turn a door mounted on self-closing hinge into a soft closing door.

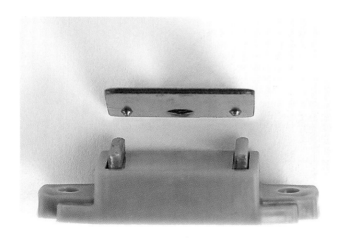

A magnet catch is the standard catch to use with any door that is not mounted on a self-closing hinge.

A touch latch pops open the door with a gentle tap on the front of the door – no knob or pulls necessary.

Built-Ins
for the Kitchen

Most kitchens already have more built-ins than any other room in the house—at least in North America, where wall-hung and base cabinets are installed as permanent fixtures in our houses. In much of Europe (although this is changing) the kitchen cabinets resemble home furnishings more than built-ins. Armoires and simple shelving carry the burden of storing pots, pans, dishes, and dry goods. But the opportunities for using built-ins in your kitchen go far beyond basic cabinets and countertops. A kitchen island (even one that rolls instead of being fixed) is probably the quintessential built-in. In this chapter you'll see how to fashion an island from a couple of base cabinets and some stock countertop. We'll also demonstrate a project that combines extreme functionality and economy with green remodeling, creating a rolling island from a salvaged metal cabinet and two slabs of granite.

In addition to cabinetry and islands, many kitchens contain (or have the potential to contain) pantries that are perfectly suited for built-in storage features.

But perhaps the most appealing kitchen built-in is the breakfast bar or banquette. In many cases installing a truly roomy one involves annexing some space from an adjoining room or even adding a small bump-out addition to your house. But installing a dedicated dining/relaxing/homework/newspaper-reading spot in a corner of your kitchen is an extremely popular project with great payback in coziness and utility. We show you two distinct but equally appealing ways to go about it.

In this chapter:

- Stock Cabinet Island
- Reclaimed Island
- Pull-out Pantry
- Banquette
- Country Diner

Stock Cabinet Island

Kitchen islands can be created using a whole range of methods, from repurposing an old table to fine, custom woodworking. But perhaps the easiest (and most fail-safe) way to add the conveniences and conviviality of a kitchen island is to make one from stock base cabinets. The cabinets and countertops don't have to match your kitchen cabinetry, but that is certainly an option you should consider. When designing and positioning your new island, be sure to maintain a minimum distance of 3 ft. between the island and other cabinets (4 ft. or more is better).

Tools & Materials ▶

Marker
Drill/driver
2 × 4 cleats
Pneumatic nailer and
　2" finish nails or
　hammer and 6d
　finish nails

2 base cabinets
　(approx. 36"
　wide × 24" deep)
Countertop
Drywall screws
Eye and ear protection
Work gloves

Two base cabinets arranged side-to-side make a sturdy kitchen island base that's easy to install. When made with the same style cabinets and countertops as the rest of the kitchen, the island is a perfect match.

How to Create a Stock Cabinet Island

1

Set two base cabinets side-to-side in position on the floor and outline the cabinet corners onto the flooring. Remove the cabinets and draw a new outline inside of the one you just created to allow for the thickness of the cabinet sides (usually ¾").

2

Cut 2 × 4 cleats to fit inside the inner outline to provide nailing surfaces for the cabinets. Attach the cleats to the floor with screws or nails. *Tip: Create an L-shaped cleat for each inside corner.*

3

Join the two base cabinets together by driving 1¼" drywall screws through the nailing strips on the backs of the cabinets from each direction. Make sure the cabinet sides are flush and aligned. Lower the base cabinets over the cleats. Check the cabinets for level, and shim underneath the edges of the base if necessary.

4

Attach the cabinets to the floor cleats using 6d finish nails. Drill pilot holes for nails, and recess the nail heads with a nail set. Make a countertop and install it on top of the cabinets. If your cabinets do not have back panels, cut them from ¼"-thick cabinet-grade plywood. Attach with brads and cover the edges with trim.

Reclaimed Island

A built-in, or any kind of cabinet, may be new to you without being new to the world. In these days of green building practices, repurposing salvaged material is regarded as perhaps the greenest way to build. And finding salvageable materials is easier than ever. Websites that allow buyer and seller to find each other directly make it possible to locate materials like flooring and cabinets almost instantly. Condition is a very important factor when you're shopping for used materials. The metal cabinet we eventually found for this project needed some clean-up, but was well-built and heavy with very little rust or damage. The fact that it is only 22" deep meant that it would fit nicely with the two 12"-wide granite slabs that will be used for the countertop.

Not every kitchen is large enough to accommodate an island. You should have roughly 36" of space between the island and the nearest wall or cabinet; you'll need more space if two people will regularly work on that side of the island. One way to make an island more versatile is to build it on wheels. An island that can be moved allows you to create more space when it's needed on any side of the island.

If you are using a wood cabinet or two to create a kitchen island, choose cabinets with face frames. They offer more options for adding paneling and they tend to be much sturdier.

Tools & Materials ▶

Base cabinet	Casters
Countertop	Spray paint
Corbels	Drill/driver with bits and
(shelf brackets)	wire brush attachment
Clear adhesive	Epoxy
Masonry screws	Eye and ear protection
Door hardware	Work gloves

A base and a countertop are the basic elements of a kitchen island made from salvaged material. Here, the parts that were located included a very sturdy metal cabinet that needed only a little sanding and a little paint to be a perfect base for the island. The countertop was fashioned by laying two narrow granite slabs together across the top. The resulting 1½"-thick countertop measures 24 × 48", and the overall height of the island, after casters were added to the base, is 38".

How to Make a Kitchen Island from Salvaged Materials

It should go without saying that any kitchen island you may cobble together from salvaged material will look and feel very different from the one seen here. So naturally, the techniques and strategies that make sense for your project will differ by an equal amount. Nevertheless, we've attempted to break this project down into general strategies that should have application in just about any effort to convert a base cabinet and a countertop into a functional, attractive island.

DISASSEMBLE & CLEAN

In most cases, the more you can break a cabinet down into its fundamental components, the easier it is to do a thorough job of rehabbing it. Stop short of breaking glued joints, but if a face frame can be removed and reattached easily after you sand it, then go for it. At a minimum, remove the drawers and doors and then pull off all the old hardware (photo 1) so it can be replaced or cleaned and reinstalled after the doors, cabinet and drawer boxes are refurbished.

On a metal cabinet such as this, you'll be cleaning with a wire wheel mounted in a drill (photo 2), not sandpaper. If you find a lot of rust, use a larger wheel than the one shown here and chuck it into a corded drill—you'll be at it for a while. If you find that the metal has rusted through at any point, you should probably reconsider investing any more time in that cabinet. Be sure to wear eye protection and a particle mask when cleaning metal with a wire wheel.

REPAIRS & IMPROVEMENTS

Now is the time to fix repairable problems and make modifications to the cabinet. This cabinet required little in the way of repairs, but we did add a pair of 5" shelf brackets at each side to function as corbels.

Remove the cabinet drawers, shelves, and hardware for cleaning and reconditioning.

Prepare the cabinet for painting or finishing by cleaning, sanding, or brushing off rust or loose paint. All of the failing material must be removed. Wipe down the cabinet with mineral spirits and a rag and let it dry completely before you begin paint application.

These help stabilize the countertop overhang, but their contribution to the island is mostly visual. Because the cabinet sides are metal, small bolts were inserted into guide holes and secured with nuts to fasten the brackets (photo 3).

PAINT OR REFINISH THE CABINET

A fresh coat of paint goes a long way toward improving the look of any cabinet. If you're using a solid wood cabinet, you also have the option of refinishing it. But if the cabinet sides are thin veneer over particleboard, painting is probably a better option. Whenever you paint metal, applying primer first is a good idea. Primers are more effective at inhibiting rust and corrosion than paint—even paint that's formulated for metal. And applying paint to metal is best done by spraying. For smaller jobs you can pick up a couple of cans of spray paint, but for larger jobs buy metal paint in cans and apply it with a sprayer such as an HVLP sprayer. Always wear eye protection and a respirator when spraying paint, and work in a well-ventilated space. Apply a coat of primer first (photo 4). Choose a tinted primer that's as close to the finished color as possible. Once the primer has dried, apply several thin coats of paint for the finish (photo 5).

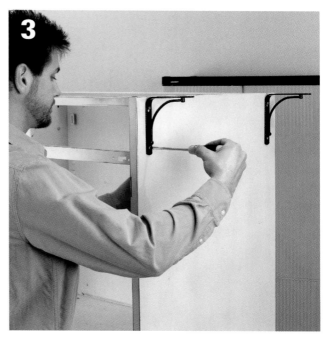

Make repairs or additions to the cabinet before finishing it. Here, metal shelf brackets are being attached to the sides of the cabinet to create a mounting surface for the countertop. Resembling corbels, the brackets also add decorative appeal. For this metal-sided cabinet, nuts and bolts were used to attach the brackets. If your cabinet has no back panel, add one.

Prime the cabinet carcase, doors, and drawer fronts with metal primer. On metal cabinets, you'll get the best results if you use spray-on primer formulated for metal, or if you use a power sprayer such as an HVLP sprayer. Spray paint only in a well-ventilated workspace. Apply at least one base coat of primer.

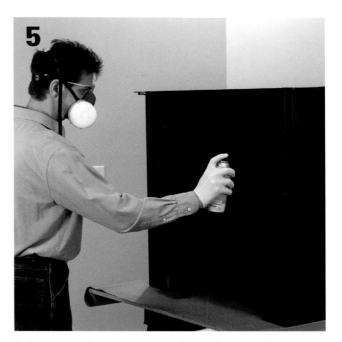

Paint the cabinet. For best results, apply several thin coats and use a paint formulated for metal (if your cabinet is metal).

(continued)

COMPLETE THE CABINET PREPARATIONS

If you plan to add casters or wheels to the island, now is the time to do it. The casters have a couple of advantages: they make the island easier to move out of the way if you need the floorspace, and they raise the height a couple of inches. This extra height can make the island more comfortable for use with bar stools, and the higher surface makes it stand out from the kitchen cabinets. The cabinet we used here was predrilled for wheels, so we simply found stem-type wheels that fit and installed them (photo 6).

Lastly, the cabinet doors need to be rehung (photo 7) and the drawers reinstalled with all hardware in place.

INSTALL THE COUNTERTOP

As much as the cabinet you use is likely to vary, the countertop for the island will differ even more from project to project. As with the cabinet, however, the strategy is simply to disassemble where you can, repair and improve the material, and secure it in place.

And keep in mind that you are by no means bound to using salvaged materials. Many island cabinet projects are made with an all-new material, often a slab of granite or another higher-end material that can be used as a featured surface in the kitchen.

The countertop we used is made from salvaged material: two 1½ × 12 × 48" slabs of granite. The slabs were in fairly good condition, so the only preparation they really needed was a nice buffing with a diamond-pad polishing wheel fitted onto an angle grinder (photo 8). Wear a respirator and goggles for this job.

Because our kitchen island is of the rolling variety, securing the countertop is important. The flanges at the top of the cabinet were in good condition, so we simply applied a thick bead of clear polyurethane adhesive caulk to the flanges and set the slabs into the caulk bed (photo 9). We also ran a bead of caulk along the seam where the slabs join and used padded bar clamps to draw the slabs together as the caulk set (photo 10). Finally, we used small masonry screws to secure the ends of the slabs to the metal brackets (photo 11).

Install casters or wheels to the cabinet base so it can be moved around the kitchen as needed. The casters also raise the height of the countertop an inch or two, which is generally a desirable effect.

Attach hardware, including drawer pulls, and reinstall the cabinet doors.

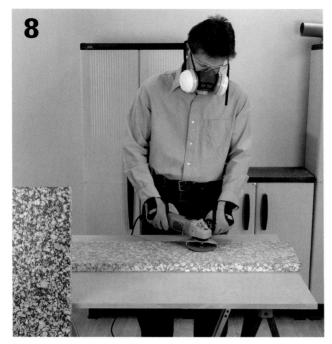

8

Clean up and rehabilitate the salvaged countertop. Here, two 12"-wide strips of 1½" thick granite are seamed together to create the countertop. Before installation, the top surface and edges of each strips are polished with a diamond wheel mounted in an angle grinder. Wear a respirator and eye/ear protection and work in a well-ventilated area.

9

Position one countertop strip on the cabinet with the overhangs roughly equal at the sides. Apply a bead of clear polyurethane sealant to the mating edge of the first strip.

10

Place the second countertop strip on the cabinet and press it firmly against the first. Use padded bar or pipe clamps to draw the strips together.

11

Anchor the countertop to the corbels (or to the mounting strips or flanges at the cabinet top). Use a masonry bit to drill holes for masonry screws. Apply a few drops of epoxy into the screw holes before driving for added holding power.

Pull-out Pantry

You can transform a small walk-in closet into a highly efficient pull-out pantry by replacing ordinary shelving with slide-out drawers. This is a great way to customize your kitchen and make it more user-friendly. You can find slide-out drawers for do-it-yourself installation at online sellers. Look for shelves and rollers that are rated to 75 or 100 pounds so you don't have to worry about overload.

There are many options when planning a project such as this. You can purchase shelf rollers that mount to the back of the closet and to the doorframe, or you can purchase shelf rollers that attach to the closet walls of the pantry. Each requires some modification to the closet structure. This project uses side-mounted rollers. If you have a pantry with sides that are set back from the door to accommodate shelves along the sides as well, you will need to build out the wall surfaces of the side walls to be flush with the door frame. It is best to create a solid wall surface, rather than simply framing. A solid wall surface prevents items from falling off shelves. Closet pantries come in many shapes and sizes. The pantry we are remodeling is a 24 × 24" pantry with only a slight setback and shelves only along the back.

Tools & Materials ▸

Stud finder	Lattice trim
Tape measure	Shelves
Level	Roller hardware
Table saw	Eye and ear protection
1 × 4	Work gloves
2 × 4	

A group of pull-out pantry trays dramatically increases the storage capabilities of the former closet.

How to Install a Pull-out Pantry

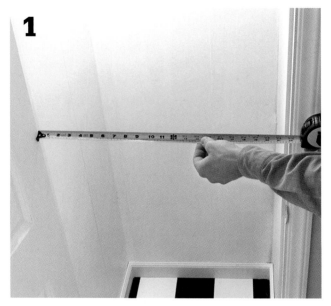

1

2

Remove any existing shelves from the closet. Use a stud finder to locate the studs on the side walls. Mark the locations of the studs. Measure the width of the door opening. Make sure to measure at more than one location in case the door opening is not true. Use this measurement to order the sliding shelves.

Mark the hardware locations. First, measure the setback of the wall from the door frame on each side. Include the doorstop trim in your measurement. This depth equals the thickness of the spacers you will need for mounting the roller hardware. Mark the locations of each shelf on the side walls. Use a carpenter's level or laser level to make sure your shelf marks are level.

3

4

Install spacer blocks. Cut the spacers to length from material of the appropriate thickness, as determined by your measurements. If you have a table saw, you can rip spacers to thickness, otherwise use combinations of 1 × 4, 2 × 4, and lattice trim to achieve the desired depth. Mount the spacers to the studs, centered over the shelf height lines.

Assemble and install the shelves. Mount the roller hardware to the spacers. Check for level using a carpenter's level or torpedo level. Install the shelves on the rollers.

Banquette

Almost everyone loves sitting in a booth at a restaurant—why not have one at home? Aside from providing an intimate, cozy setting for eating, games, or homework, a banquette or booth solves a critical space issue. An L-shaped booth eliminates the space needed to pull out chairs on two sides, plus, it allows children to sit closer together. Three kids can occupy booth space that is smaller than that required for two kids on two chairs. This project can create even more usable space if you add a roll-out storage unit under the booth seats.

This project creates an L-shaped, built-in booth in a kitchen corner. It does not show you how to redirect air vents or electrical outlets. Make sure you take into account the thickness of cushion foam if you plan on upholstering the backs. The plans assume you'll use 2" foam for seat cushions and back cushions. Thicker cushions will make the bench too shallow. Booth seating is most comfortable if the seats are 16 to 19" deep. The total height for the seat should be 18 to 19" to fit a standard 29"-tall table.

This project is designed to be painted, but if you wish to match your wood kitchen cabinets, you can use veneer plywood. Before beginning to build the booth, carefully remove the base shoe or molding

along both walls using a pry bar. Using a stud finder, mark the stud locations along both walls. Use masking tape to mark the stud locations to avoid marking on the wall surface.

Tools & Materials ▶

Tape measure	2 × 4 lumber
Stud finder	1 × 2 lumber
Pry bar	#8 screws
Circular saw	(1⅝", 2", 2½", 3")
Cordless screwdriver	1½" finish
Carpenter's square	head screws
Level	Finish nails
Bevel gauge	Edge banding
Compass	Trim molding
Jigsaw	Painter's caulk
Hammer	Wood putty
¾" paintable interior	Paint
plywood	Eye and ear protection
Masking tape	Work gloves

How to Build a Banquette

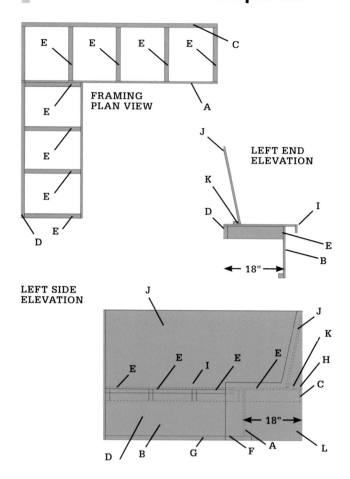

FRAMING PLAN VIEW

LEFT SIDE ELEVATION

LEFT END ELEVATION

Cutting List ▶

KEY	PART	SIZE	MATERIAL	NO.
A	Kickboard, long	15½" × 60"	¾" plywood	1
B	Kickboard, short	15½" × 42"	¾" plywood	1
C	Ledger, long	60"	2 × 4	1
D	Ledger, short	42"	2 × 4	1
E	Braces	16½"	2 × 4	8
F	Cleat, long	60"	2 × 2	1
G	Cleat, short	42"	2 × 2	1
H	Seat, long	22" × 60"	¾" plywood	1
I	Seat, short	22" × 38"*	¾" plywood	1
J	Seat backs	60" × 24"	¾" plywood	2
K	Seat cleats	60"*	1 × 2	2
L	End pieces	20" × 40"*	¾" plywood	2

* cut to fit

1

Cut the kickboards, ledgers, and braces to length.
Attach braces at each end of a ledger using two 2½" screws.
Evenly space the other braces and attach. Attach the
kickboard to the braces using 1⅝" screws. Use a carpenter's or
combination square to make sure all joints are squared.

2

Cut the long cleat to length. Measure 18" out from the
wall and draw a line parallel to the wall. Align the cleat with
the inside edge of the line and attach to the floor using
2½" screws.

(continued)

3

Turn the brace and the kickboard assembly right side up and place against the wall and cleat. Check for level and make sure that the kickboard butts firmly against the cleat. Attach the ledger to the studs using two 3" screws per stud. Attach the kickboard to the cleat using 1⅝" screws.

4

Assemble the short bench and attach it to the studs and cleat following steps 1 through 3. Make sure the second bench butts firmly against the first bench.

5

Attach the long bench top using 1⅝" screws. Center the screws over the braces and not the kickboard. Measure from the edge of the long bench to the outside edge of the brace for the exact length of the short bench. Cut and attach the short bench top.

6

Lean one seat back against the wall so the bottom edge is 6" from the wall. Slide the long back cleat behind the back and mark its location. Use a bevel gauge to determine the edge bevel for the back. Remove the back and bevel the edge with a circular saw or table saw.

7

Attach the cleat to the seat top, using 1⅝" screws. Make sure the cleat is parallel to the wall. Apply edge banding to the top edge of the back. Replace the back and attach it to the cleat using 1⅝" screws. Attach it to the wall studs using 2" screws.

8

Lean the second back against the wall with its base 6" from the wall. Slide the short back cleat behind the back and mark its location. Use a compass to scribe the angle of the long back onto the short back. Cut along this mark using a circular saw. Attach the cleat and seat back as in step 7.

9

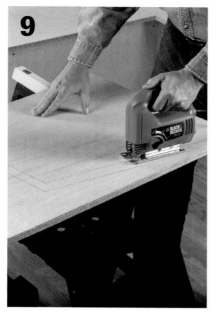

Place the end blanks against each end and trace the bench profile. Create a rounded or angular bench end that extends at least 1½" beyond the bench profile. This "lip" will prevent the cushions from slipping off the end. Cut the bench ends using a jigsaw.

10

Before attaching the ends, use a sander to break the pointed bench ends. Apply wood glue to the ends of the bench backs, kickboard, and bench tops. Attach the ends to the braces and bench using finish head screws every 6" to 8". Apply edge banding to the bench ends.

11

Attach the molding of your choice to the front edges of the bench with finish nails. Reattach the base molding if desired, or use trim molding to create panels, as pictured here. Fill all screw holes with wood putty, and sand smooth. Run a bead of painter's caulk along the joint between the bench top and back, the joint where the two bench backs meet, and between the bench back and wall. Smooth with a wet finger. Paint with a high-quality wood primer and satin, semigloss, or gloss paint. Make cushions, if desired.

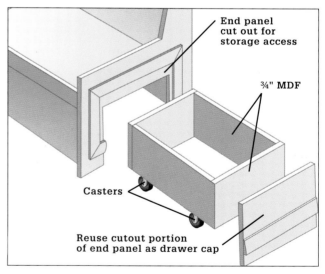

End panel cut out for storage access

¾" MDF

Casters

Reuse cutout portion of end panel as drawer cap

Variation: A wheeled drawer can add some storage space to your banquette. Before attaching the bench end, cut out an opening. Create a box with wheels and a drawer front to fit the opening.

Country Diner

Diners are traditional morning and late-night gathering spots, well-loved for being bright, friendly, and upbeat. They have been graciously kicking off our days for generations with hot food, great coffee, and warm company.

At home, breakfast nooks emulating diner booth designs and ambience are traditional gathering spots for morning coffee, preparing for the day ahead, or quiet evening conversations with the family. But at-home breakfast nooks have traditionally been interpreted as dark-stained, hard-edged plywood and somewhat monolithic designs. They lack the spunk, pop, and zip of the local diner and can overpower a small space.

The Country Diner combines the feel of the small-town diner with a modern flare that keeps up with your family. While we've used plywood for the bench supports, we wrapped it in warmer white pine that can be left clear, painted, or pickled. The seatboards and tabletop are made from edge-glued pine, but you can choose other materials if you prefer.

The tongue-and-groove pine paneling wrapping the benches adds contour and shadow lines while the bench's back grows right out of the seat. The ascending modern line delivers a sleek shape while the wide bench cap provides a nice capital along with a flat surface. The modern surface looks like it might once have supported white ceramic coffee cups and short-stacks back when diners looked like train cars, yet it's modern and tough enough to stand up to busy families that will use the country diner for a lot more than breakfast.

Tools, Materials & Cutting List

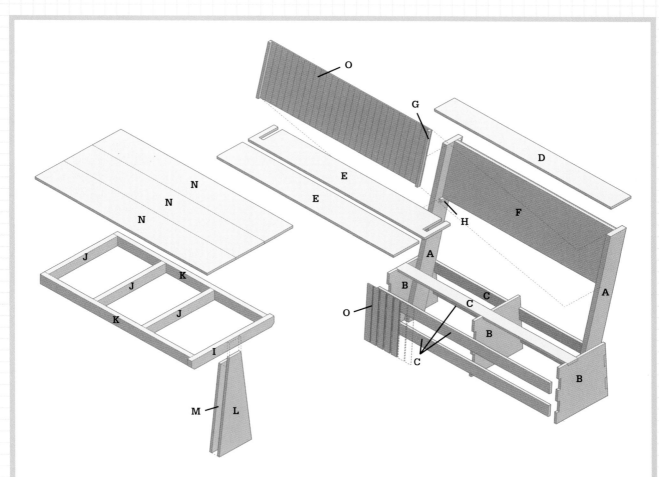

Tablesaw

Circular saw and
 shooting board

Jigsaw

Tape measure

Cordless drill/driver

Countersink bit

Combination square

Framing square

Miter saw

Table saw

Finish materials

(6) tabletop clips

(2) metal L-brackets

Screws

Nails

Glue

2) 2 × 8" × 10 ft. pine

4) 2 × 4" × 8 ft. pine

2) ¾ × 4 ft. × 8 ft. plywood

10) 1 × 4" × 8 ft. pine

2) 1 × 8" × 8 ft. pine

7) 1 × 10" × 8 ft. pine

1) 1 × 12" × 8 ft. pine

7) ⅜ × 3½" × 8 ft. pine
 bead-board

Eye and ear protection

Work gloves

KEY	PART	NO.	SIZE	MATERIAL
A	Bench upright	4	1½ × 5½ × 50	Rip from 2 × 8
B	Bench support	6	¾ × 18 × 18	Plywood
C	Bench strut	10	¾ × 3½ × 60	1 × 4
D	Seat back cap	2	¾ × 7 × 61½	1 × 8
E	Seat boards	4	¾ × 9 × 61½	1 × 10 (edge glue)
F	Back panel	2	¾ × 18 × 57	Plywood
G	Back cleat	8	¾ × ¾ × 18	Pine
H	Back cleat	4	¾ × ¾ × 2¼	Pine

KEY	PART	NO.	SIZE	MATERIAL
I	Table strut/front	1	1½ × 3 × 28	Rip from 2 × 4
J	Table strut/ledger	3	1½ × 3 × 24	Rip from 2 × 4
K	Apron	2	¾ × 3 × 52¼	Rip from 1 × 4
L	Table leg-front	1	¾ × 11¼ × 29¼	Cut from 1 × 12
M	Table leg-back	1	¾ × 11¼ × 26¼	Cut from 1 × 12
N	Tabletop boards	3	¾ × 10 × 60	Cut from 1 × 12
O	T&G cladding		⅜ × 6 × cut to fit	Beadboard

How to Build a Country Diner

MAKE THE BENCH FRAMES

The framework for the diner benches is made by fabricating six identical bench supports from plywood (three per bench). The supports are notched to accept five 1 × 4 struts that tie the supports together and provide nailing surfaces for the tongue-and-groove cladding. It's important that the bench supports be identical so the notches align correctly (otherwise the benches won't be square). The best way to make this happen is by fabricating a pattern that will serve as the template for cutting the other pieces. For greatest accuracy, use a router and a template bit to cut the bench supports. But if you are reasonably handy with a circular saw and jigsaw, you can use the first bench support as a pattern for marking and cutting the others.

Cut ten 3½" by 5-ft.-long struts from 1 × 4 pine. Then, to make the legs, cut ¾" plywood into six identical 18 × 18" blanks. Taper one of the blanks 1" at each side, so the top edge is 16" long (photo 1).

Lay out the ¾ × 3½" notches for the struts according to the diagram on page 85. Cut the notches with a jigsaw (photo 2). Clean up cut edges on the first bench support with a sander, then use the first support as a pattern for laying out the taper lines and notches on the rest of the workpieces.

Use a circular saw and straightedge guide to make taper cuts on the first bench support.

Carefully cut strut notches using a jigsaw. See drawing for locations. Using a cut-off from a strut as a tracing pattern will help you get accurate cuts.

Starting with the top strut, attach the struts to the bench supports, spacing the middle bench support exactly midway in each bench frame (photo 3). Use glue and wood screws driven in countersunk pilot holes to attach the struts to the bench supports.

Finally, cut the uprights. As shown, they are sized to be rip-cut to finished size (1½ × 5½") from 2 × 8 stock. Make sure to take stock from each side so you remove the slight bullnose edges that are cut at the lumber mill. Set your power miter saw to make 12 degree cuts. Trim the ends in parallel cuts to cut the uprights to length (photo 4). Attach the uprights to the inside faces of the outer bench supports, according to the placement information on page 85.

Assemble the frames for the benches by attaching the struts to the bench supports with glue and screws. Take care to keep everything square.

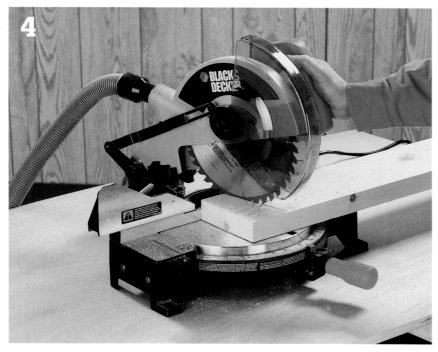

Use a miter saw to cleanly cut the angled seat upright prior to installation.

(continued)

ADD THE BENCH BACKS

The backs of the benches are made by installing a plywood back board between the uprights and then cladding the backboard on both faces with tongue-and-groove paneling. Start by cutting the cleat that you'll use to anchor the back board from 1× stock. Cut eight cleats (4 for each bench) to 18" and cut four to 2¼". Install a short cleat and a long cleat in an L-shape on the inside face of each upright (photo 5). The top of the long cleat should be flush with the top of the upright.

Using a table saw or a circular saw and shooting board, cut the back panels to size. Apply a bead of wood glue or adhesive and lay the panels into the L-shaped brackets created by the two cleats (photo 6). Drive countersunk 1¼" screws through the back panel and into the long cleat. Install the remaining trim pieces around the plywood seat backer.

CLAD THE BENCHES

The bases and backs of the benches are clad with pine tongue-and-groove paneling (sometimes called carsiding). Because the paneling on the ends of the benches that face the room conceals their edges, install the paneling that's attached to the bench

Fabricate an L-shape to accept the plywood bench back, then attach it to a bench upright.

A plywood backer gives the bench back its rigidity. Install the backer using adhesive and fasteners.

along its length first. Cut the first paneling board to length so the bottom end is slightly above the floor and the top ends are flush with the tops of the bench supports (the top ends will be concealed by the seatboard overhang). Then, trim off the groove to create a solid wood edge at the end of the bench. If you own a pneumatic nailer, use it to drive nails through the tongue of the first paneling board. Otherwise, hand-nail with 4d or 6d finish nails and set the heads with a nail set. Drive at least one nail into each strut that the paneling board is positioned over (photo 7).

Apply paneling to the front and back of the bench base. To clad the bench ends (you only need to clad the end that will face the room), hold a paneling board up against the end and trace the angled edge onto the back side of the paneling (photo 8). Cut along this line. Install this piece flush to the bench end. Fasten and complete paneling installation for the bench base. Also install tongue-and-groove paneling boards on the front and back sides of each back panel. The boards should be flush with the top and bottom of the plywood back panel.

Begin installing the tongue-and-groove cladding on the base of the bench. You'll find many options, but ⅜"-thick paneling (sold in 14 sq. ft. packages) is an economical choice.

Trace the angle of the tapered bench onto the back side of a piece of paneling and trim it to fit.

(continued)

Edge-glue two 9"-wide boards to make each seat board, and glue up three 10" boards for the tabletop. Use a biscuit joiner to help ensure that the boards are aligned and level.

Mark the cutout locations for the uprights onto the seatboard and cut them with a jigsaw.

Cut the seat back cap to length from 1 × 8 stock and attach it to the tops of the uprights and to the top of the bench back using glue and nails. The cap should overhang the front upright by about 1½" and be flush with the end of the bench that goes against the wall.

MAKE THE SEATBOARDS & TABLETOP

Both the seatboards and the tabletop are constructed by edge-gluing pine boards together. If you have access to a woodworking shop, you'll want to join the edges of the boards before you glue them together. Otherwise, make a nice, clean rip-cut along each edge with a sharp circular saw blade. For strength,

it is not necessary to use splines, biscuits, or dowels to reinforce the edge-glued joints, but any of these devices will assist with alignment. We used a biscuit joiner to align the glue-ups for both benches and the tabletop. Use at least three or four pipe clamps with jaw padding to clamp each glue-up together (photo 9).

After the glue has dried overnight, remove the clamps and sand the glue-ups to remove any dried glue squeeze-out.

The seat board must be notched to fit around the uprights. Position the boards on the seat base, flush at the wall end and overhanging about 1½" on the room-side end. Mark the location of the uprights onto

11

Attach the seatboards to the bench base with tabletop clips that secure glued-up panels but also allow for some wood movement.

There are many tricks you can use to conceal the gap at the bottom of the cladding, as well as the ragged ends of the tongue-and-groove boards. A skilled woodworker would bevel-rip trim moldings and install them with compound miter joints.

12

the seatboards, then remove them and make cutouts with a jigsaw (photo 10).

Tip the bench so the end that goes against the wall is flat on the floor. Attach a pair of tabletop clips to the inside of the bench base near each end, and a couple more on each side. (Tabletop clips are sold at woodworking stores and in woodworking catalogs. They offer a means for fastening tabletops and benchtops, while still allowing for some wood movement.) Attach the seatboard from underneath using the tabletop clips (photo 11).

Set the benches back down in their correct orientation. Cut filler strips of ¾"-thick pine and glue them into the gaps between the uprights and

the backs of the benches. Make sure the wood grain on the filler strips has the same orientation as the seatboards.

As a last finishing detail for the benches (other than sanding, painting, or staining), attach some type of wood trim to conceal the gap between the tongue-and-groove boards and the floor. If you use very small molding, such as screen retainer or very narrow base shoe, you can probably get away with attaching the molding as is, using butt joints at the corners. But for larger moldings (and for a more professional appearance) you'll need to bevel-rip the molding to allow for the taper of the bench base, as well as make compound miter joints at the corners (photo 12).

(continued)

Cut two identical leg halves, then trim 3" off the back one and face glue it with the front half to make a laminated table leg.

Attach the ledger for the tabletop to the wall with heavy-duty fasteners, such as counterbored lag screws driven at stud locations.

MAKE & INSTALL THE TABLE

The Country Diner table is designed to be affixed to a wall, supported by a ledger board on the wall side while a leg runs to the floor on the entry side. The length and width of the table are adjustable to suit your particular set-up but the fabrication techniques are the same. The dimensions specified in the drawing are 30" wide and 5 ft. long. The top of the table surface is 30" above the floor. Struts cut from 2 × 4 pine are added beneath the table for both looks and stability. We chose to glue up a rustic pine tabletop (which should get many coats of polyurethane varnish). You may prefer to have a tabletop fabricated from solid-surfacing, quartz, or natural stone.

Lay out and cut the leg from 1 × 12 pine. The front half of the face-glued leg should run full height

(29¼"), tapering from 4" at the top to the full width of the 1 × 12 (11¼") at the bottom. Make the back half of the laminated leg identical to the front, but then trim off the top 3" to create a ledge for the front tabletop strut (photo 13). Attach the ledgers (photo 14).

Rip 2 × 4 pine stock to 3" wide to make all four tabletop struts. Also rip-cut some 1 × 4 stock for the two aprons. Cut the front strut to 28" long and then clip the bottom corners to give the table both some "lift" and to create leg room as you enter the booth. Cut the ledger and the inner struts to 24" long. Also cut the aprons to 52¼" long from the 1 × 4 stock. Locate exactly where your table will be fastened to your wall by arranging the location of your benches and then centering the table between them. Using a cardboard cut-out to tailor exactly where you want the

15

Assemble the table frame all at once on a flat surface.

16

Clamp the table leg to the front strut temporarily and check the tabletop for level. Attach the leg to the strut with glue and screws.

table and benches also will help you customize your diner. Once you find the center of the table location, find the center of the ledger board and mark it. When installing the ledger board, line up these two marks for a perfect fit. At the ledger board location, strike a level line 29¼" above the floor. Find and mark the wall stud locations—try to locate the ledger so it spans two studs. Install the ledger on layout using glue and the proper fasteners (photo 14). Ideally, use a ⅜" × 3½" counterbored lag screw driven through the ledger and into wall studs, plus additional screws and/or toggles to stabilize the ledger.

On a flat surface, assemble the table frame by capturing the short struts between the aprons (photo 15). The front strut should be attached to the aprons with L-brackets on the inside joint.

Attach the tabletop to the struts with one tabletop clip near each end of each strut. Clamp the leg to the front strut and rest the other end of the tabletop on the wall ledger, which should fit between the free ends of the aprons (photo 16). Adjust the height of the leg if necessary, and then attach it to the front strut with glue and screws. Drive screws through the aprons into the ends of the ledger.

APPLY FINISH, POUR COFFEE
The Country Diner is shown here with a light wood stain and high gloss polyurethane finish, for ease of cleaning. Let all adhesives, finish and paint dry thoroughly before sitting down at the Country Diner for a slow home-cooked breakfast and time well-spent with family and friends.

Bathroom and Laundry

The bathroom may not be the first room you think of when planning a built-in. But with floor space almost always at a real premium, the bathroom can benefit nicely from a well-selected and well-designed built-in. Cabinetry and seating are the most obvious opportunities for built-ins in a bathroom. Other possibilities include shelving and customized tub aprons or jetted tub platforms.

Because bathrooms are high-humidity areas, select your materials and finishes wisely. Avoid particleboard, which can swell from moisture. Plywoods generally are fine as long as you make sure you do not end up with any exposed edges. Always choose better grades of plywood when making any built-in. Painted finishes are good choices in bathrooms. Glossier paints generally stand up better. For stained wood finishes, apply a polymerized topcoat such as polyurethane varnish.

Built-ins for laundry areas should be designed with the same basic parameters discussed for bathrooms above. In basement laundry rooms, make sure any wood panels are installed so their bottom edges are at least ½" or so above the floor.

In this chapter:

- Bathroom Window Seat
- Towel Tower
- Full-height Medicine Cabinet
- Bathroom Wall Cabinet
- Custom Laundry Center
- Compact Laundry Center

Bathroom Window Seat

Two things that many bathrooms don't have are adequate storage and a comfortable place to sit. This built-in, window-seat style bench is designed especially for use in a bathroom and will address both inadequacies. The drawer is deep enough to hold three or four large towels or a family-sized collection of toiletries. The bench is just the right height for taking a seat while you get dressed, and with the addition of a seat cushion is very comfortable. You can build the bench to fit a common cushion size or you can make your own cushion to fit the bench.

This bench design will work best in your bathroom if you customize it to fit the space you have. This will mean taking some measurements and calculating the dimensions for your project based on your available space. Also, some parts are optional depending on where the bench is installed. For example, if the bench is installed with a vanity directly against one side but the other side is open and exposed, then you will need to make a seat side edge piece and a side finished panel. But if the bench is captured between two taller objects, such as a vanity and a tub with a high sidewall, then you won't see the sides and do not need the side trim or finished panel.

Tools & Materials ▸

- Table saw or circular saw
- Router table or table saw
- Drill/driver
- No. 8 pilot and countersink drill bit
- Pneumatic brad nail gun and compressor (or hammer)
- Wood glue
- ¼"-dia. straight router bit or ¼"-wide dado blade set
- (1) ¼ × 2 × 4, birch veneer plywood (cabinet back)
- (1) ¾ × 4 × 8, birch veneer plywood (bench cabinet sides, top and bottom)
- (1) ½ × 4 × 4, Baltic birch plywood
- (1) 1× 6 × 8, solid wood (face frames)
- (1) 1 × 2 × 8, solid wood (seat edge)
- (1 pr.) 18" drawer slides
- 1¼" wood screws
- 2" wood screws
- 1" panhead screws and washers
- 1" brad nails
- 1½" brad nails
- Optional:
- (1) ¼ × 2 × 4, veneer plywood (finish end; same species as solid wood)
- Eye and ear protection
- Work gloves

This built-in bench tucks in snugly next to a vanity cabinet and in front of a window. Fitted with a comfortable cushion, it provides convenient seating for getting dressed, and the ample storage is always a welcome addition to a bathroom.

Cutting List

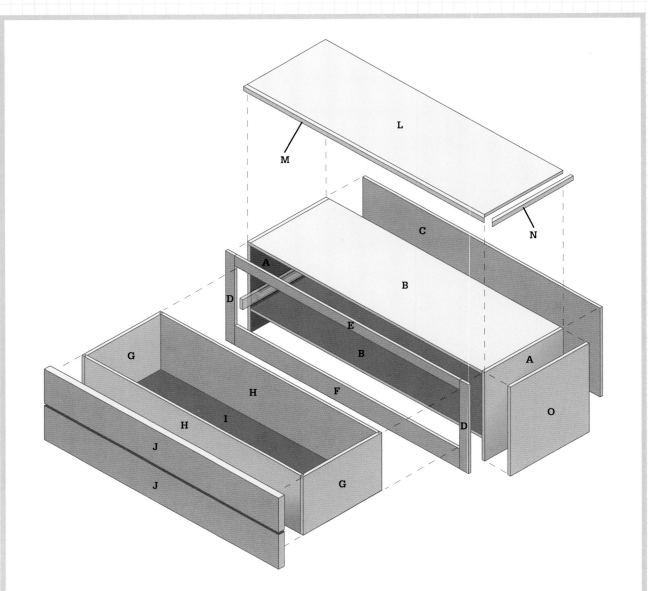

KEY	NO.	PART	DIMENSION
A	2	Cabinet sides	¾ × 16 × 18½"
B	2	Cabinet top/bottom	¾ × 18½ × (Y − 2)"
C	1	Back	¼ × 12¾ × (Y − 2)"
D	2	Stiles	¾ × 1¾ × 16"
E	1	Top rail	¾ × 1¾ × (Y − (3½))"
F	1	Bottom rail	¾ × 4 × (Y − (3½))"
G	2	Drawer box sides	½ × 9 × 18"
H	2	Drawer box front/back	½ × 9 × (Y − 5)"
I	1	Drawer box bottom	½ × 17½ × (Y − 5)"

KEY	NO.	PART	DIMENSION
J	2	Drawer fronts	¾ × 5½ × (Y − (2¾))"
K	2	Drawer slide cleats	¾ × 2 × 18¼"
L	1	Seat (without side trim)	¾ × 19½ × (Y + ¼)"
M	1	Seat front edge	¾ × 1 × (cut to fit)"
N	1	Seat side edge (Opt.)	¾ × 1 × 20"
O	1	Side finished panel (Opt.)	¼ × 16 × 18½"

* Y = width of opening for built-in (see step 1, next page)

How To Build a Bathroom Window Seat

ADJUST PROJECT DIMENSIONS (IF NEEDED)

Measure the width of the space where you intend to install the bench if you wish or need it to be sized differently than the project seen here (photo 1). To alter the width of the project cabinet, adjust the length (by a consistent amount) of the cabinet top, bottom and back panels, the top and bottom rails, the seat and the drawer widths.

Identify obstacles, such as electrical outlets or HVAC registers, that will have to be removed or relocated in order for the bench to be installed. Consult a qualified contractor if you are not comfortable making the necessary changes.

BUILD THE CABINET

Use a table saw or circular saw and straightedge guide to cut the cabinet sides, top, bottom, and back to size. Place the top, bottom, and sides on a flat work surface with the front edge down. Align the top face of the top with the top edges of the sides and position the top face of the bottom so it is 4" from the bottom edge of the sides. Attach the sides to the top and bottom with 2" flathead wood screws. Drill a pilot hole and countersink at each screw location. Adjust the cabinet so it is square and then attach the back with glue and 1" brads or 18-ga. pneumatic nails (photo 2).

Cut the face frame rails and stiles to size. Assemble the face frame. You can assemble the face frame with pocket screws (photo 3), dowels, or loose tenons. Attach the face frame to the cabinet with glue and 1½" brads. The outside edges of the face frame overhang the bench cabinet sides by ¼". The inside edges of the face frame overhang the inside faces of the cabinet sides by ¾".

Measure the width of the space where you plan to install the bench. Measure in several places and record the smallest measurement. Plug this measurement in as Y in the cutting list equations to determine your part dimensions.

Apply glue to the back edges of the top and bottom. Then place the back between the sides on the back edges of the top and bottom. Attach the back with 1" brads or 18-ga. pneumatic nails.

Use a pocket-hole jig and drill bit to bore the pocket holes in the rails. Then assemble the face frame with pocket screws.

(continued)

Place the drawer side face down on the router table and use a miter gauge to guide the piece through the cut. Cut a ¼ × ¼" dado located ¼" from each end of the inside face.

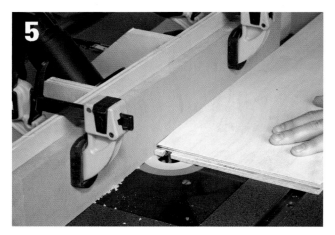

Cut the ½"-wide × ¼"-deep grooves that will contain the bottom in the front, back and side pieces. Cut the groove in two passes. Move the fence over ¼" for the second pass.

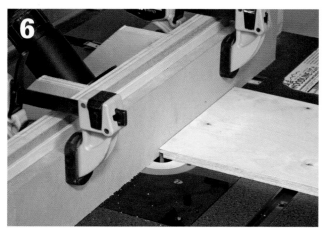

Cut the ¼ × ¼" rabbets in the ends of the front and back pieces. Place each piece face down and use a miter gauge to push it through the cut.

BUILD THE DRAWER

The drawers are constructed with ½"-thick Baltic birch plywood. The sides, front, and back are joined with dado-and-rabbet corner joints. These joints are easy to make with a router table and ¼" straight bit. You can also follow the same construction process and make these joints with a table saw and ¼"-wide dado blade set.

First, cut the dadoes in the ends of the drawer sides. Set the router table fence ¼" away from the edge of the bit. Set the bit height so the top is ¼" above the table. Cut dadoes across the ends of the inside faces of the drawer sides (photo 4).

It's common to use ¼"-thick stock for drawer bottoms, but for these wide drawers go ahead and use the same ½" plywood that is used to build the rest of the drawer parts. Cut the ½"-wide grooves that will contain the drawer bottom. These grooves should be cut in two passes. Set the fence ½" away from the edge of the bit. Cut a groove near the bottom of the inside face of each drawer side. Move the fence out ¼", so that it is now ¾" from the edge of the bit. Make another pass, widening the grooves to ½" (photo 5). Test the fit of the drawer bottom in the groove. If the groove is too narrow, then move the fence out slightly and make another pass to widen the groove.

The last cut for the drawer box joinery is the ¼ × ¼" rabbet in the ends of the drawer front and back pieces. Attach a sacrificial fence to the permanent router table fence. A sacrificial fence is a scrap piece of wood that protects the face of the permanent fence. Slide the fence in so that it is just touching the tip of the router bit blade.

Use a miter gauge to guide each workpiece through the cut. Test-cut a rabbet in a scrap piece first, to check how well the rabbet fits in the drawer side piece dado. Adjust the bit height to change the width of the rabbet and adjust the fence to change depth of the rabbet. Once you're satisfied with the fit, cut rabbets across the ends of the front and back (photo 6).

Dry-assemble the drawer, using clamps to hold the parts, to make sure all the parts fit together well. Then, re-assemble the drawer box using glue on the joints (photo 7).

MOUNT THE DRAWER

Next, cut and install the drawer slide cleats inside the bench cabinet. Attach them to the bottom of the cabinet sides with glue. The faces of the cleats should be flush with the inside edge of the face frames.

Mount the drawer slides on the cleats and drawer box. The front edge of the slide is flush with the front of the face frame. Mount the drawer box ¼" above the bottom of the bench cabinet.

Two narrow drawer faces are attached to the drawer box rather than one large face. Use a router and edge profile bit to shape the edges around the drawer faces. Choose a profile that matches or is similar to the profiles on your vanity or other bathroom moldings.

Use double-sided tape to hold the drawer faces in position against the drawer box. The drawer faces should overlay the face frame by ⅜" on all sides. Drive 1" panhead screws and washers through the inside of the drawer box front to attach the faces (photo 8).

MAKE THE SEAT

Place the cabinet in position, but do not secure it to anything yet.

Cut the seat ¼" wider than the finished width and ¼" longer from front to back than the cabinet. Making the seat a little oversize gives you the ability to scribe (trim to fit) the seat to fit any inconsistencies in the wall or other adjacent surfaces.

Next, rip cut 1"-wide strips of ¾"-thick stock for the edging pieces. If only the front edge of the bench seat will be exposed, then you only need one piece of seat edging. Cut the ends so that the front edging is flush with the sides of the seat. If you use side edging, then miter cut the ends of the edging where the front and side edging pieces connect. Attach the edging with glue and 1½" brad nails, aligning the top edge flush with the top of the seat.

FINISH & INSTALL THE BENCH

Once you are satisfied with the fit, return the bench cabinet and seat to the shop. Sand all surfaces smooth. Remove the drawer faces and apply three coats of water-base polyurethane to the drawer box. Apply finish to the cabinet, seat, and drawer faces. If you apply paint, choose a satin or semi-gloss sheen. If you choose to apply a stain or other natural finish, then apply a little on some scrap wood from the same batch to test the color before you apply it to the actual workpieces.

After the finish is dry, return the bench cabinet and seat to the bathroom. Use shims to fill any gaps between the side of the bench and the vanity or other flat surface and attach the cabinet to the vanity with 1½" screws. Be careful not to drive the screws completely through the vanity side. Finally, drive 1¼" screws up through the underside of the bench cabinet top to attach the seat (photo 9).

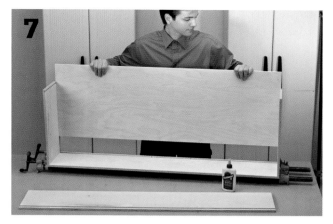

Assemble the drawer with glue, adjusting the parts and clamps as necessary to make them square (perpendicular and parallel) to each other.

Attach faces–Bore ³⁄₁₆"-dia. pilot holes through the drawer box fronts. Then attach the drawer faces with No. 8 × 1" panhead screws and washers. Use 4 to 6 screws per drawer face, depending on how large the faces are.

Attach the top to the bench with 1¼" screws. An optional final step that will make the bench look more integrated with the vanity is to wrap the base with the same base molding that is used on the walls.

Towel Tower

If there's one place in the house that collects everybody's stuff, it's the bathroom. Towels, clothes, cleaning supplies, even laundry. But some fancy design work using a refrigerator wall cabinet and some cool carpentry create a niche spot that can provide a central location for all kinds of different items. Suitable even for small bathrooms, this towel tower also adds texture and color to the space. Another added benefit to this project is the seating provided by the seatboard top on the cabinet.

The beadboard backing for this project is made with painted ⅜"-thick tongue-and-groove pine, sometimes called carsiding. More advanced carpenters may prefer to make their own custom beadboard from hardwood and give it a custom wood finish.

The base for this project is an over-the-fridge-size wall cabinet (sometimes called a bridge cabinet). At 15" high, it is within the range of comfortable seating heights. But if you prefer a slightly higher seat (and many people do), build a 2 × 4 curb for the cabinet to rest on (see the Window Seat project on pages 96 to 101 for information on how to install a seat in a 2 × 4 curb).

To conceal the seam where the towel tower meets the floor, we trimmed around the base with base shoe trim, mitering the corners. We used the same trim stock to conceal the gap where the seatboard meets the tongue-and-groove paneling. Here, however, we added small miter returns to the ends of the base shoe.

Tools, Materials & Cutting List

Router and bits
Drill/driver and bits
Circular saw
Straightedge
Level
Caulk gun
Hammer
Pneumatic nailer (optional)
32 sq. ft. tongue-and-groove paneling
(2) 1 × 6 × 8 ft. pine
3 ft. crown molding
½ sheet ¾"-thick MDF
12 ft. quarter-round molding
Towel hooks
Fasteners
Eye and ear protection
Work gloves

KEY	NO.	DESCRIPTION	SIZE	MATERIAL
A	1	Over-fridge cabinet	15h × 30w × 24d	
B	1	Seatboard	¾ × 25 × 32*	MDF
C	8	T&G paneling	⅜ × 5½ × 71½"**	Pine
D	2	Towel hook backers	¾ × 5½ × 27"	Pine 1 × 6
E	3 lin. ft.	Crown molding	Cut to fit (w/miters)	Pine
F	12 lin. ft.	¼-round molding	Cut to fit	Pine

* Finished size: requires slightly larger board
  for machining
** Length equals distance from top of seatboard to
  ceiling minus ½"

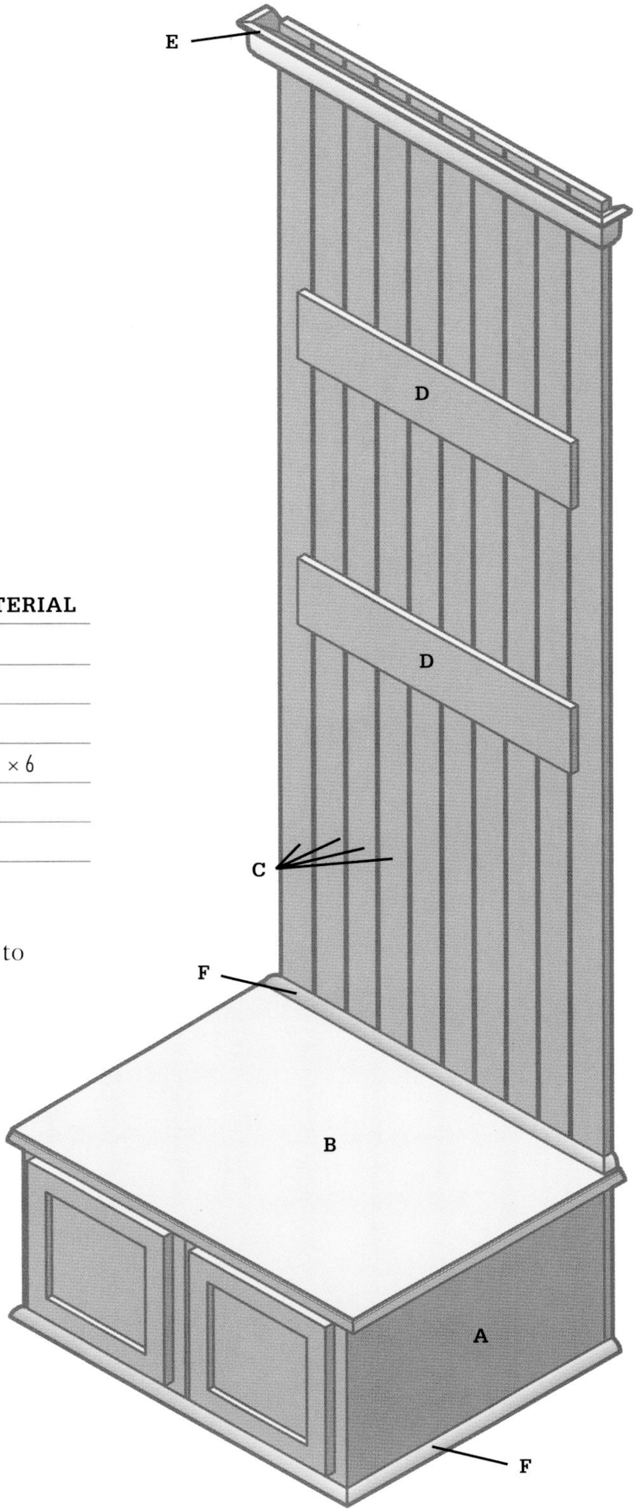

How to Build a Towel Tower

INSTALL THE BASE CABINET

Begin by making the seatboard that tops the refrigerator cabinet. Cut a piece of medium density fiberboard (MDF) so it is 1" wider than the cabinet and a couple of inches longer front-to-back (make it about 26" if using a 24" cabinet as shown here). Mount a piloted ogee or roundover bit (or other profiling bit of your choice) into your router and shape the front and side edges (photo 1). You'll probably get a little bit of blow-out at the back edge, which is why it's recommended that you make the workpiece a couple of inches too long. Once you've routed the profiles, trim the back edge so the front overhangs the cabinet by 1". Coat all faces and edges with primer and at least two coats of paint.

Attach the seatboard with screws driven through the mounting strips on the cabinet top and into the underside of the seatboard. The back edge of the seatboard should be flush with the back edge of the cabinet and the overhang should be equal on the sides. Since this cabinet is small, it might be best to clamp the blank in location on the cabinet, then turn the cabinet on its back so you can access the fastener locations more easily (photo 2).

Install the cabinet in the project location. Baseboard and any other obstructions should be removed from the project area. Slip shims below and behind the cabinet as needed to make sure it is level and plumb. Attach the cabinet to the wall by driving 2" wallboard screws through the cabinet back at wall stud locations (photo 3).

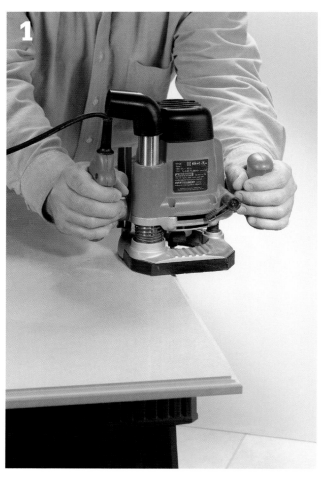

Rout a profile, such as an ogee or roundover, into the sides and front of the seatboard. Use a router table if you have one, otherwise hand-machine it with a piloted profiling bit.

Flip the cabinet upside-down so you can more easily attach the seatboard with screws.

3

Drive screws through the back of the cabinet at the marked wall stud locations.

INSTALL THE PANELING

The backer board for the towel tower can be made from a number of building materials, while retaining the beadboard appearance that lends a bit of country style to this project. The easiest and cheapest product you can use is beadboard paneling: thin sheet stock that comes in 4 × 8 ft. panels. You'll find a wide range of colors, patterns, and qualities in the beadboard sheet stock, including some that is presized to around 42" for installation as wainscoting. The cheapest material has a printed pattern layer laminated over hardboard. The better quality material has hardwood veneer over a plywood or lauan backing. We chose real tongue-and-groove boards made from pine. With actual dimensions of ⅜ × 5½", the carsiding product we used has enough depth to create a convincing profile but is still relatively inexpensive.

Because it is very unlikely that the strips of carsiding will be exactly the same width as your base cabinet once they're installed, you'll need to rip-cut the outside boards to fit the project area (it is better to rip-cut both outer boards an equal amount than to take everything out of one of the boards). To gauge where to make your cuts, assemble enough boards to cover the width of the cabinet and lay them out on a flat surface (photo 4). Mark the centerpoint of the middle board and measure out half the distance in each direction. Make rip-cut lines at these points.

4

Midpoint

Lay out the tongue-and-groove carsiding boards in a row, with the tongues fitted into grooves. Measure out in one direction (half the width of base cabinet) from a midpoint line in the center board.

(continued)

5

Clamp a straightedge over a tongue-and-groove board, placing a piece of scrap plywood underneath as a backer. Rip-cut the board to the correct thickness for the filler piece.

6

Press the trimmed filler board to the wall, seating it in construction adhesive, at the left edge of the panel area.

Before ripping the boards, trim all of your carsiding stock so it is ¼" to ½" shorter than the distance from the seatboard to the ceiling. Then, trim the outer carsiding boards to width using a table saw (make sure you are trimming off the correct edge, be it tongue or groove). If you have access to a tablesaw, use it to make the cuts. Otherwise, use a circular saw and a straightedge cutting guide. With thin stock like this, cutting a scrap wood backer board along with the workpiece will result in a cleaner cut. Make the rip cuts (photo 5) and sand the edges if necessary to smooth out the cuts.

Use a 4-ft. level to extend plumb lines directly up the wall from the outside edges of the seatboard. Then, mark the wall stud locations on the seatboard and ceiling with tape. Begin installing the carsiding on the left side, with the left trimmed board. In most cases, the tongue will be preserved on this board and should be oriented inward (photo 6). Apply a heavy bead of construction adhesive to the back of the board and stick it to the wall. If it happens to fall over a wall stud, nail it in place by driving a finish nail (or, preferably, a pneumatic brad) through the tongue at an angle. The nails should be countersunk enough that they do not obstruct the groove of the adjoining board.

Continue installing boards until you reach the right edge (photo 7). Use plenty of adhesive and drive several nails when you hit a wall stud. If none of the wall studs align beneath carsiding joints, tack the board that falls over a wall stud by face-nailing once at the top and once at the bottom. In most cases, you should be able to tack each board at the top too, nailing through the face and into the stud wall cap plate (this will be concealed by crown molding anyway). *Note: The mounting boards for the towel hooks will help hold the carsiding in place once they are attached at stud locations.*

Cut the towel hook backer boards to length from 1 × 6 stock. For a more decorative effect, cut a chamfer profile into the edges (or just the top and bottom edges) with a router and chamfering bit.

Install the backer board by driving 2½" deck screws, countersunk, at wall stud locations. Fill the screw holes with wood putty.

Install quarter-round molding around the bottom of the cabinet to conceal the gap where it meets the floor. Also install quarter-round to conceal the gap where the carsiding meets the cabinet seatboard (photo 8). Make mitered returns at the end for a more finished appearance.

Attach crown molding to the top of the project (photo 9), also making a mitered return to finish the ends of the molding.

Sand all wood surfaces and fill nail holes, screw holes and visible gaps with wood putty. Paint the project with primer and at least two coats of enamel paint. Finally, attach the towel hooks to the towel hook backers.

Drive a pneumatic brad through the tongue of one of the far-right boards, and into a marked wall stud.

Install quarter-round or base shoe molding at the top edge of the seatboard where it meets the carsiding. Tie the molding back to the wall with mitered returns.

Attach crown molding at the top of the project, creating mitered returns at the ends. Mark the ceiling joists with tape.

Full-height Medicine Cabinet

A classic medicine chest is a great storage solution for several reasons. First, it keeps your stuff right where you need it, near the sink. Second, its multiple shallow shelves store small items in plain view, so there's no digging around for everyday necessities. Built-in medicine cabinets are recessed into the wall, minimizing the use of precious room space. And finally, most medicine chests serve a dual purpose in the bathroom by having mirrored doors.

Indeed, the basic medicine chest design leaves little room for improvement. That's why the bathroom cabinet in this project takes the same great features and simply makes more of them. This built-in cabinet has a 3½"-deep storage space yet projects only ¾" from the wall (not counting the overhead crown molding). Inside, it's loaded with adjustable shelves, so it can hold not only prescription bottles and toiletries, but also taller things like shampoo bottles and cleaning supplies. And the cabinet's door is tall enough to accommodate a full-length mirror—a great convenience feature for any bathroom.

The box of this medicine cabinet is sized to fit into a standard 14½"-wide space between wall studs. With the drywall cut away, the box slips into place and mounts directly to the studs. Then you trim out the cabinet to fit the style of your bathroom. The traditional molding treatment shown here is only one way to do it; you can add any type of molding and extras you like using the same techniques. Another option is to build a similar cabinet that mounts to the surface of the wall, as shown in the Variation on page 113. With this design, you're not limited by the width and depth of a stud cavity, but the cabinet does occupy a small amount of floor space.

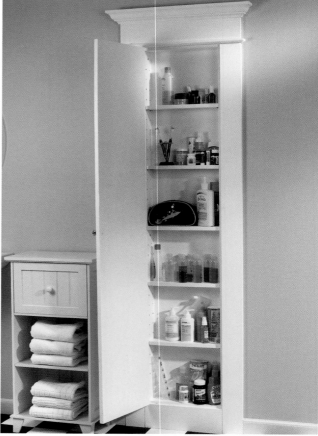

Using less than two feet of wall space, this built-in cabinet offers more than enough room for a household's medicines, toiletries, and backup bathroom supplies.

Tools & Materials

Work gloves
Eye and ear protection
Tape measure
Circular saw
Miter Saw
Drill/driver
Clamps
Chisel
Mallet
Drywall saw
Putty knife
Level
Drill guide
Paint Brush
Caulk Gun
AC plywood (¼", ¾")
Poplar (1 × 4, 1 × 6)
Shims
Pegboard
Shelf pins
Door catch
Finish nails (1½, 2¼")
Construction adhesive
Mirror (approx. 10 × 48")
Wood putty
Finishing materials
Crown molding

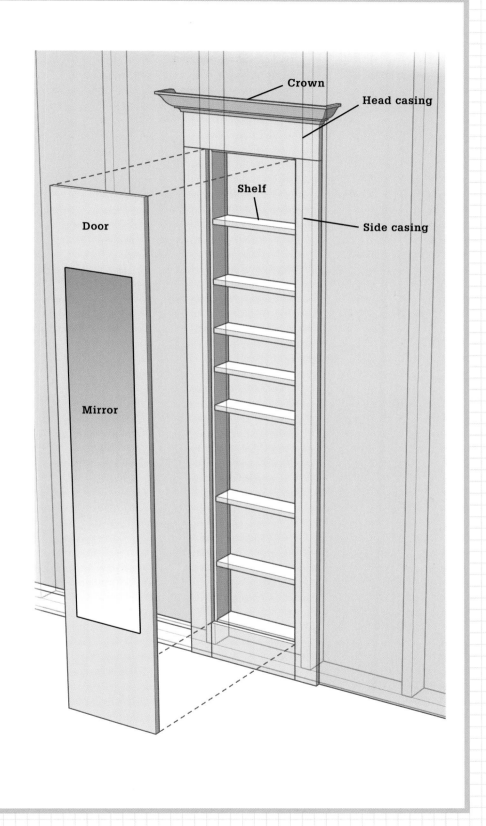

How to Install a Full-height Medicine Cabinet

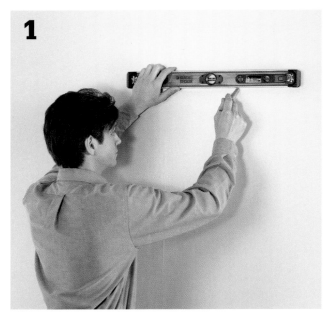

1

Determine the overall height of the finished cabinet (with trim), then subtract the height of the trim assembly above the door. Add ¼" to find the height of the cabinet box. Measure up from the floor and draw a level at the installed box height between two wall studs where the cabinet will go.

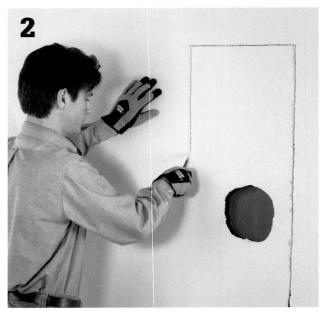

2

Cut one or more exploratory holes in the drywall between the host studs, then examine the stud cavity to make sure that no electrical cables, plumbing pipes, or other elements intersect the cavity. Cut out the drywall between the studs, up to the level line.

3

Measure between the studs to determine the overall width of the cabinet box. *Tip: If the studs aren't plumb, leave some extra room for adjusting the cabinet when you install it (see step 8, on page 111).*

4

Cut the two side pieces for the cabinet box to length, 1½" shorter than the floor-to-top dimension from step 1. Cut the top piece, middle shelf, and bottom shelf 1½" shorter than the overall cabinet width. Cut the adjustable shelves ³⁄₁₆" shorter than the fixed shelves. Cut the back panel equal to the overall width of the cabinet and the same length as the sides.

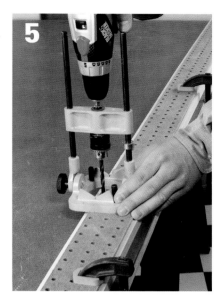

Drill holes into the box sides for the adjustable shelf pins using pegboard with ¼" holes as a drilling guide. Align the pegboard so the hole pairs are evenly spaced across each side piece, and drill the holes to the depth of the pin plus the hardboard using a stop collar on the bit. Make sure the hole pairs are matched on both pieces so the shelves will hang level.

Assemble the cabinet box by fastening the sides over the ends of the top and bottom and middle shelves using glue and 2" screws. Position the bottom shelf so its top face is 4½" from the ends of the sides. Position the top piece flush with the top ends of the sides, and position the middle shelf roughly halfway in between.

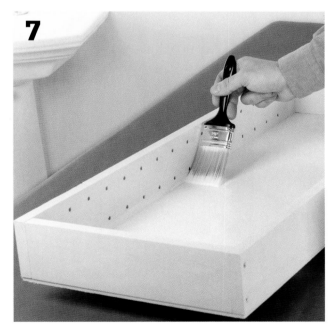

Fasten the back panel to the assembly with 1" screws. Align the box sides and top with the panel edges as you work to ensure the assembly is square. Prime all sides of the box, including the back, and then add two top coats of paint to the box interior and front edges of the side pieces.

Set the box into place between the wall studs and check it for plumb. Use cedar shims to fill any gaps along the studs and to adjust for plumb. Fasten the box sides to the studs with 2" screws so the front edges of the sides are flush with the surface of the drywall.

(continued)

Cut, prime, and install the 1 × 4 side trim and 1 × 6 base trim with 2¼" finish nails, overlapping the sides of the box by ¼". Add the bead and head trim over the ends of the side trim. Install the crown molding over the head trim with 1½" finish nails, mitering the corners and adding return pieces back to the wall. Measure the opening created by the trim pieces and cut the door panel ⅛" narrower and shorter than the opening.

Fill any voids in the panel edges with wood putty or auto body filler, then sand the panel smooth and prime and paint the panel. Paint the cabinet trim, and fill and paint over the screw heads inside the cabinet box.

Mount the door to the side trim with three small butt hinges or a single piano hinge. Mortise-in butt hinges for a flush fit. Install a drawer pull or knob, then add a magnetic door catch onto the door and cabinet box side.

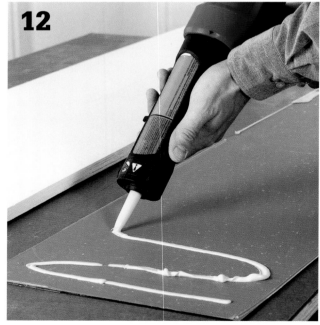

Have the mirror cut to the desired size by a glass dealer. Secure the mirror to the front of the door panel with a recommended adhesive (you can remove the door if you used butt hinges). If desired, add trim around the edges of the mirror. Install the adjustable shelves.

Variation: Surface-mount Cabinet ▶

This surface-mount cabinet is a freestanding unit that you secure to the wall for stability. You can use this design if a recessed cabinet is impractical or undesirable for your situation. The basic construction steps are similar to those of the recessed unit:

1. Assemble the cabinet box with a fixed top, middle shelf, bottom shelf, and back panel. If you want a deeper cabinet, you can substitute 1 × 6 lumber for the box sides, top, and shelves.

2. Add 1 × 2 side trim pieces to the front of the box, then add a 1 × 4 head trim piece and a 1 × 6 base trim piece between the side trim. Cut the door to fit between the side, head, and base trim pieces.

3. Add the crown molding, then prime and paint all parts. Hang the door with hinges secured to the side trim.

4. Secure the cabinet to a wall stud with screws driven through the back panel. Wrap the base of the cabinet with baseboard trim for a built-in look. Add quarter-round molding along the cabinet sides to hide the edges of the back panel and any gapping caused by wall contours.

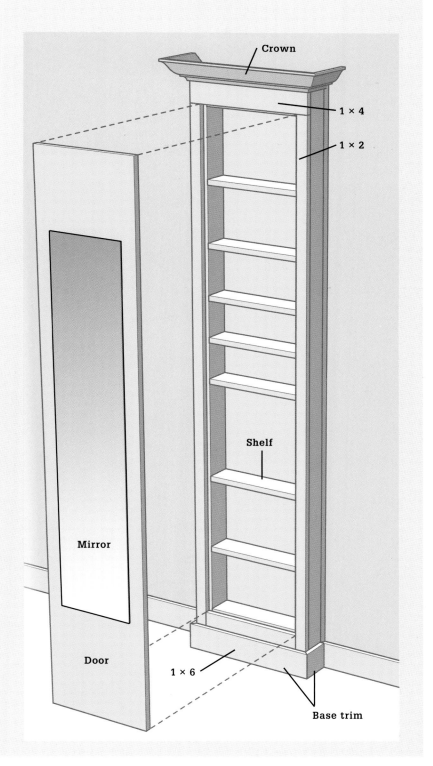

Bathroom Wall Cabinet

Cabinetry and casework are fundamental to making built-ins and bookcases. This small wall-hung cabinet is a useful item for bathroom or kitchen, and it is a great project for a beginning carpenter to develop some basic cabinetry skills. It is also extremely inexpensive to make. The entire case, including the top, can be built from an 8-ft.-long piece of 1 × 10 wood (you'll need a little extra material for the shelving and the towel rod). The mitered frames applied to the fronts of the door give the look and feel of a raised panel door, without any of the fuss.

We built the version of the cabinet you see here out of No. 2 and better pine and then gave it an orangey maple finish. You can choose any lumber you like for this, even sheet stock such as MDF, and apply a clear or a painted finish. For a traditional look, choose a white enamel paint. Be sure and apply several thin coats of polyurethane varnish, especially if the cabinet will be installed in a wet area like a bathroom.

Tools, Materials & Cutting List

Eye and ear protection
Work gloves
Pencil
Tape measure
Combination square
Router, profiling bit
Circular saw
Miter saw
Jigsaw
Clamps
Hammers
Drill/driver
¾" Spade bit
(1) 8 ft. 1 × 10
(1) 4 ft. 1 × 8
(1) ¾" Dowel
(1) Screen retainer
   molding (10 lineal ft.)
(2) Door knobs
(2) Touch latches
(2) Hinges
Drywall or deck screws
Finish nails
Finishing materials

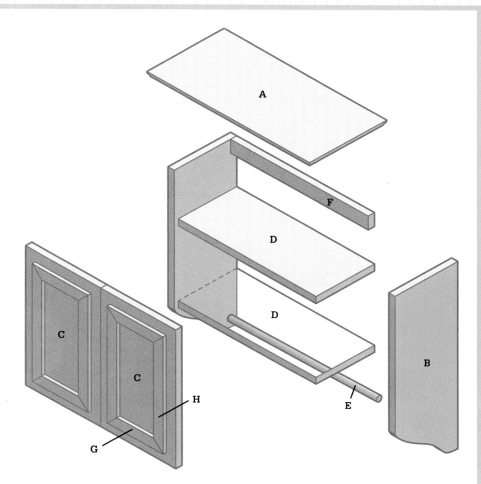

PART	NO.	DESC.	SIZE	MATERIAL
A	1	Top	¾ × 9¼ × 19½"	1 × 10 pine
B	2	Sides	¾ × 7½ × 20¼"	1 × 10 or 1 × 8 pine
C	2	Doors	¾ × 9 × 15"	1 × 10 pine
D	2	Shelves	¾ × 7 × 16½"	1 × 8 pine
E	1	Towel rod	¾ × 18"	Dowel
F	1	Wall cleat	¾ × 1½ × 16½"	1 × 2 pine
G		Door molding (short)	¼ × ¾" × cut to fit	Retainer molding
H		Door molding (long)	¼ × ¾" × cut to fit	Retainer molding

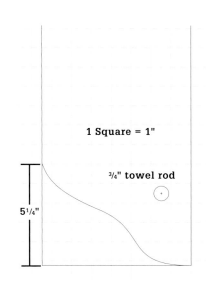

1 Square = 1"

¾" towel rod

5¹/₄"

How to Build a Bath Cabinet

PREPARE THE STOCK

This bathroom cabinet can be made almost entirely from a single 8-ft. 1 × 10 using basic tools. (If you buy a 10-footer you'll have enough stock to make all but the middle shelf, which can easily be made from another piece of wood or even glass.) At your local lumberyard or building center, hand-select a board (pine or another wood: No. 2 or better pine is much cheaper than other types in most areas). Look for a board that's straight and free from defects like large knots or waney (bark-like) edges. When you get the board home, trim around ¼" off each end (never trust the factory ends—they're seldom squarely cut).

Cut the top board to 19½". Then, cut an ogee profile into the front edge and the side edges using a piloted ogee bit (photo 1). Be sure to attach blocking at the back edges to prevent the router bit from turning the corner and cutting into the back edge. If you don't own a router, you can simply hand-sand a roundover on the bottom edges or you can try cutting a chamfer profile with a hand plane (a tricky job, but a good skill to develop).

Next, cut the stock for both doors to length, plus a little bit (cut a piece around 30½" long) and either rip-cut the edges to get a clean surface on both sides or sand them or plane them smooth (photo 2). The final width of the material should be 9". Once the stock is prepared, cut the doors to length.

Shape a decorative profile into the top using a router and piloted ogee bit. Do not remove more than ¾" of material along the bottom edges.

Use a tablesaw, circular saw, plane, or sander to get straight, crisp edges on the cabinet door stock.

Cut the stock for the cabinet sides to width (7½") or select a piece of 1 × 8 stock and simply sand the edges. Then enlarge the pattern on page 115 using a photocopier to make a hardboard template of the curved shape. Trace the profile on one side, referencing up from the bottom of the board (photo 3).

Clamp the two sides together so the ends and edges all are flush. Then, cut out the profile in both pieces at once using a jigsaw (photo 4). Make your cuts just short of the cutting line. When the cut is finished, do not unclamp the ganged sides. Use a sander or a round file to smooth the cuts and remove waste wood exactly up to the cutting lines. An oscillating spindle sander is the best tool here. Another good idea is to mount a drum sander in a drill

press. Lastly, before you unclamp the sides, locate the centerpoint for drilling the ¾"-dia. dowel hole for the towel rod. Drill the hole with a ¾" spade bit, making sure to slip a backer board underneath the bottom board to prevent tearout when the bit exits the workpiece (photo 5).

ASSEMBLE THE CABINET

Assembling your bathroom cabinet is a simple process of gluing, clamping, and nailing. It is worth investing in a couple of 24" bar clamps or pipe clamps if you don't own them already, although another option is to use screws instead of nails to fasten the parts, relying on the screws to provide clamp-like pressure to the glue joints. Only do this if you are painting the cabinet.

Photocopy the pattern on page 157 and use it to make a hardboard template guide to trace the profile onto the bottom of one cabinet side.

Cut both side profiles at the same time, staying just outside the cutting line so you can sand precisely up to the cutting line.

Still with the sides ganged together, drill a ¾"-dia. hole for the towel rod, using a backer board under the bottom side.

(continued)

Press the two shelves and the cleat between the cabinet sides after applying glue to the ends.

Reinforce the glued joints with 6d finish nails driven into pilot holes.

Glue the ends of the towel rod into the holes in the cabinet sides and then pin it in place with a finish nail driven through the back edge of each side.

Miter the corners of screen retainer molding and nail and glue decorative frames to the door fronts.

Lay the side boards on a flat surface, lying parallel and on their back edges. Cut the 1 × 2 cleat and the 7"-wide shelves to length (16½"). *Note: The shelves are ½" narrower than the sides to provide clearance for the doors. Position the cleat and the shelves between the cabinet sides, making sure everything fits squarely. Then, apply wood glue to the ends of all three parts and clamp them between the cabinet sides (photo 6). Then, clamp the sides with bar clamps and check with a framing square to make sure the sides are square to the shelves. Also make sure the middle shelf is perpendicular to the sides.*

Before the glue sets (about 15 minutes) drive three 6d finish nails through the cabinet sides and into each shelf end. Drive a pair of nails into the wall cleat (photo 7). It is always a good idea to drill pilot holes

for nailing. Insert the towel rod into the holes in the cabinet sides. Once it is in position, push it inward ½" or so on one side and apply glue to the inside surfaces of the dowel hole. Then, press the rod from the other side to reveal about ½" of the hole and apply glue. Push the rod so the ends are flush with the cabinet sides and the drive one 4d finish nail through the back edge of each cabinet side and into the dowel to pin it in place (photo 8).

HANG THE DOORS

Cut strips of half-round screen retainer molding to make decorative frames for the fronts of the cabinet doors. Miter the corners (photo 9). The frames should be inset 1" or so from the door edges on all sides. Attach the frames to the door fronts with glue and a few ½" wire brads.

Note: Now is a good time to finish or paint your bathroom cabinet. Be sure to sand all the surfaces well and make sure you remove any dried glue—the stain and finish won't stick to it. We used a gel-type Swedish maple stain on our pine cabinet because it imparts a rich color (it resembles orange shellac) and disguises the fact that pine has very little wood grain. We added three thin coats of wipe-on varnish after the stain dried (photo 10).

Hang the cabinet doors with 1½" brushed chrome or nickel butt hinges (photo 11). In most cases, you'll need to cut shallow mortises in the cabinet sides and door for the hinges. Center the cabinet top so the overhang is equal on the side and the back is flush with the cabinet back. Attach the top by driving a few finish nails through it and into the top edges of the cabinet sides, as well as into the top edges of the wall cleat (photo 12). You're better off not using glue to attach the top.

Install a touch latch at the top of each door opening.

HANG THE CABINET

Locate wall studs in the installation area. Where possible, position the cabinet so it hits two studs. Attach the cabinet with wood screws driven through the wall cleat and into the studs (photo 13). If you only have one stud available, drill a ¼" hole through the cleat, as far from stud location as you can get and still have access. Position the cabinet against the wall and mark the hole onto the wall by inserting a finish nail into the hole. Remove the cabinet and install a plastic screw insert at the hole location. Replace the cabinet and drive a screw so it catches the insert. Then re-level the cabinet and screw the wall cleat to the wall at the stud location. Drill pilot holes in the doors and install door knobs with screws.

Apply your finish or paint the cabinet before you hang the doors and install the cabinet top.

Hang the doors. Use care to position the doors so the outside edges are flush with the outer faces of the cabinets sides. The tops should be about ⅛" below the top edges of the cabinet sides.

Attach the finished cabinet top to the cabinet sides with 4d finish nails.

Hang the cabinet. If you don't have access to two wall studs, use a plastic screw insert or other hanging hardware in addition to fastening the wall cleat to a wall stud.

Custom Laundry Center

Many of the areas where we do our laundry lack two important features: organization and lighting. This laundry center is a self-contained built-in that functions like a room within a room, adding both storage space and task lighting for what can otherwise be a disagreeable task. It is built from a base cabinet and butcher block countertop on one side of a 24"-wide, 7 ft.-tall stub wall, and a bank of wall cabinets on the other side of the wall. The cabinets are designed to fit above a washer and dryer combo. The structure includes a ceiling with light fixtures mounted over both sides, and a switch wired into the stub wall to control the lights. The walls are built from inexpensive wall sheathing and, along with the ceiling, are clad with easy-to-wash tileboard that adds brightness while contrasting with the maple wood of the cabinets. The edges of the center are trimmed with clear maple.

If you are creating your built-in laundry center in a room that did not previously house your washer and dryer, arrange for and have installed the hookups for both appliances before you build. If you are not experienced with plumbing and wiring, hire a plumber and electrician to run any new drain, supply, dryer vent, or electrical service lines. Also make sure to identify potential sources for electrical service to power the lights (in the version seen here, we installed recessed canister lights over the countertop and above the washer and dryer).

Tools, Materials & Cutting List

Tape measure
Level
Pencil
Square
Drill/driver & bits
Powder-actuated nailer
Hammer or
    pneumatic nailer
Jigsaw
Circular saw
Miter saw
Eye and ear protection
Work gloves

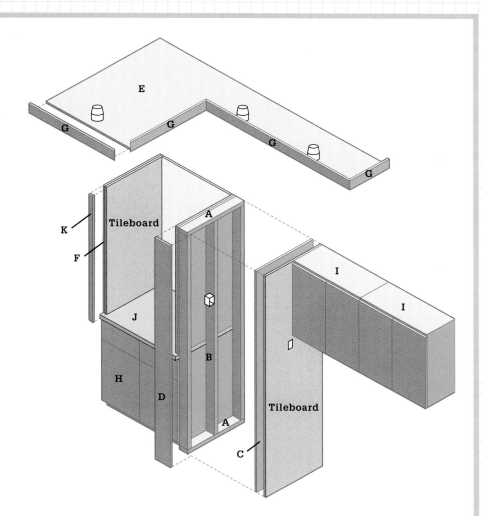

(1) 4 × 8 × ½ plywood or OSB (wall sheathing)
(1) 4 × 8 × ¾ plywood or OSB (ceiling)
(3) 4 × 8 sheets tileboard with an 8-ft. inside corner
    strip and panel adhesive
(3) Recessed canister light with trim kit
(1) Clothes rod (24") with mounting hardware
1 × 2, 1 × 4 and 1 × 6 maple for trim
32" wide base cabinet
Butcher block countertop for base cabinet
(2) 30" 2-door uppers
Electrical box, switch, 14/2 romex, switch plate
End panel for upper cabinets (if unfinished)
Panel adhesive
Drywall or deck screws
Nails
(4) 1½ × 3½ × 96 pine

PART	NO.	DESC.	SIZE	MATERIAL
A	2	Cap/sill plate	1½ × 3½ × 23¾"	2 × 4
B	3	Stud	1½ × 3½ × 79"	2 × 4
C	1	Full wall	½ × 23¾ × 81¾"	Sheathing
D	1	Wall cap	¾ × 5½ × 79"	Maple 1 × 6
E	1	Ceiling	¾ × 24 × 100"*	Sheathing
F	2	Half wall	½ × 23¾ × 43"	Sheathing
G	4	Top trim	¾ × 5½ × cut to fit	Maple 1 × 6
H	1	Base cabinet	34½" h × 36" w	Stock cabinet
I	2	Wall cabinets	12 × 30 × 30"	Stock cabinets
J	1	Countertop	1½ × 25 × 36	Countertop
K	1	Trim	¾ × 1½ × 43"	1 × 2

*Can be pieced together from two boards joined
    above A

How to Build a Laundry Center

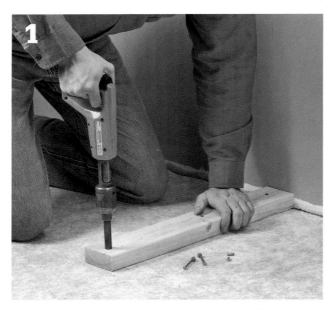

Attach the base plate for the stub wall perpendicular to the wall, allowing space between the stub wall and the corner for your base cabinet. Use pressure-treated wood if your laundry is in the basement.

After toenailing the studs to the base plate (and facenailing the stud next to the wall if possible) attach the cap plate, making sure the studs are vertical.

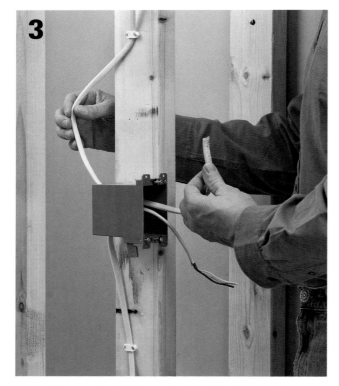

Run cable and install boxes for the light fixtures. Hire an electrician to do this if you are not experienced with home wiring. (Note that you will need to apply for a permit and have your wiring inspected.)

FRAME THE STUB WALL

This built-in laundry center is anchored by a 7-ft.-tall, 24"-wide stub wall, so start by framing the wall. Measure out from the corner the width of your base cabinet (36" here) and draw a 24"-long reference line perpendicular to the wall. Cut a 2 × 4 wall plate to 23¾" and attach it to the floor. If you are building in a basement with a concrete floor, use pressure-treated lumber for the base plate and attach it by driving concrete nails with a powder-actuated nailer (photo 1).

Cut three 2 × 4s to 79" long and attach them to the base plate by toe-nailing (reinforce connections with L-brackets if you wish). Then, cut a 23¾"-long cap plate and nail it to the free ends of the studs with 16d common nails (photo 2). If you are installing overhead lighting, run cable from the power source (don't hook up the wires yet) through the studs and to an electrical switch box mounted to the wall frame (photo 3). Also run sheathed cable from the electrical box and out through a hole in the wall cap plate. Run enough cable to reach the light fixtures. We wired the fixtures in series: the power lead goes to the canister light over the counter first, then runs to the other lights. If you prefer to switch the light independently, install a double gang box and cable for two switched circuits.

INSTALL THE BASE CABINET

We designed this laundry center with matching base and upper cabinets. Install the base cabinet between the stub wall and the corner (photo 4). You can use just about any type of countertop material you wish. We selected maple butcher block because it can resist water and heat, requires very little maintenance, and makes a nice surface for folding laundry. Plus, it matches the maple cabinets and trim boards. To secure butcher block, you need to drill extra-large guide holes through the nailing strips on the base cabinet and attach the countertop with a short screws and washers (photo 5). This allows the material to move as it expands and contracts, which butcher block will do.

INSTALL THE WALLS

At the very least, you'll need to cover both sides of the stub wall for your laundry center. If the walls in your installation area are fit for covering with tileboard, you won't need to create any additional wall surfaces. In part to create an attachment surface for the clothes rod, we also installed a wall surface on the left side of the project area. The wall surfaces are created by attaching sheathing to the wall studs and then bonding water-resistant tileboard over the faces of the sheathing with panel adhesive. Cut a piece of wall sheathing that's the same width as the stub wall and reaches the same height when placed on the countertop surface. Attach the sheathing to the side of the countertop area (photo 6). Insert a couple of

Install the base cabinet between the stub wall and the corner, making sure it is level and securely attached to at least one wall.

Attach the countertop material (butcher block is seen here). The countertop should be flush against both walls and it should overhang the base cabinet slightly.

(continued)

furring strips between the sheathing and the wall to create airspace.

Clad the stub wall on both sides with wall sheathing (photo 7). Make a cutout for the switch box. The sheathing on the countertop side should rest on the countertop. Slip a couple of shims underneath the wall sheathing on the washer and dryer side so the sheathing does not contact the floor, which can lead to wicking of water.

Cut pieces of tileboard to fit the wall surfaces and attach them with panel adhesive. Attach inside corner strips cut to fit at the inside corners of the countertop area (photo 8). Rub the tileboard surfaces aggressively with balled-up towels to help seat the tileboard into the adhesive.

HANG THE UPPER CABINETS

The upper cabinets should be mounted on the walls so their tops are flush with the top of the stub wall and they butt up against the stub wall at the side. Attach with a ledger system or by driving cabinet screws through the mounting strips and into the wall at stud locations (photo 9). If the exposed cabinet end is not finished, purchase and install an end panel to match the cabinet type (or, make one from ¼" plywood).

MAKE & INSTALL THE CEILING

You'll find that it's easiest to cut the ceiling board, attach the tileboard, and mount the light fixtures all before you attach the ceiling assembly to the stub wall and cabinets. Start by cutting the ceiling board to size and shape from a piece of 4 × 8 sheathing (photo 10). We designed the ceiling to be 24" wide above the cabinet, then to cut back to 18" wide over the wall cabinets, which creates a 6" overhang above the cabinets so an undercabinet light fixture can be mounted if you wish. As shown, the side-to-side width of the structure is over 96", so a single piece of 4 × 8 ft. wall sheathing won't cover it. You'll need to make the ceiling in two pieces, so size the pieces so the seam falls in the middle of the top plate for the stub wall.

Attach wall sheathing to the wall to create a nailing surface at the wall end of the countertop area.

Clad the stub wall on both sides with wall sheathing, making sure to cut out accurately for the switch box.

Cover the wall surfaces with tileboard, which is attached with panel adhesive and set by rubbing with a rag.

Install the wall cabinets so they are level and their tops are flush with the top of the stub wall.

Cut the ceiling to size and shape from a piece of sheathing (you'll need multiple pieces if your project is more than 8 ft. long).

(continued)

11

Mount the hardware and box for the light fixture to the ceiling panel before you install the ceiling.

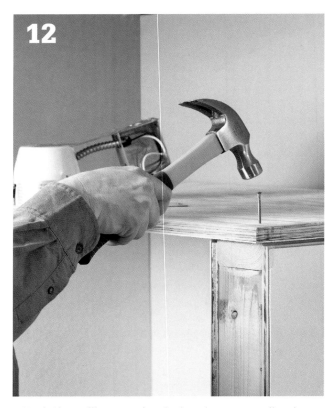

12

Attach the ceiling panel to the laundry center wall and the cabinets.

13a

13b

Make the wiring connections at the light fixtures (left) and at the switch (right).

Attach tileboard to the ceiling panel on the face that will be facing downward. Then, plot out the locations for the light fixtures and mount the housings and ceiling boxes to the back of the ceiling panel as needed (photo 11). Set the ceiling panel over the laundry center and attach it with nails or screws driven into the top plate of the stub wall and the cabinet sides (photo 12).

HOOK UP LIGHTS & INSTALL TRIM

Be sure the power source is turned off and make the wiring connections at the light fixtures and at the switch (photos 13a and 13b). Consult an electrician according to your skill and comfort level with wiring. You will need to have a wiring inspection before making the final hookup at the power source.

Cut pieces of 1 × 4" maple to make the top trim. Miter the outside and inside corners as you install the trim. Use a pneumatic nailer to attach the trim if you have access to one (photo 14). Attach the vertical trim members to cover the wall at the left side of the project and the end of the stub wall (photo 15). Scribe as necessary and rip the stub wall trim to fit. For a more finished look, round over the edges of the vertical trim pieces slightly.

Finally, slide in, level, and hook up your washer and dryer (photo 16). Make sure to follow local codes for water and drain supply and for venting your dryer.

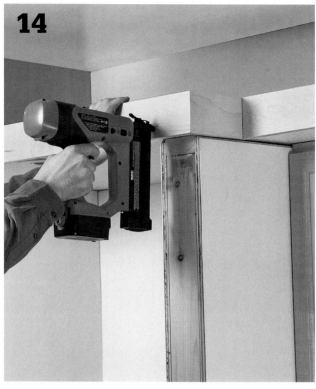

Trim out the top of the structure with 1 × 4 hardwood to conceal the gap beneath the ceiling panel. If you prefer, you can use crown molding here.

Attach the vertical trim boards, butting them up against the top trim and keeping the bottom slightly above the floor. Apply a finish and top coat to the trim boards as desired.

Install your washer and dryer (or have your appliance dealer install them for you).

Compact Laundry Center

While there may be no scientific evidence to prove it, we all know that there's a direct correlation between the quality of a laundry room space and how much we dread doing the laundry. Cramped, cluttered, or poorly arranged rooms slow the work and add a general sense of unpleasantness. And things get complicated when you can't complete the laundry tasks in the laundry room—you have to hang up your sweaters to dry over the bathtub and do all the folding on the kitchen table.

If this sounds familiar, you'll be glad to know that it doesn't take much to turn an ordinary laundry area into an efficient storage and work center. Nor does it take a lot of space. The project shown here requires only about nine feet of wall area, including where the washer and dryer go. And with a few extra feet available on a nearby wall, you can add a hideaway ironing board that folds up into a recessed cabinet when not in use.

Tools & Materials ▸

Work gloves
Eye and ear protection
4 ft. level
Drill
Circular saw and
    straightedge guide
Drywall saw
Plumb bob
Stud finder
Household iron

30"w × 24"h
    and 36"w × 30"h
    melamine-laminate
    wall cabinets
3½" heavy-duty
    wood screws
¾" melamine-covered
    particleboard
    (laminated on
    both sides)

Polyurethane glue
Coarse-thread drywall
    screws (1¼", 2")
Melamine-laminate edge
    tape and stickers
Hanger rod with
    mounting brackets
Lumber (1 × 2, 2 × 2)
Deck screws (3½", 2½")
2¼" finish nails

48"-long post-formed
    laminate countertop
    (straight section)
Countertop end cap kit
¾" particleboard
Wood glue
Ironing board cabinet
    for recessed
    wall mounting
Drop hook (optional)

What every laundry room needs: dedicated areas for ironing, hanging, folding, and stacking clothes, plus convenient spaces for holding point-of-use supplies and for stored items that you want to keep clean.

How to Create a Laundry Center

1

Mark the cabinet locations onto the wall, including level lines to represent the cabinets' top edges. Standard cabinet height is 84" above the floor, but make sure the washer door won't block the hanging shelf. Locate and mark all of the wall studs behind the cabinet locations.

2

Assemble the cabinets, if necessary. Position each cabinet with its top edge flush to the level line, drill pilot holes, and fasten through the back panel and into the wall studs with at least four 3½" heavy-duty wood screws (or install according to the manufacturer's directions).

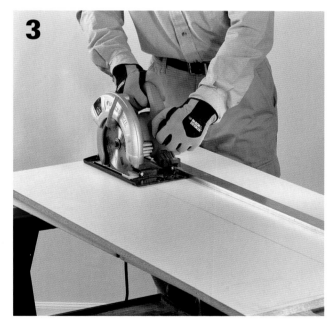

3

Cut pieces of ¾" melamine-covered particleboard for the hanging shelf. Cut the top and bottom pieces equal to the cabinet depth × the cabinet width minus 1½". Cut the side pieces equal to the cabinet depth × the overall shelf height (as desired). Cut the back panel equal to the cabinet depth × the shelf height minus 1½" in both directions.

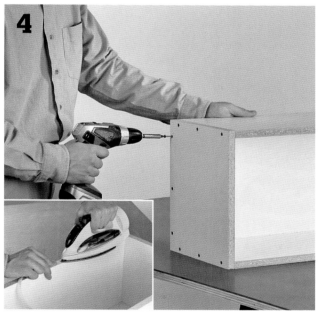

4

Assemble the shelf with polyurethane glue and 2" coarse-thread drywall screws or particleboard screws. Cover any exposed front edges and screw heads with melamine-laminate edge tape and cosmetic stickers (inset). When the glue has cured, mount the shelf to the bottom cabinet panel with 1¼" coarse-thread drywall screws driven through pilot holes.

(continued)

5

Mount the hanger rod to the sides of the cabinets using the provided screws. Locate the rod as close as possible to the front edge of the cabinets (without hindering door operation) and as high as you can comfortably reach.

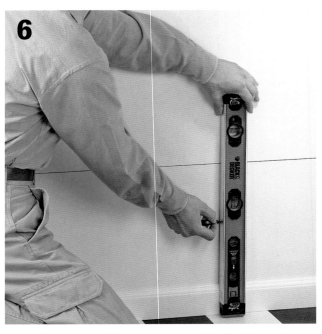

6

Mark the layout of the countertop and shelf unit onto the wall. Draw level lines at 34½" and at the desired height for the shelf top minus ¾". Draw plumb lines for the end panel at 46½ and 47¼" from the side wall and for the shelf support at 22⅞ and 23⅝" from the side wall. Also mark all wall studs in the area.

7

Following the layout lines, cut and install 2 × 2 wall cleats for the countertop along the back and side walls. Fasten the cleats to the wall studs with 3½" deck screws. Cut and install 1 × 2 cleats for the shelf, shelf support, and end panel using 2½" deck screws or drywall screws.

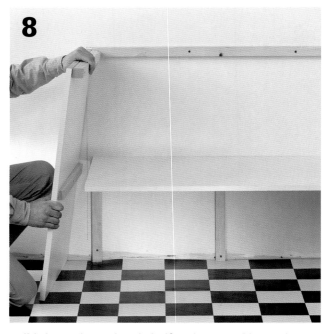

8

Build the end panel and shelf to size at 34½" long × the countertop depth minus ¾". Cut the shelf at 46½" long × the same width as the end panel. Add a 2 × 2 cleat flush with the top edge of the end panel. Fasten the shelf and end panel to the wall cleats with polyurethane glue and 2¼" finish nails. Fasten through the end panel and into the shelf edge with 2" screws.

9

Cut the shelf support to fit underneath the shelf. Notch the back edge to fit around the 1 × 2 wall cleat, then install the support to the cleat and shelf with glue and 2¼" finish nails.

10

Prepare the countertop by cutting a stiffener panel from ¾" particleboard to fit inside the edges on the underside of the countertop. Fasten the panel with wood glue and 1¼" screws. If desired, install an end cap kit onto the end opposite the side wall following the manufacturer's directions. Set the countertop in place and secure it to the 2 × 2 cleats with 2" screws.

11

Begin the ironing board cabinet installation by locating two adjacent wall studs and drawing level lines to mark the top and bottom of the wall opening. Make sure there's no wiring or plumbing inside the wall cavity, then cut the drywall along the stud edges and the level lines using a drywall saw.

12

Fit the cabinet into the wall opening and secure it to the wall studs using the recommended screws. *Tip: Add a drop hook on the inside of the cabinet door for hanging up ironed clothes (inset). The hook drops down against the door when not in use.*

Bedroom & Spare Room Built-Ins

Cabinets and loft beds are natural built-ins for a bedroom. But because spare bedrooms so frequently are used for purposes other than (or in addition to) sleeping, more task-specific built-ins also come into play. A home office or a craft center are two good examples where built-ins convert a spare bedroom into a task room, but still can leave the space usable as a guest room.

Closet space is critical in a bedroom. A clever built-in can provide all new organized storage space, as with the closet cabinets project or the kneewall cabinet, where a dresser is set into the dead space behind a half-height kneewall on a second floor. Built-in techniques also can be used to organize an existing closet so the space is used more efficiently.

For the ultimate in bedroom built-ins, create a loft bed. With some smart planning and careful work you can build a loft that creates open workspace below without making your bedroom feel like a dormitory.

In this chapter:

- Closet Cabinets
- Bed Surround
- Loft Bed
- Closet Organizing System
- Closet Home Office
- Kneewall Cabinet
- Hobby Center

Closet Cabinets

More closet space is at the top of the wish list for many homeowners. Adding more square footage isn't the only solution; sometimes the best approach is to reconfigure the space you already have. The side recess inside many closets is a space with potential that is often overlooked. This area can be difficult to access behind the things you have hanging or stacked in the main closet opening. A great way to improve the usefulness of this space and add an architectural element to your bedroom is to open up the wall next to the closet door and install a built-in cabinet.

This version combines a top cabinet area with adjustable shelves and five drawers underneath. You can substitute a door or drawer front style to match your décor.

If you plan to apply a natural wood finish, then select solid wood and veneered plywood that are the same species. If you plan to paint your cabinet, then select paint-grade plywood, such as birch, and solid wood that is easy to machine and takes paint well, such as poplar. The cutting list and materials list for this project provide the materials necessary to build one cabinet. If your cabinet will be less than 17" wide, then you can cut all four parts from a single 4 × 8 sheet of plywood or other cabinet grade sheet good.

Note: This project involves removing wall framing. Submit building plans to your municipal inspections department for approval and to obtain a permit.

Tools & Materials ▸

Table saw
Drill/driver
Miter saw
Edge-banding iron or old household iron
Random orbit or finish sander
¾" × 2 × 4 plywood (door)
¾" × 4 × 8 plywood (cabinet)
½" × 4 × 8 plywood (drawer sides)
¼" × 4 × 8 plywood (cabinet back, drawer
   bottoms and side base trim)
(2) 1 × 4 × 8-ft. solid wood
(1) 1 × 6 × 8-ft.
2" flat-head wood screws
(10) No. 6 × 1" pan head screws
18 ga. × 1" brad nails
(1 pr.) inset European hinges
(5 prs.) 22" full extension drawer slides
Eye and ear protection
Work gloves

Cutting List

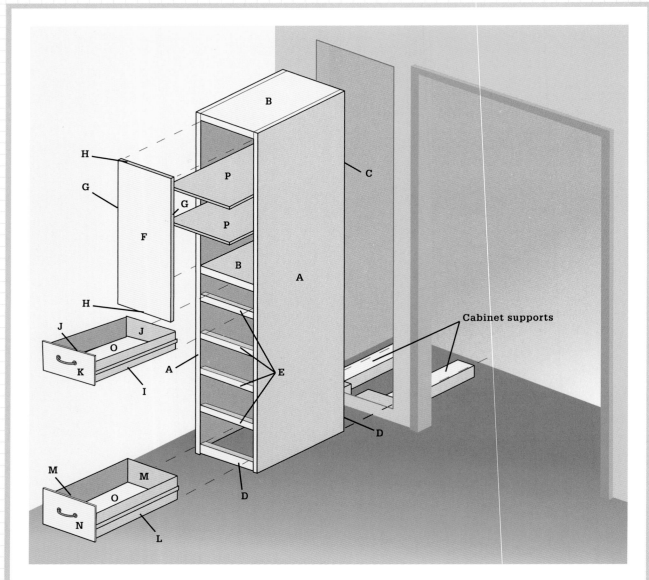

KEY	NO.	DESCRIPTION	DIMENSIONS
A	2	Cabinet sides	¾ × 23¾ ×
B	2	Cabinet top/shelf	¾ × (Y-2) × 23"
C	1	Cabinet back	¼ × (Y-½) × 77½"
D	2	Bottom rails	¾ × 1¾ × (Y-2)"
E	4	Narrow rails	¾ × 1¼ × (Y-2)"
F	1	Door panel	¾ × (Y-(2¾)) × 30"
G	2	Door side edging	¼ × ¾ × 30"
H	2	Door top/bottom edging	¼ × ¾ × (Y-(2-4))"

KEY	NO.	DESCRIPTION	DIMENSIONS
I	2	Short drawer sides	½ × 4 × 22"
J	2	Short drawer front/back	½ × 4 × (Y-(3½))"
K	1	Short drawer face	¾ × 5¼ × (Y-(2¼))"
L	8	Tall drawer sides	½ × 6½ × 22"
M	8	Tall drawer fronts/backs	½ × 6½ × (Y-(3½))"
N	4	Tall drawer faces	¾ × 7¾ × (Y-(2¼))"
O	5	Drawer bottoms	¼ × (Y-(3½)) × 21½"
P	2	Adjustable shelves	¾ × (Y-(2¼)) × 20"

* Y = width of rough opening

How to Build Closet Cabinets

CREATE THE ROUGH OPENING

The first step is to determine the dimensions of the rough opening in the wall next to your closet. Locate the wall studs. Typically, you'll find two studs directly next to the closet side jamb. One side of the rough opening should be flush against the closet-frame studs. The other side is roughly 3" from the side wall of the closet (the thickness of two 2 × 4s). The bottom of the rough opening is 3" off the floor and the top is 81¾" up from the floor (assuming the ceiling is a least 8 ft. high). Mark the rough opening area on the wall. Check for utilities (wires or pipes) in the wall before cutting the rough opening. If there are obstructions, contact a qualified contractor to move the utilities that are in the way. When you're sure the wall area is clear, cut the opening along the outlines using a utility knife (photo 1). Cut all the way through and then remove the drywall. (If you don't mind the dust you can use a reciprocating saw or jigsaw for this once you've scored a line—just be sure to wear a dust mask).

Next, install new framing as needed around the opening (photo 2). The new framing should be flush with the cut drywall edges. Secure the drywall to the new framing members with drywall screws.

BUILD THE CABINET

Cut the cabinet sides, top, and divider. The widths of the top and divider are based on the width of the rough opening. Only the front edge of each side panel is visible after the cabinet is installed. Attach heat-activated edge banding to the front edges of the side panels (photo 3).

Cut the rough opening after making sure there are no utilities in the wall. Draw cutting lines on the wall and score the drywall with a utility knife. Finish cutting through the drywall with the utility knife or a reciprocating saw.

Install new studs where necessary, placing them flush with the edges of the rough opening. Install support blocks on top of the base plate to bring it level with the bottom of the rough opening. Attach blocks to fill in the top openings.

Attach heat-activated veneer edge band to the front edges of the side panels. A household iron works well for heating the edge band. Protect the base of the iron with foil. Press the hot edge band down with a roller. After the edge band has cooled, trim any excess with a sharp knife or chisel.

(continued)

Bore ¼"-dia. shelf pin holes. Using pegboard as a guide, make two rows of aligned holes. Locate each row 3" from the front and back edge of the side panels. Attach tape or a manufactured depth guide at the depth of the pin plus the hardboard to mark the depth you will drill.

Attach the wide rails to the top and divider. Align the top edge of the rail with the top of the panel. Attach the rails with glue and a few 1½" brad nails.

Place the two side panels with the outside faces down and the front edge of each panel touching. Measure and mark the positions of the bottom edge of each rail on the inside face of each side panel.

Attach the top panel and divider panel. Drive four screws through the outside face of each side to attach the top and divider. Bore a countersink and pilot hole for each screw.

Next, bore two rows of shelf-pin holes in the upper cabinet section of each side panel. Use a piece of perforated hardboard (pegboard) as a guide for laying out the holes (photo 4). Pegboard features ¼"-dia. holes that are spaced 1" apart. Sand the inside face and front edge of each side panel.

Next, cut the wide and narrow rail pieces. These parts can all be cut from 1 × 4 stock. Rip the 1 × 4 down to 1¾"-wide strips for the wide rails and then rip the remaining stock down to 1¼"-wide for the narrow rails. Cut the rail pieces to the same length as the width of the top and divider panels.

Attach one wide rail to the front edge of the top and one to the front edge of the divider (photo 5). Sand the panel and rail seam smooth after the glue has cured.

Rails are typically attached to face frame stiles or to the cabinet sides with hidden fasteners such as tenons, dowels, biscuits, or pocket screws. But, because the sides of this cabinet will be hidden after it is installed, the rails, top, and divider are attached by driving screws through the cabinet sides. It doesn't matter that the screw heads are visible on the outside face of the cabinet sides because the sides will be concealed inside the closet.

Mark the location of the bottom edge of each rail on the inside face of the cabinet sides (Photo 6). Place each cabinet side front-edge down on a flat work surface. Position the top and the divider between the sides and clamp the cabinet assembly together. Check that each piece is square to the side panels and that the spacing is correct. Bore countersink and pilot holes and attach the top and divider to the sides (photo 7). Next, attach the rails (photo 8). Attach the back bottom rail last.

Cut the back to size. Attach the back to the cabinet sides, top and back bottom rail with glue and 1" brads or 18-ga. pneumatic nails. Make sure the cabinet is square as you attach the back panel.

BUILD THE DOOR & SHELVES

Cut plywood door and shelf pieces. You could use heat-activated edging to conceal the door and shelf edges, but because these edges are subject to more contact, you're better off attaching thicker, solid-wood edging. Rip ¼"-thick × ¾"-wide strips of solid wood for the edging. Cut two pieces that are slightly longer than the height of the door. Attach these pieces to the door-side edges with glue, leaving a little excess to hang over each end. Trim the overhang flush with the top and bottom of the door. Then cut two pieces that are slightly longer than the width of the door (including the side edging pieces). Attach these pieces to the top and bottom of the door with glue and brads (photo 9). Then cut two pieces for the front edges of the shelves and attach them in the same way.

After the glue has dried, sand the cabinet and door surfaces and edging smooth, being careful not to sand through the plywood veneer. Apply finish to the cabinet. In this case an oil based stain was applied, followed by three coats of water-base polyurethane. Lightly sand the surfaces with extra-fine grit sandpaper after each coat is dry.

Hang the door after the finish has dried. Use European-style inset hinges (photo 10) to hang the door. Follow the installation instructions and diagrams included with the hinges.

BUILD & INSTALL THE DRAWERS

The drawers are constructed with ½"-thick Baltic birch plywood. The drawer sides, front, and back have rabbet joints, which are easy to cut with a router table or a table saw. If using a table saw, you can use a single blade to make the cuts; or, you can speed up the cutting by substituting a dado-blade set that's adjusted to ¼"-wide. You can also follow the same construction process using a router table and straight bit.

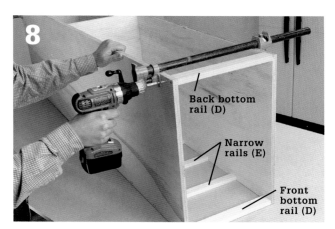

Back bottom rail (D)

Narrow rails (E)

Front bottom rail (D)

Use two screws to attach each end of each rail. Space the screws ⅜" from the edges. Be especially careful when locating the screws on the narrow rails. You must drill pilot holes or you may split the rails.

Attach the door edge with glue. Secure the edge with 1" brad nails while the glue dries. Trim the excess with a saw and sand the seams smooth.

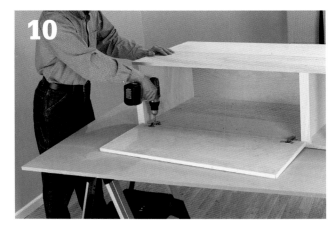

Hang the door with cup-style inset hinges. There are several models of these hinges available. Most feature adjustment screws that let you move the door slightly for a perfect fit in the cabinet opening after installation.

(continued)

First, cut all the drawer parts to size. Then cut the ¼ and ½"-deep rabbets in the ends of the drawer sides by making two passes (photos 11, 12). Next, cut the ¼"-wide grooves that will house the drawer bottom (photos 13, 14).

Sand all the drawer box parts smooth before assembling them. Dry-assemble the drawer to make sure all the parts fit together well. Then, assemble the drawer box with glue and brads (photo 15). Remove the clamps, clean up any dried excess glue and apply two coats of water-base polyurethane to the drawer boxes.

Next, mount drawers in the cabinet. Install the drawer slides on the cabinet sides and drawer box so that when the drawer is closed the front of the drawer box is ¾" inside the front of the cabinet.

This creates the necessary set-back so that when the drawer face is attached it will be flush with the front of the cabinet.

Make the drawer faces. If you don't have wide enough stock you must make the tall drawer faces by edge-gluing two pieces. Cut the drawer faces to size and sand them smooth. Finish the drawer faces with the same finishes you used on the cabinet.

Use double stick tape to position the drawer faces on the drawer box. The drawer faces are centered in the opening between the rails and cabinet sides. Carefully open the drawer and attach a clamp to secure the face. Then attach the drawer face with screws (photo 16). Finally, attach handles or pulls to the drawers and door.

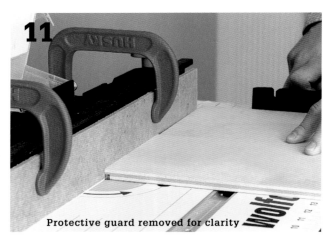

Make the initial pass for cutting the rabbets on a router table or table saw. Rabbets and dadoes should be made in multiple passes of deepening cuts—don't try and make the entire cut in one pass.

Reposition the fence and make the second pass on each rabbet. The width of the rabbet should equal the thickness of the plywood.

Finish cutting all rabbets and dadoes in the drawer box parts.

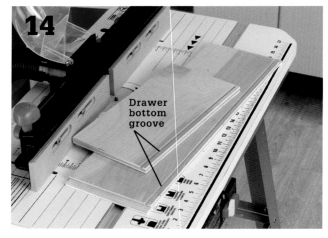

Cut the drawer bottom groove in the front, back, and side pieces.

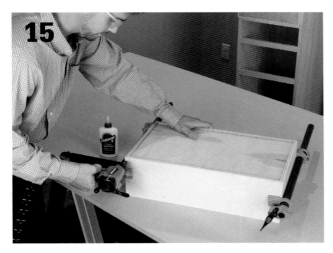

Assemble the drawer with glue and clamps. Adjust the drawer as needed so it is square. Then secure the sides by driving a couple 1" brad nails through the side rabbets into the front and back pieces.

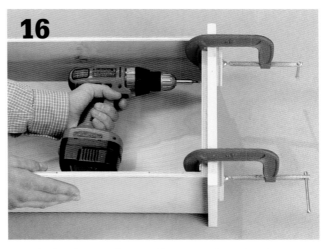

Attach the drawer faces with No. 6 × 1" pan-head screws and washers. Bore a ³⁄₁₆"-dia. pilot hole through the drawer box front, but not into the face, for each screw.

Secure the cabinet in the rough opening. Drive 2" screws through the cabinet bottom into the supports and through the cabinet sides into the side framing at shim locations.

Conceal the gaps around the cabinet and closet with trim. Reuse pieces of the old closet casing and cut new pieces of matching trim. In this case, wide gaps are covered with ¼"-thick plywood or solid stock.

INSTALL THE CABINET

First, build a set of supports for the cabinet inside the closet. The supports must be the same height as the bottom of the rough opening and roughly 20" long. Place the supports on the floor of the closet, spacing them apart no wider than the cabinet. Then slide the cabinet into the rough opening, center it, and insert shims to fill any gaps between the framing and the cabinet. Secure the cabinet to the rough opening framing and supports with 2" screws (photo 17).

Install trim around the cabinet and closet doors. Trim the outside edges with casing that matches the existing door and window case molding. The top casing will look best if it runs the full width across the cabinet and closet. There are several ways you can trim the interior seams. In this case a strip of ¼"-thick plywood is used to cover the wide space between the closet-door frame and cabinet side and the space below the bottom drawer (photo 18). The plywood edges are so narrow that it is difficult to distinguish them as plywood after they are sanded and stained or painted. You can also plane down solid stock or combine manufactured moldings to trim out the closet and cabinet.

Bed Surround

Headboards aren't the only way to adorn the head of a bed. Indeed, it can be dressed not only with form but with terrific function. Combining cabinets of differing sizes and shapes provides both the finish to a bed—that is often the sole domain of the attractive but purely decorative headboard—and the utility of cabinets that double as both decoration and much-needed storage.

The cabinets' clean, defined lines lend this Bed Surround a modern feel, while the option for above-bed lighting creates the halo of a warm and calm space for starting and ending the day or tucking away for a quick nap.

Before getting started, determine if you want the option of cabinet-mounted lights. If so, rough-in the wires and switch(es) prior to installing the cabinets. Once the cabinets are on site, prep them before hanging by drilling the appropriate holes to accommodate the wires and house the light fixtures.

Tools, Materials & Cutting List

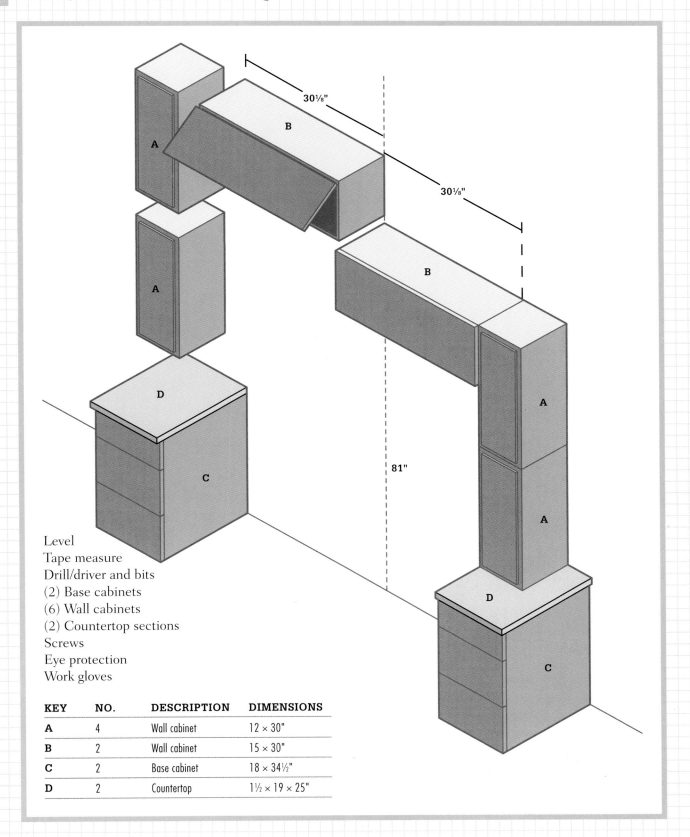

Level
Tape measure
Drill/driver and bits
(2) Base cabinets
(6) Wall cabinets
(2) Countertop sections
Screws
Eye protection
Work gloves

KEY	NO.	DESCRIPTION	DIMENSIONS
A	4	Wall cabinet	12 × 30"
B	2	Wall cabinet	15 × 30"
C	2	Base cabinet	18 × 34½"
D	2	Countertop	1½ × 19 × 25"

How to Build a Bed Surround

LAY OUT THE PROJECT

Choose the exact location for your bed surround. Mark the left and right edges of the project area based on your bed size, and then find the centerline. Be very exact. Using a 4 ft. level, plumb up from the center point. Mark a plumb line (photo 1). This is the control point from which you map out the rest of the layout. Measure 30⅛" left and right of the center point to mark the outside edges of the horizontal uppers (photo 2). Drive a 6-penny nail right on the centerline to hold your tape.

INSTALL THE UPPER CABINETS

Install a temporary ledger at the location of the bottom edges of the horizontal cabinets (81" above the floor in our project). Carefully install the horizontal uppers by resting them in position on the temporary ledgers and then driving screws through the cabinet backs and into wall studs (photo 3). If you discover gaps between upper cabinets, create filler strips to insert between the cabinets (photo 4) and conceal the gaps.

From the outside edges of the installed horizontal upper assembly, plumb down to the floor with a 4-ft. level. With the uppers installed, you now have rock solid control points to plumb down to the floor from. These lines enable you to place the lower cabinets accurately and keep all face frames tight. Measure the base cabinets' width to the left and right of the plumb lines and mark the baseboard for removal (photo 5). Using a combination square and pull saw, mark and remove the base molding. Be careful not to damage the drywall when removing the base molding.

INSTALL THE VERTICAL ELEMENTS

The base cabinets will need some type of countertop surface so they can function as nightstands and also support the vertical upper cabinets. We made particleboard countertops with plastic laminate applied to the tops and edges. Because the sizes are relatively small, this project also presents a good opportunity to experiment with some high-end countertop materials, such as granite or quartz. Install the countertops before installing the base cabinets in the project area (photo 6). Install the left base cabinet tight to the plumb line (photo 7).

Draw a plumb reference line in the exact center of the project area.

Mark vertical reference lines ⅛" further out from the centerline than the horizontal cabinet height.

3

Move the upper cabinets into position and fasten them to the wall at stand locations using screws.

4

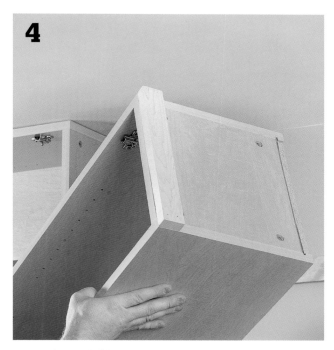

Cut and attach filler strips to the edge of one of the cabinets if there is a gap between it and its neighbor.

5

From the plumb line, measure out the exact width of the base cabinet carcass and mark the base molding for removal.

(continued)

6

Install the laminate countertop on the base cabinet prior to installation. Make sure it is flush to the inside edge and back of the base cabinets and overhangs the front and outside edges.

7

Install the left base cabinet tight to the plumb line. Drive screws into a stud at both the top and bottom of the cabinet carcase.

On top of the left base cabinet, mount the first vertical upper tight to the plumb line. Be careful of the laminate countertop during installation. Mount the second vertical upper tight to the first. Make sure the face frames are flush. Shim the back as necessary and make sure to catch wall studs with the fasteners (photo 8). Repeat these steps for the base cabinet on the right side.

JOIN THE CABINETS

The horizontal uppers and vertical uppers should be at the same height. If so, flush up and fasten the face frames (photo 9).

If the cabinet gangs are not flush, adjust the horizontal uppers to mate with the left and right vertical gangs. Once flush in all directions, fasten the face frames and secure to the wall (photo 10).

Install (or have installed) the light fixtures and switches. Remove the temporary ledger, patch drywall, caulk, and trim cabinet bases as required. Sand and spot-touch the finishes.

Sometimes shims are required to keep face frames tight and flush, due to irregularities in the wall surface. Insert shims behind the cabinets as needed and remove excess shim material after installation.

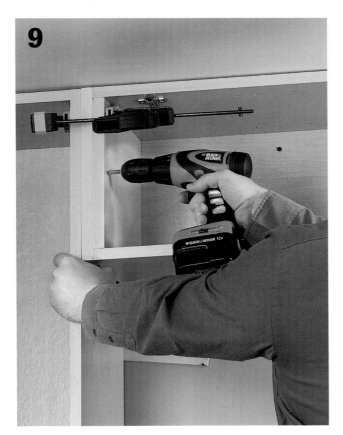

Fasten the face frames of the vertical uppers to the horizontal uppers. Predrill and countersink before driving screws.

Once the face frames are fastened together, attach the wall cabinets securely to the wall with screws driven through the cabinet backs at stud locations.

Loft Bed

If you had—or wanted—a loft bed back in college or in your first apartment, then this is a project you're going to like. But your kids will probably like it more because it's cool, fun, and their friends probably won't have one.

This loft bed is designed to open up floor space usually consumed by a bed. It also provides a location underneath it for a kid or kids to play, do activities or set up a desk. And, because it ties in with the wall, it can work for kids of all ages.

Because you attach it to the wall, this loft bed probably has a little more oomph than the one you might have built with your old roommate. A built-in safety rail adds an extra layer of protection for younger kids. While you can make the bed to your own specifications following the techniques below, the bed design here is based on a twin-sized mattress, which is 39" × 75".

The outside dimensions of the bed frame are 49½" × 81½", which allows room up top for books, a drink, and a little extra room for the bedding to drape when the bed is made. Your little princess or prince will love climbing the ladder to get into bed.

Safety note: Never attach hooks or handles to the loft bed and do not hang items from it, including rope and belts. Children can catch themselves on these items when playing or in the event that an accidental fall occurs.

Tools, Materials & Cutting List

Eye and ear protection
Work gloves
Miter saw
Table saw
Circular saw
Drill/driver
Level
Stud finder
Hammer
Tape measure
Nail set
Pneumatic nailer/compressor
Router and bits
Sander
Carpenter's square
Shooting board or straightedge
(2) ¾" × 4 × 8 ft. maple plywood
(6) 1 × 2 × 8 ft. maple
(4) 1 × 6 × 8 ft. maple
(3) 2 × 2 × 8 ft. pine
Brass screws
   with grommet washers
Deck screws
Trim head wood screws
Finishing materials

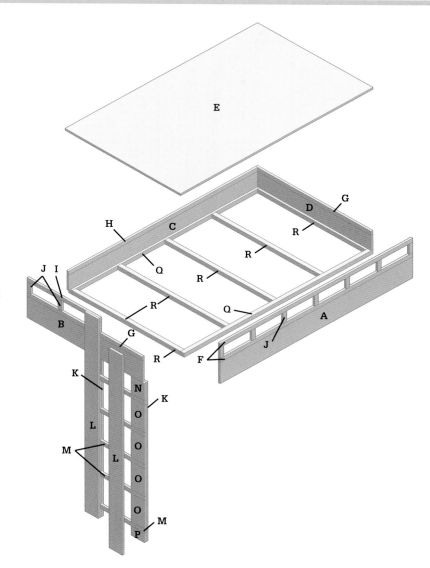

KEY	NO.	DESC.	DIMENSIONS	MATERIAL
A	1	Box front	¾ × 8 × 80¾"	Maple plywood
B	1	Box end—left	¾ × 8 × 48"	Maple plywood
C	1	Box back	¾ × 5¾ × 79¼"	Maple plywood
D	1	Box end—right	¾ × 5¾ × 48"	Maple plywood
E	1	Box bottom	¾ × 48 × 80"	Maple plywood
F	2	Box/rail cap—front	¾ × 1½ × 80¾"	1 × 2 maple
G	2	Box cap—end	¾ × 1½ × 48"	1 × 2 maple
H	1	Box cap—back	¾ × 1½ × 79¼"	1 × 2 maple
I	1	Rail cap—end	¾ × 1½ × 30¼"	1 × 2 maple

KEY	NO.	DESC.	DIMENSIONS	MATERIAL
J	10	Rail post	¾ × 1½ × 4"	1 × 2 maple
K	2	Ladder leg—short	¾ × 5½ × 59½"	1 × 6 maple
L	2	Ladder leg—long	¾ × 5½ × 74½"	1 × 6 maple
M	6	Ladder rung	¾ × 1½ × 24"	1 × 2 maple
N	2	Ladder filler	¾ × 5½ × 6½"	1 × 6 maple
O	8	Ladder filler	¾ × 5½ × 10½"	1 × 6 maple
P	2	Ladder filler	¾ × 5½ × 3½"	1 × 6 maple
Q	2	Cleat—long	1½ × 1½ × 80"	2 × 2 maple (or pine)
R	5	Cleat—short	1½ × 1½ × 45"	2 × 2 maple (or pine)

How to Build a Loft Bed

Once you've determined the height you want the mattress to be, strike a level line indicating the bottom of the mattress support box.

Cut stock using a circular saw and straightedge guide, and stack it neatly. Label each piece (magic marker on blue painter's tape works) to make identifying it later easier.

LAY OUT THE WALL CLEATS

Determine the length, width, and location of the bed frame. Plan your layout so that once the mattress is in, you have 4" to 6" all the way around it inside the mattress box, providing room for bedding and other things. Mark a level line on both walls at the bottom of the mattress box (photo 1). Leave rougly 30" or more of space above the mattress. (Our plan is for a room with a 102" celing; lower the ladder height by 6" for an 8 ft. ceiling.)

BUILD THE MATTRESS BOX

The mattress box is fabricated from ¾"-thick maple plywood, which creates a clean, modern look once installed and finished. Maple is also a very stable material that delivers dependable mechanical connections for assembly. And, because we can make panels larger than with dimensional lumber, we create a nest for the mattress to set inside that results in a curb that will help keep children safe at night. The box should be assembled as completely as possible on the ground (in your shop) and then hoisted into position on the wall cleats when you've taken it as far as it makes sense to go. The two sides of the box that face out into the room are wider than the two that go against the walls because the room-side of the box needs to conceal the cleats that support the plywood box bottom. These cleats (the room side ones) are attached to the frame first and the other two are attached to the walls first. The plywood bottom is butted against the room sides of the box frame, and is flush with the outside edges of the wall sides of the frame. The top edges of the box are covered with 1 × 2 maple on-edge, which also serves as the bottom rail of the railing on the room sides.

Rip-cut the four box frame sides from ¾" maple plywood, using a tablesaw or a circular saw and straightedge cutting guide (photo 2).

The fastener scheme we chose for this bed is to tack the parts together with glue and pneumatic nails, then reinforce with brass screws and grommet-style washers once things are squared up (the brass screws only need to be used on visible surfaces). Join the corners of the box with glue and screws (photo 3). The two exposed sides should conceal the end grain of the side they're attached to. Work on a large, flat surface with the box sides upside-down so their top edges are even.

Cut the cleats to length from 2 × 2 pine stock. Attach cleats to the bottom inside faces of the exposed box sides, flush with the bottom edges of the box (photo 4). Use glue and brass wood screws driven at 8" intervals to secure the cleats.

Once the cleats are in place, cut the mattress box bottom to size and attach it to the cleats that are connected to the room sides of the box. Drive 2" deck screws through the plywood bottom and into the cleats, spaced no more than 12" apart (photo 5). At the wall-sides of the box, the plywood bottom should be flush with the outside edges of the box. Also drive 2" deck or drywall screws into the plywood box edges on this side.

Cut three 2 × 2 stiffeners and position them on the undersides of the plywood. The ends should be flush against the room side cleat. Tack in place and then attach by driving screws through the top of the plywood.

Join the corners of the mattress box with glue and a few nails or with glue and clamps, and then reinforce each joint with three #8 × 2½" brass wood screws. Space the screws evenly. We added decorative grommet-style brass washers instead of counterboring and plugging the screw holes.

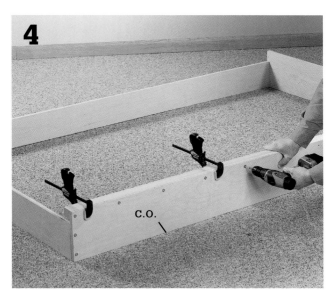

Attach the cleats that support the mattress box bottom to the two sides of the box that face the room.

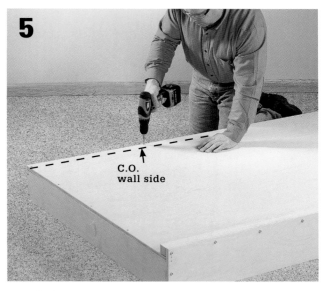

Attach the plywood mattress box bottom by driving screws through the plywood and into the two cleats mounted inside the box. Also drive screws through the box bottom and into the back and right end edges of the box.

(continued)

Run the top edges of the 1 × 2 maple stock for the railing and edge caps parts through a router table fitted with a ¼" roundover bit. Cut the box caps, cap rails and rail posts to length (use a stop block on your power miter saw to make uniform length pieces). Attach the 1 × 2 caps to the back edge and right end (the wall sides) with glue and finish nails (drill pilot hole for the finish nails if hand-driving them). Before attaching the front and left side box caps, lay out positions for the railing posts according to the diagram on page 149 (photo 6). For best accuracy, gang-mark the post locations on the rail caps and box caps.

Attach each post to the box caps at marked locations, using glue and two 3" deck screws or wood screws driven up through pilot holes in the box cap and into the bottom ends of the posts. Then, attach the box caps with attached posts to the front and left sides of the mattress box, using glue and 3" trim-head wood screws driven down through the top edges of the box caps and into the box at 12" intervals (photo 7).

Next, attach the railing caps to the tops of the railing posts with glue and trimhead wood screws driven down through the rail caps and into the posts. Make sure the posts are aligned with the reference lines you marked for their positions. Finish-sand the mattress box (you may want to back out the screws a ways to get underneath the grommets). It's best to wait until all parts are built so you can apply finish at the same time

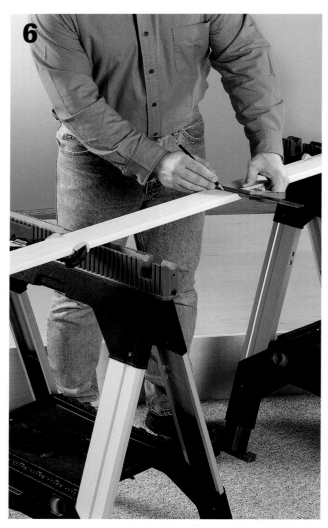

Lay out the locations for the railing posts on the mating rail and box caps so you'll be sure they're aligned perfectly.

After screwing the railing posts to the box caps, attach the assemblies to the front and left sides of the mattress box using counterbored trim-head wood screws.

Shape the bullnose profiles into the top edges of your 1 × 2 rung stock before cutting the rungs to length.

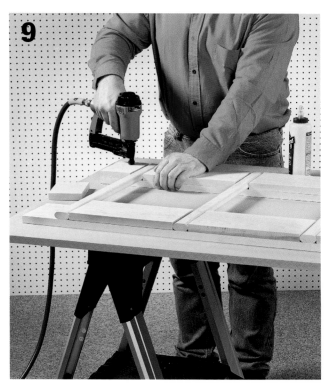

The ladder is a 3-ply assembly. The short leg is the first layer. Next come the ladder blocks that run parallel to the leg. After you install a ladder block, you install a rung perpendicular to it, working your way down the ladder—block, rung, block, rung, etc. Make sure the blocks are flush to the edges of the leg and that the rungs are held tight to the blocks. Use glue and screws (or pneumatic nails).

Adding a Ceiling ▸

The bottom edges of the front side and left end of the mattress box are still exposed plywood edge grain. There are a couple of ways of dealing with this. One is to conceal the edges with heat-activated maple veneer tape. Or, you can tack on additional strips of maple 1 × 2. But we chose to create a "ceiling" for the area underneath the loft bed by attaching a sheet of tempered ¼" hardboard to the underside of the box.

MAKE THE LADDER

The ladder/post is made from built-up 1 × 6 maple boards. The rungs are 1 × 2 maple boards with bull-nosed edges. To simplify the machining, cut the bullnoses by profiling all four edges of your 8-ft. 1 × 2 stock on a router table fitted with a ⅜" roundover bit (photo 8). The rungs should have a more pronounced bullnose than the top of the 1 × 2 box caps. Then cut the rungs to length with a miter saw or power miter saw (a stop block is a good idea for ensuring uniform lengths).

Cut the ladder legs and ladder blocks to length from 1 × 6 maple stock. Arrange the shorter legs on a flat surface with the outside edges 24" apart and the end flush. Make sure legs stay parallel at all times. Install the 6½" blocks first flush with the top ends of the legs. Use glue and a couple of finish nails or pneumatic nails to secure the blocks. Then begin working downward, adding rungs and blocks according to the diagram on page 149 (photo 9).

(continued)

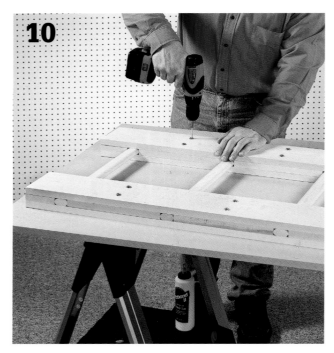

Attach the long outer legs to the blocks, rungs, and short legs, ensuring that the bottoms and sides are flush. Glue and screw securely with flathead brass wood screws and decorative grommet-type washers.

Fasten the longer legs over the assembly, sandwiching the blocks and rung ends between 1 × 6 legs (photo 10). The extra 15" of length should be at the top of the longer legs.

INSTALL THE LOFT BED

Before installing the loft bed, apply your finish of choice (a few coats of durable polyurethane varnish is a good option). Preassemble the long side cleat and short side cleat into an L-shape, using glue and 3" deck screws. Attach the cleat to the wall at the mattress box layout lines. Apply panel adhesive to the back faces of the cleats before installing. Attach with ⅜ × 3½" countersunk lag screws with washer at each stud location (photo 11).

Clamp a long 2 × 4 to the front face of the mattress box so the 2 × 4 will support the front at roughly the correct height when it is installed. With a couple of helpers (or more), raise the box and rest the back and right end on the wall cleats, making sure the box is square to the corners and flush against the walls. Place a level on the box and adjust the clamp and 2 × 4 brace so the box is level (photo 12).

Preassemble the wall cleats into an L-shape and fasten them to the wall studs with lag screws and adhesive.

Check with a 4 ft. level across the corner of the box near the ladder location to make sure the box is level on both sides.

13

Position the ladder at the corner of the front and left side edges. The rung layer and short leg layer should fit snugly underneath the box, since the ladder will serve as a corner support post. Attach the ladder to the mattress box.

14

Secure the bottom of the ladder/corner post by attaching a cleat to the floor behind the ladder legs.

Once the mattress box is level, face-nail through the front and left ends of the box and into the wall cleats to hold the bed in place. After the ladder is secured and attached to the bed it will be safe enough to go topside and drive some nails through the box bottom and into the wall cleats.

INSTALL THE LADDER

Position the ladder under the mattress support box. Make sure that the right side of the ladder is flush with the long, outside edge of the mattress support box. Plumb it and fasten using glue and screws. The short legs of the ladder create a ledge to help support the free end of the box.

Drive 2½" brass screws with grommet washers through the ladder leg and upper ladder block at 8" intervals to secure the ladder (which functions as

a post) to the mattress box (photo 13). Locate the screws so they hit the 2 × 2 cleat at the bottom, inside edge of the box. Also drive a few countersunk 2" screws down through the plywood box bottom and into the top ends of the short legs.

Double check the ladder to make sure it is plumb and then screw the sixth ladder rung to the floor, directly behind the bottom of the ladder, lying flat (photo 14). The ends of the rungs should be flush with the outside faces of the ladder legs. Drive screws or nails through the rungs and into the bottoms of the legs to prevent the ladder from moving. Also attach the top ends of the long ladder legs to the top railing caps with trim-head screws. Drive a few extra nails through the box bottom and into the cleats, remove the temporary 2 × 4 brace, and add your mattress.

Closet Organizing System

An adjustable closet system puts clothes and accessories within reach for people of all sizes. Build your own closet system to attain accessibility features like roll-under space, as well as adjustable shelves and rods. Add closet accessories, such as hooks, additional rods or shelves, pull-out drawers, baskets, slide-out belt and shoe racks, and fold-down pants racks to customize your system.

The closet organizer shown here can be adapted to fit almost any closet. It is a simple plywood cabinet with three adjustable shelves and space above and below for additional storage and easy access. Use finish-grade plywood for the cabinet and support piece. Then paint, stain, or protect the wood with a clear finish. Solid wood trim covers the plywood edges and lends strength to the shelves. For this, you can use clear pine or a hardwood such as poplar, oak, or maple. The shelves shown in this project are 11" deep. You may want to make them deeper. Just keep in mind that shelves longer than 36" may require additional support to prevent sagging.

This complete closet organizing system has a place for practically every stitch of your wardrobe.

Tools, Materials & Cutting List

Work gloves
Eye and ear protection
Tape measure
Circular saw
Straightedge cutting guide
Drill/driver
Router w/straight bit
Framing square
Stud finder
Level
Clamps
Hammer
Nail set
Pine or hardwood trim
   (1 × 1, 1 × 2)
¾" finish grade plywood
2" coarse-thread
   drywall screws
4d finish nails
Wood glue
Wood finishing materials
1¼"-dia. × 6 ft. closet rod
Shelf standards and clips

KEY	PART	DIMENSION
A	(1) Cabinet back	½ × 37½ × 77¼" plywood
B	(2) Cabinet sides	¾ × 11⅞ × 77¼" plywood
C	(1) Side support	¾ × 11⅞ × 77¼" plywood
D	(1) Cabinet top	¾ × 12½ × 37½" plywood
E	(1) Cabinet bottom	¾ × 11⅞ × 36" plywood
F	(3) Shelves	¾ × 11⅞ × 35⅞" plywood
G	(7) Trim	1 × 2* pine

* Cut to fit

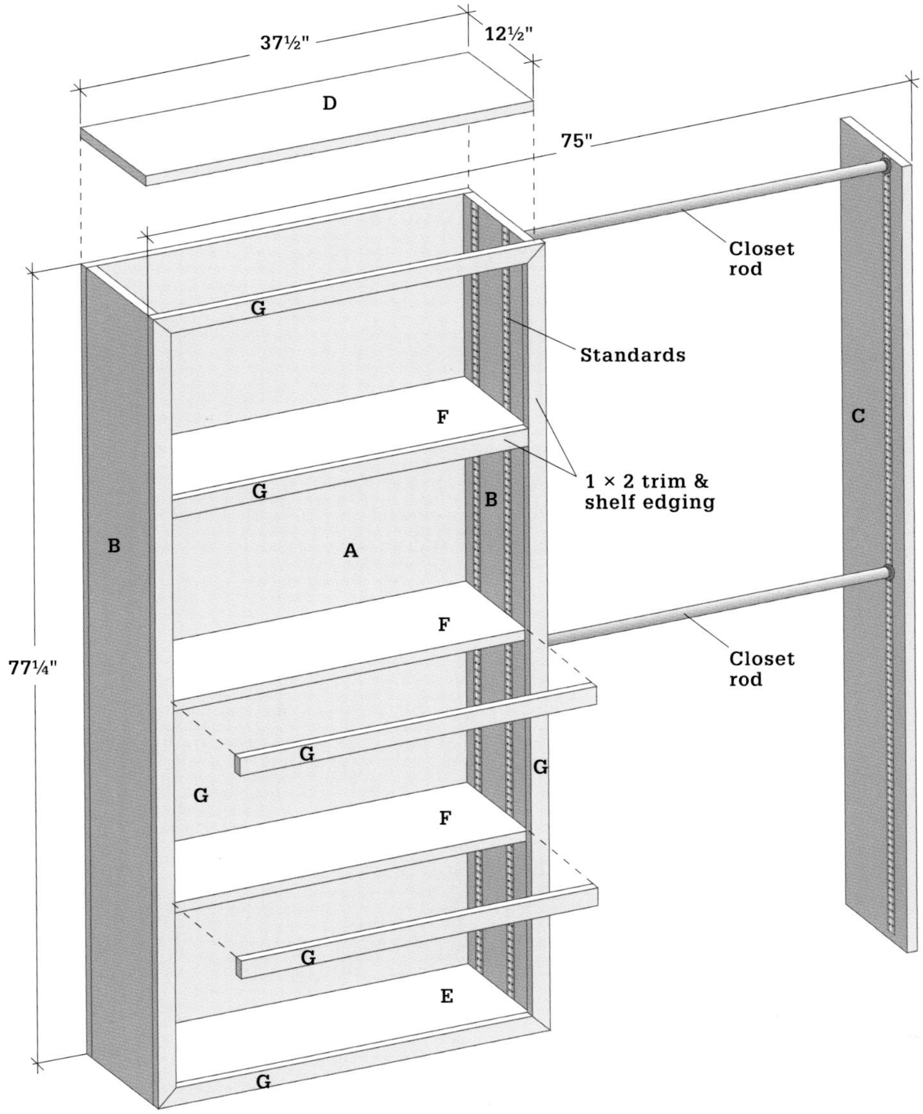

37½"
12½"
D
75"
Closet rod
Standards
G
F
C
G
1 × 2 trim & shelf edging
B
B
A
F
Closet rod
F
G
G
G
77¼"
G
F
G
E
G

How to Build an Adjustable Closet Organizing System

Cut the plywood into narrow strips to create the cabinet sides and the shelves. A circular saw and a straightedge cutting guide work well for this task. If you have a table saw or a panel-cutting saw, you'll probably want to use one of those.

Cut grooves in the cabinet sides to accept the shelf standards. A router with a straight bit and cutting guide is a good tool choice here. Do not try to make the cuts in a single pass; use several passes of increasing depth.

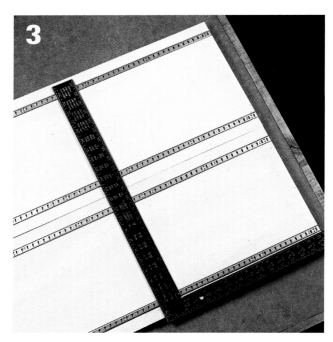

Lay the metal shelf standard strips into the grooves with the numbers and holes matched up. Check alignment with a square, and then trim off the top. Install the standards.

Assemble the cabinet. Glue the cabinet top and bottom pieces between the ends of the cabinet sides. Make sure the outside faces of the top and bottom are flush with the ends of the sides. Before the glue dries, fasten the back panel to the cabinet using 2" coarse-thread drywall screws driven every 12".

5

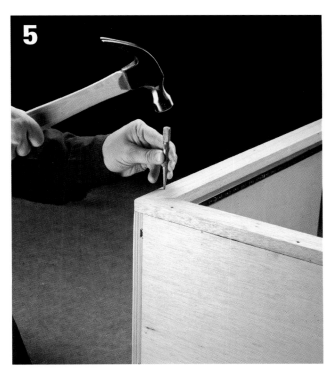

Install the face frame. Cut trim pieces as well as the shelf edging. Attach the face frame members to the front edge of the cabinet with glue and 4d finish nails driven into pilot holes. Set the nail heads with a nail set.

6

Mount the cabinet to the back wall of the closet by driving screws through the back panel and into wall studs. Set the cabinet up on blocking to create storage space below. Make sure the cabinet is level before attaching it.

7

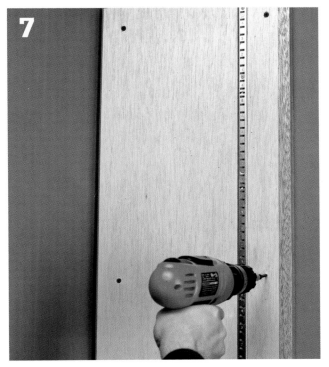

Install side supports and any other system parts, fastening into wall studs wherever possible. Add closet rods and other accessories.

Shelf Supports ▶

Shelf support pegs, pins, and clips come in a very wide range of styles and sizes. Make sure the hardware you are planning to use is designed to work with the standards you've already installed. The clips seen here provide good holding power and are easy to remove and relocate.

Closet Home Office

When you need a dedicated office space and don't have a den or an extra bedroom available, the conventional option is to set up shop in some other room, such as the living room. But sharing a space has its drawbacks. Busy living spaces aren't always conducive to work. On the flip side, office equipment and file storage aren't exactly dazzling décor for living spaces. Office areas that aren't well-defined also tend to collect other kinds of paperwork or, worse, general household clutter.

A good option for your new office space just might be a closet. Tucked away in its own discreet nook, a closet office is nicely contained and clearly separated from other activities. The office itself requires no extra living space—all you need is a little room for a chair when you're working at the desk. Perhaps best of all, the office and all of its contents are out of sight (and mind) as soon as you close the closet doors. This office design is simple and easy to build yet provides all of the necessary basics for both tasks and storage in a modern work space.

Tools & Materials ▶

Work gloves
Eye protection
Caulk gun
Circular saw and straightedge guide
Level
Drill with bits
Hacksaw
Wrench
Sander
Stud finder
Hammer
Clamps
Construction adhesive
Finish nails (1¼", 2")
3½" wood screws
2¼" trimhead screws
⁵⁄₁₆" all-thread rod
Hardwood-veneer MDF-core plywood (finish-grade on one side) (¼", ¾")
Hanger bolts
Coupling nuts
Flat washers
Hex nuts
Hardwood lumber (1 × 1, 1 × 2)
¾" particleboard with plastic laminate (on one side) for desktop
Wood glue
1¼" coarse-thread drywall screws
Finishing materials

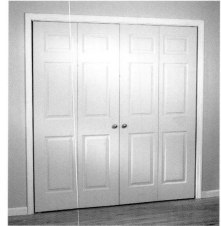

Closets are prime real estate in any home, but if you can manage to clear one out, you can create a private, efficient office space that's instantly hidden behind closed doors.

How to Transform a Closet Into an Office

Power ▸

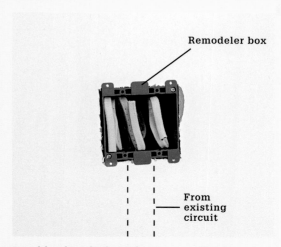

Remodeler box

From existing circuit

Provide electrical service to your office by branching off of an existing circuit. Here, boxes for a light fixture and a wall receptacle were added and wired to a room circuit. Patches for the drywall cut to route the wiring will be hidden by the panel and don't need a complete finish. Consult an electrician according to your skill and comfort level with wiring.

1

Prepare the walls for the paneling by removing any baseboard or other moldings. Make sure the wall is smooth and dust free. Locate and mark the wall studs to guide the installation; the panel seams should fall over stud centers.

Option: If you intend to panel the ceiling, locate the ceiling joists in the closet, and then map out their locations onto paper. The joists will support the suspended bookshelves, and it would be difficult to locate the joists once the paneling is up. If you're not paneling the ceiling, find and mark the joists after step 6 on page 162.

2

Finish the good side of the paneling stock as desired. Cut the first panel to length, cutting from the back side with a circular saw to prevent splintering. Apply beads of construction adhesive to the back of the panel, and press the panel against the wall so the side edges are centered over studs.

(continued)

Adjust the panel so it's perfectly plumb, then nail it to the wall studs with 1¼" finish nails. Use the nails sparingly; you need only enough to ensure the panel stays flat and the edges are securely and evenly adhered.

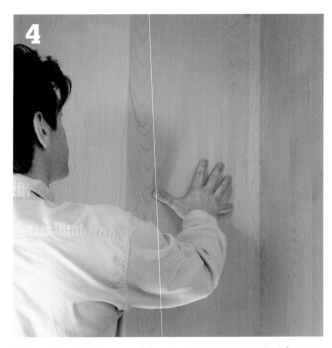

Cut and install the remaining panels. Use the straight factory edges for the butted seams. At the inside corners, place the second (perpendicular) panel with its factory edge butted against the first panel. If the seams are tight, you don't need to hide them with molding.

Plan the bookshelf spacing as desired, then draw level lines onto the walls to represent the bottom edge of each shelf. Cut and install 1 × 1 shelf cleats so their top edges are flush with the level lines. Fasten the cleats with 2¼" trimhead screws driven into wall studs.

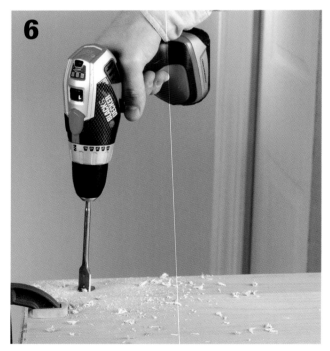

Cut the shelves from ¾" plywood. The top and middle shelves are L-shaped, 11" deep along the back wall, with an 18"-long, full-depth leg at one end. The bottom shelf matches the leg dimensions. If desired, drill a hole near the back corner of each shelf for routing power cords.

Drill holes for the all-thread hangers following the ceiling joist layout. Finish the shelves as desired.

Draw level lines to represent the top edges of the desktop cleats: these are 1½" below the desk surface. *Tip: Standard desktop height is 29 to 30" from the floor, while typing surfaces are typically 26 to 27".* Cut and install the 1 × 2 cleats flush with the lines using a 3½" wood screw driven into each wall stud.

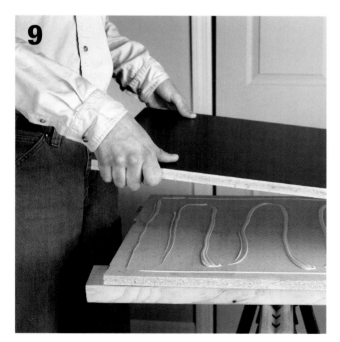

Cut two identical pieces of desktop stock to fit the closet dimensions, with a little bit of wiggle room for getting it in place (be sure to account for the ¾" thickness of the 1 × 2 nosing). Glue the pieces together on their bare faces using wood glue and a few 1¼" screws to clamp them together while the glue dries. Make sure the pieces are perfectly flush at their front edges.

Install the desktop. If desired, drill a large hole (1½"-dia. or so) through the desktop for routing cords. Cut, sand, and finish 1 × 2 stock for the decorative nosing. Install the nosing with wood glue and 2" finish nails, keeping it flush with the desk surface. Set the desktop onto the cleats; its weight will keep it securely in place.

Kneewall Cabinet

A kneewall is a short wall that meets the slope of the roofline in an upstairs room. By cutting a hole in a kneewall and installing a recessed cabinet, you can turn the wasted space behind it into a useful storage area.

Because the body (carcase) of a kneewall cabinet is not visible, it can be built using ordinary plywood and simple butt joints. The face frame and drawer faces, however, should be built with hardwood, and finished carefully.

The project shown here fits in a space that is 30" wide—the standard width of two adjacent stud cavities with a center stud removed. Before beginning work, check the spacing of studs and the location of electrical or plumbing lines behind your kneewall. Your kneewall may have a removable access panel, which makes it easy to check behind the wall.

You can make the cabinet wider or narrower to fit your wall stud spacing, but regardless of size, be sure to leave a few inches of space between the back of the cabinet and the rafters. Also, you'll need to cover the back of the cabinet with vapor barrier and insulation if the kneewall is insulated.

Tools, Materials & Cutting List

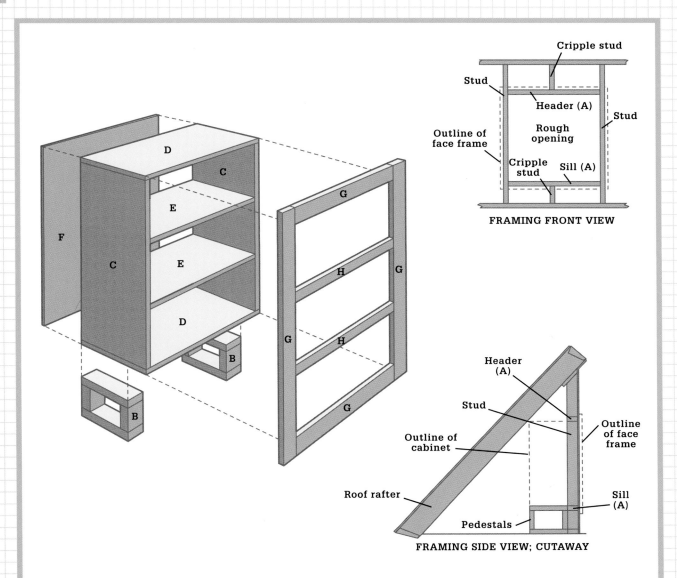

FRAMING FRONT VIEW

Cripple stud

Stud

Header (A)

Stud

Outline of face frame

Rough opening

Cripple stud

Sill (A)

FRAMING SIDE VIEW; CUTAWAY

Header (A)

Stud

Outline of face frame

Outline of cabinet

Roof rafter

Sill (A)

Pedestals

Level
Circular saw or jigsaw
Flat pry bar
Reciprocating saw
Drill
Tape measure
Bar or pipe clamps
Hammer
Nail set
Miter saw

Drywall or deck screws (1", 2", 3")
Finish nails (1½", 2", 3")
Wood glue
Finishing materials
Drawer hardware
Eye and ear protection
Work gloves

KEY	NO.	DESC.	SIZE	MATERIAL
A	2	Header and sill	6 linear ft.	2 × 4s
B	2	Pedestals	14" × 15"	2 × 4s
C	2	Sides	19" × 28½"	¾" plywood
D	2	Top and bottom	19" × 30"	¾" plywood
E	2	Shelves	19" × 28½"	¾" plywood
F	1	Back panel	30" × 30"	¼" plywood
G	2	Face frame	11 linear ft.	1 × 4 oak
H	2	Shelf rails	5 linear ft.	1 × 2 oak
I	3	Drawers	see pages 38 to 51	

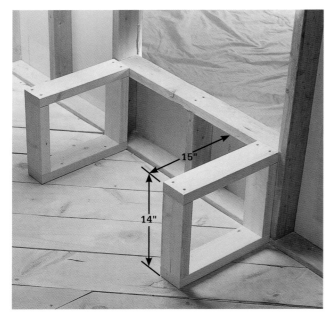

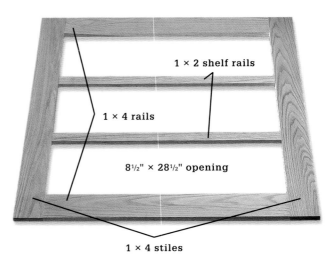

Pedestals installed behind the kneewall create a sturdy base for the cabinet. Built from 2 × 4s, the pedestals raise the cabinet so it fits above the sill. Raising the cabinet also makes drawers more accessible.

Face frame is 1 × 4 hardwood, which will cover the rough edges of the wall opening. The shelf rails are made from 1 × 2 hardwood to maximize the size of the drawer openings.

How to Build a Kneewall Cabinet

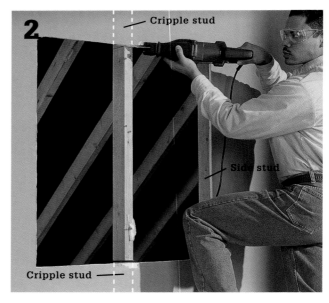

Locate wall studs in area where cabinet will be installed. Mark the cutout on the wall, using a level as a guide. Bottom of cutout should be at least 3" above baseboard, and sides of cutout should follow edges of wall studs. Height of cutout should be 3¼" taller than overall height of cabinet, to allow space for a header and sill. *Caution: Check for wiring, pipes, and ductwork before cutting into any wall.*

Cut away the center stud at the top and bottom of the opening, using a reciprocating saw. Remove the stud. Remaining portions of cut studs are called "cripple" studs.

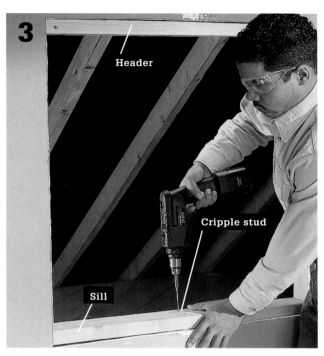

3

Header

Cripple stud

Sill

Measure and cut a 2 × 4 header and sill to fit snugly between side studs. Position in opening, check for level, and shim if necessary. Attach the header and sill to the cripple studs and side studs, using 3" screws.

4

Measure the distance from the floor behind the opening to the top of the sill, and build two 2 × 4 pedestals to this height. Join pedestal pieces together with glue and 3" screws.

5

Set the pedestals on the floor inside the wall opening, even with the sides of the framed opening. Check to make sure pedestals are level, and shim between the pedestals and the floor if necessary. Attach pedestals to the floor, using 3" screws.

6

Measure width and height of the rough opening between framing members. Cut side panels 2" shorter than the height of rough opening. Cut top and bottom panels ½" shorter than the width of rough opening. Cut shelves the length of the top and bottom panels, minus the width of the side panels (usually ¹³⁄₁₆").

(continued)

Attach drawer slide tracks to the center of the bottom panel and the shelves, following manufacturer's directions.

Clamp and glue the shelves to the side panels to form butt joints. Reinforce the joints with 2" screws driven through the side panels and into the edges of shelves.

Clamp and glue the top and bottom panels to the side panels, then reinforce the joints with 2" screws.

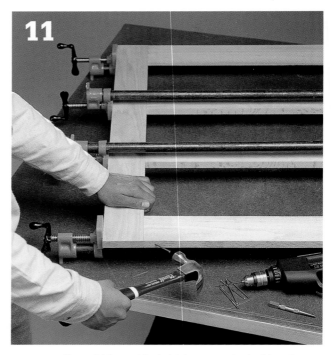

Measure and cut ¼" plywood panel to cover the back of the cabinet. Attach with 1" screws or wire nails driven through the back and into the side, top, and bottom panels.

Measure the width and height between the inside edges of the cabinet. Cut the rails to the width. Cut the stiles to the height plus 7". Clamp and glue rails between stiles, and reinforce joints by toenailing 3" finish nails through the rails and into the stiles.

12

Apply glue to the edges of the cabinet, then position the face frame over the cabinet so the inside edges of the face frame are flush with the top, bottom, and side panels. Attach the face frame by drilling pilot holes and driving 1½" finish nails into the cabinet every 8". Use a nail set to countersink the nail heads.

13

Slide the cabinet into the opening so it rests on the pedestals and the face frame is against the wall surface.

14

Anchor the cabinet by drilling pilot holes and driving 3" finish nails through the face frame and into the wall framing members. Also, drive 3" finish nails through the bottom of the cabinet and into the sill.

15

Sand and finish the cabinet face frame, then build, finish, and install overlay drawers (pages 38 to 51).

Hobby Center

If you or someone in your family enjoys a hobby or activity, whether it's computing, scrapbooking, drawing, or anything else that involves pleasant time seated and engaged in your avocation, you deserve to have a special place set aside for that activity. And here, it is important to note, "set aside" does not mean "spread out on the kitchen table between family meals." A dedicated spot with loads of storage, a pleasing appearance, and an efficient footprint are all possible. This corner hobby center provides the things you need to spend time on your activity, not managing it.

In this corner hobby center, upper and lower cabinets are combined to deliver excellent and attractive storage options. At the same time, some on-site carpentry creates a stable frame for a spacious but not overpowering L-shaped desk. The laminate desktop configuration provides not just room to spread out a project or stage supplies left and right, but also provides three access points (center, left, and right) for you to either move around a large project or for others to pull up a chair and help or just watch.

Tools, Materials & Cutting List

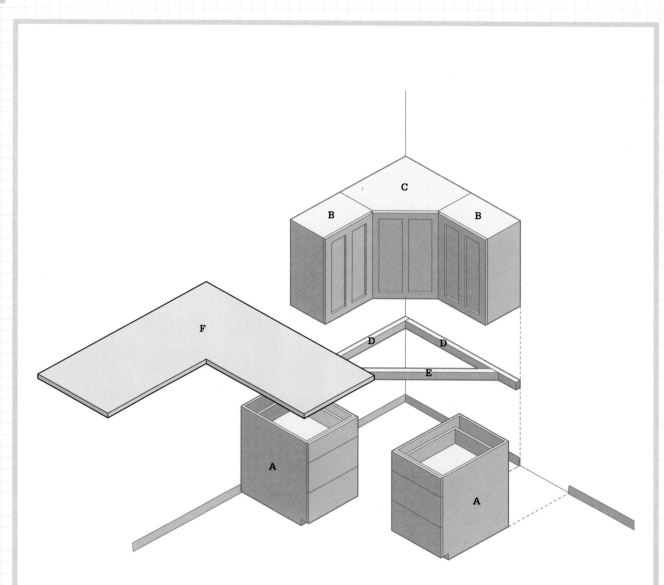

Pencil
Tape measure
Level or laser level
Drill/driver
Miter saw
Eye and ear
   protection
Work gloves

(2) Base cabinets
(2) Upper cabinets
(1) Corner cabinet
(2) 8 ft. 2 × 3
(1) Countertop
Drywall or deck screws
Finish nails
Finishing materials

KEY	NO.	DESC.	SIZE	MATERIAL
A	2	Base cabinets	24 × 34½"	
B	2	Upper cabinets	18 × 30"	
C	1	Corner cabinet	24 × 30"	
D	2	Wall cleat	1½ × 2½ × 40"	2 × 3
E	1	Diagonal cleat	1½ × 2½ × 59"	2 × 3
F	1	L-shape countertop	1½ × 25 × 72"	Custom make

How to Build a Hobby Center

LAY OUT UPPER CABINETS

Start with the upper cabinets first, then install the base units. Once the bases are set, frame the desktop supports and install the countertop. The desktop is laminate and while you can make it yourself, working with laminates is a specialty trade and it is often much easier to order the unit and have it delivered preassembled. Locate and strike the level line for the uppers 52½" above the floor. Project each line 42" out from the wall corner (photo 1).

Locate and mark the wall studs below the level line. Fasten a temporary ledger to the wall studs (photo 2). Set it below the level line to support the cabinets during installation.

LAY OUT THE BASES & DESKTOP

Measuring along the top of the base molding from the corner, make marks at 42" and 60" on the base trim. This is the location of each base cabinet. Use a combination square and mark square lines down to the floor. The 18" of base/shoe molding between the lines will be removed to accept the base cabinets. In the corner, measure up 34½" (the height of the base cabinet) from the floor and mark each side of the wall (photo 3).

Project the level line for the upper cabinets 42" out from each corner.

Fasten a ledger board for the upper cabinets just below the level line.

Extend your tape in the corner and mark each wall at 34½".

It helps to transfer the location of the wall studs to the insides of the cabinets for future reference so you're not searching for the studs while you're holding cabinets aloft (photo 4). Don't forget to subtract the width of the cabinet sides.

Transfer the stud locations to the inside surfaces of the cabinets before you lift them.

Fasten the upper cabinet to the wall studs to hold it in place, but do not drive the screws all the way (this allows for a little fine tuning).

Note: If you have a carpet floor treatment, it may be wise to place a base cabinet in position and use a 2-ft. level to transfer its height to the wall. Remember, carpet and pad will compress some once the cabinet has been loaded with items so apply a little pressure when doing this. Once height is established, strike a level line 61½" out on each wall.

The reason to strike the line out to 61½" is because the desktop extends 1½" beyond the outside edge of the base unit. Along the level line on each wall, make a mark at 42" and strike a plumb line down to the base

molding. This is the inside edge of the base cabinet and the outside edge of the desktop ledger board. Locate the wall studs and mark them along the top edge of the level line.

INSTALL THE UPPERS

Start with the center cabinet in the corner. Set it on the ledger board and then drive screws into the wall at stud locations (photo 5). Repeat for each end cabinet. Before fully sinking the wall screws, clamp the cabinets together, drill pilot holes in

(continued)

Before fully sinking wall screws, be sure the fronts of all wall cabinets are flush. Make adjustments as necessary to get them flush, clamp, pre-drill, then fasten.

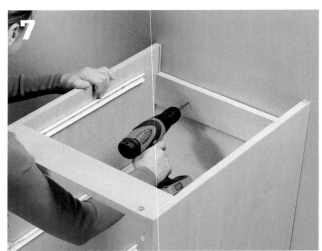

Position the base cabinets at the layout lines and fasten them to wall studs with screws.

Install ledgers below level line on wall studs. Note that the second piece overlaps the first piece and must be cut 1½" shorter to fit.

Cut the diagonal ledger brace with opposing miters. Long-point to long-point, it's 59".

the cabinet sides or face frames, and screw them together (photo 6). Complete the process by driving all wall screws tightly against the cabinet back. Add cabinet doors.

INSTALL THE BASE UNITS

Remove the base molding already marked using a pull-saw. Position the base units against the wall at the layout lines and then shim and fasten the base cabinets to the wall studs (photo 7).

ATTACH DESKTOP LEDGER

Because the desktop is only supported by cabinets on the outside edges, you must build a 3-piece ledger system that supports the desktop both along the wall and under the front edge of the desktop. Use 2 × 3s, which work well for this. Cut and install ledger pieces along the wall, fastening with two 3" screws into the wall studs (photo 8). Measure and cut the first piece to fit between the wall and the inside edge of a base cabinet. A piece just shy of 42" should fit.

Cut and install the second piece. A piece just shy of 40½" should fit.

Cut a 2 × 3 to 59" (long-to-long) with opposing miters (photo 9). Pre-drill and pre-set screws in the mitered ends of the diagonal brace then install (photo 10).

INSTALL THE DESKTOP

Have a custom desktop made to fit from particlebord and laminate, or any other suitable materials. Or, make your own (see page 163). Get a helper and place the desktop on top of the base cabinet/ledger system (photo 11). Fine-tune the desktop placement onto the layout marks and fasten from beneath. Fasten from inside the base cabinets as well as through the ledger system's diagonal brace. Fastening through the diagonal brace requires predrilling and installing screws on an angle (photo 12). Be careful not to puncture the top surface of the laminate.

APPLY YOUR FINISH

The finish details are relatively minimal on this project, since it is made out of prefinished cabinets and a pre-built desktop. You can caulk between the cabinet edges and the wall as necessary, or wrap the base cabinet bottoms with base molding as necessary (you can skip this if the floor is carpet) and prime and paint the ledger system boards the same as the wall color. One great addition is to install an undercabinet light beneath the upper cabinets to provide focused task lighting (photo 13).

Predrill (to prevent splitting) and preset screws in the mitered ends of the diagonal brace and install.

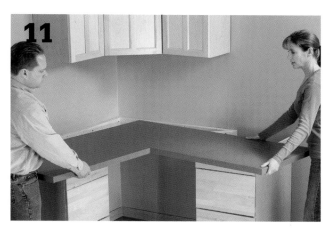

With a helper, position the desktop on the cabinets and ledger system.

Predrill then drive screws at an angle through the diagonal brace into the desktop.

Install task lighting and add convenient receptacles according to your skill and comfort level with wiring.

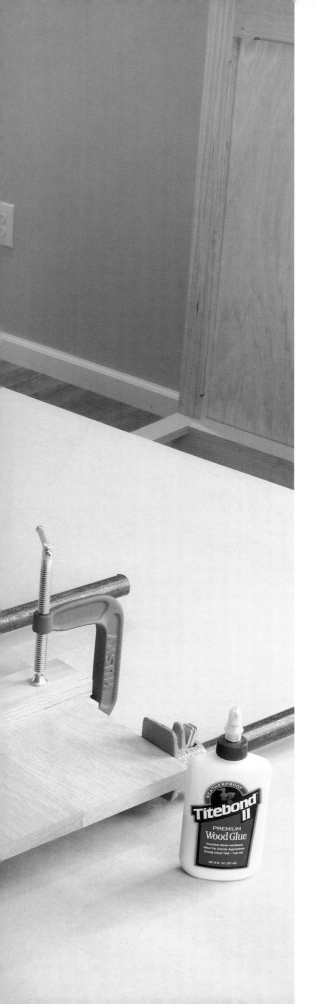

Living and Entertaining Rooms

Where built-ins for kitchens, baths and bedrooms mostly add functionality to your house, built-ins for the other rooms add fun. Living rooms, dining rooms, family and recreation rooms, even hallways and basements are all fine areas to exercise your imagination and your skill with a beautiful built-in.

Bookcases are among the most popular built-ins and you can locate one in just about any room. A formal, floor-to-ceiling bookcase will give your living room the sophistication of a private library. A less massive bookcase can fill an odd-sized space with maximum efficiency. For instance, the area next to a fireplace that has been built out from the wall is a perfect locale for a recessed, glass-door bookcase like the one in this chapter.

Another popular bookcase location is a little unorthodox but makes plenty of sense: the space beneath a staircase. A triangular, built-in bookcase here turns wasted space into a valuable storage area while adding visual interest. Do you have a favorite window but you can't find the right chair to set in front of it? Construct a built-in window seat. How about a full-wall media center for your new flat-panel TV? Or a clever wall niche tucked in between two wall studs. Do you have a basement rec room? A built-in bar will transform it into the ultimate party room. There is a world of fun to be had from simple built-in furniture.

In this chapter:

- Entry Bench/Bookcase
- Recessed Cabinet
- Window Seat
- Wall Niche
- Formal Bookcase
- Understairs Bookcase
- Media Bar
- Club Bar
- Trimwork Shelves

Entry Bench/Bookcase

A porch, foyer, or defined entry space provides a transition from the outdoors into the home that can put guests at ease and make them feel welcome. Many homes, especially those built in the middle part of the 20th century, do not have any allowance for an entry area. You might think that the only way to add such a space, if you don't have one, is to spend thousands of dollars building a small addition. But you don't necessarily need walls to define a space. You can also divide a space with a structure. This built-in entry bench and bookcase do just that.

It combines a bench where you can sit and put on your shoes, storage under the bench, and a bookcase that is just large enough to act as a virtual wall, separating the entry area from the rest of the room.

Before you begin constructing your own bench and bookcase, take a look around for potential obstructions, such as HVAC vents or electrical outlets, that may located where the project will be installed. If there are obstructions, you must relocate them in order to install this project.

This project uses oak-veneer plywood for many of the panels. Some of the panels are visible from both sides. For this reason it's best to purchase plywood with two attractive (cabinet grade or finish grade) faces. If one side of your plywood looks better than the other, then build with the best side facing the outside of the project.

Functioning as a room divider, this combination bookcase/entry bench closes off space at the room entry. This has the effect of making the living space feel much cozier by creating a transition in the foyer area between the room and the door. The built-in also offers valuable shelf space on the living area side as well as a convenient storage seat and a coat rack on the door side.

Tools & Materials ▸

Table saw	1" wood screws
Miter saw	1¼" fine thread
Drill/driver	pocket screws
Router	(6) No. 8 × 1¼"
45 degree bottom-	panhead screws
bearing chamfer bit	(6) Washers
Air compressor	Wood glue
Brad nail gun	(2) 2"-long × 1½"-
(2) 1 × 2 × 8-ft.	wide butt hinges
solid oak	¼"-dia. shelf pins
(3) 1 × 4 × 8-ft.	(1) Left mount lid
solid oak	support—Rockler
1 × 6 × 8-ft. solid oak	No. 26195
(2) ¾ × 4 × 8 oak	(4) Coat hooks
veneered plywood	Eye and ear
(1) ¼ × 4 × 8 oak	protection
veneered plywood	Work gloves
2" wood screws	

Cutting List

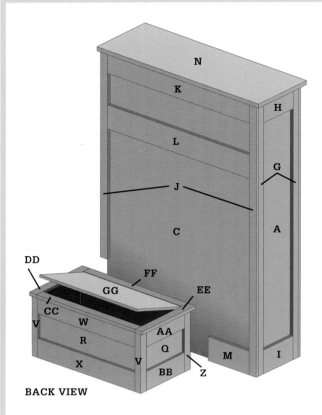

BACK VIEW

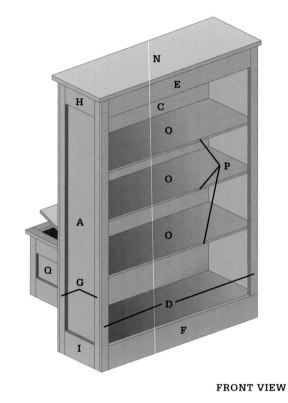

FRONT VIEW

KEY	NO.	DESCRIPTION	DIMENSION
A	2	Bookcase sides	¾ × 11 × 66"
B	2	Bookcase top and bottom	¾ × 11 × 46½"
C	1	Bookcase back	¾ × 48 × 66"
D	2	Bookcase front frame stiles	¾ × 2¼ × 66"
E	1	Bookcase front frame top rail	¾ × 3½ × 44½"
F	1	Bookcase front frame bottom rail	¾ × 5½ × 44½"
G	2	Bookcase side frame stiles	¾ × 1½ × 66"
H	1	Bookcase side frame top rail	¾ × 3½ × 8¼"
I	1	Bookcase side frame bottom rail	¾ × 5½ × 8¼"
J	2	Bookcase back frame stiles	¾ × 2¼ × 66"
K	1	Bookcase back top rail	¾ × 3½ × 44½"
L	1	Bookcase back middle rail	¾ × 5½ × 44½"
M	1	Bookcase back bottom rail	¾ × 5½ × 9"
N	1	Finished top	¾ × 13¼ × 49¼"
O	3	Shelves	¾ × 10¾ × 46¼"
P	3	Shelf edge	¾ × 1 × 46¼"
Q	2	Bench sides	¾ × 16 × 16"

KEY	NO.	DESCRIPTION	DIMENSION
R	1	Bench front	¾ × 15¼ × 35¼"
S	1	Bench back	¾ × 16 × 35¼"
T	1	Bench bottom, plywood	¾ × 14½ × 35¼"
U	1	Bench lid rail	¾ × 2¼ × 35¼"
V	2	Bench front frame stiles	¾ × 2¼ × 16"
W	1	Bench front frame top rail	¾ × 3½ × 33¼"
X	1	Bench front frame bottom rail	¾ × 5½ × 33¼"
Y	1	Bench side frame left stile	¾ × 1½ × 16"
Z	1	Bench side frame right stile	¾ × 2¼ × 16"
AA	1	Bench side frame top rail	¾ × 3½ × 12¼"
BB	1	Bench side frame bottom rail	¾ × 5½ × 12¼"
CC	1	Bench front cap	¾ × 1½ × 35¼"
DD	1	Bench left cap	¾ × 2¼ × 17"
EE	1	Bench right side cap	¾ × 2½ × 17"
FF	1	Bench back cap	¾ × 2¼ × 33¼"
GG	1	Bench lid	¾ × 14½ × 33"
HH	2	Lid support cleats	¾ × 2¼ × 3"

How to Build an Entry Bench/Bookcase

BUILD THE BOOKCASE & BENCH CABINETS

Cut the bookcase side panels to size using a table saw or circular saw and straightedge guide. Adjustable shelf pins fit into each side panel to support the shelves. Bore the shelf-pin holes in the side panels. Use a piece of ¼" pegboard as a template to space the holes 1" apart (photo 1).

Next, cut the bookcase top and bottom to size. Clamp the top and bottom between the side panels. Position the top edge of the bottom 5½" up from the bottom edge of the side panels. The top

is positioned flush with the top of the side panels. Attach the top and bottom to the sides by driving 2" screws through countersunk pilot holes in the side panels (photo 2). The face frame will conceal these screws.

Cut the back panel to size. Place the bookcase assembly face down and lay the back panel on top. Roughly align the outside edges of the shelf sides and top with the back panel. Lift up the back panel slightly and apply a thin bead of glue to the back edges of the top, bottom, and sides. Align the outside edges and attach the back with 1" brad nails.

Use a piece of ¼" perforated hardboard as a template for spacing the ¼"-dia. shelf pin holes. Mark the bit with a piece of tape to indicate the depth (the pin plus the hardboard). For maximum adjustability, drill pin holes every inch, making sure you orient the template the same way on each side of opposing panels.

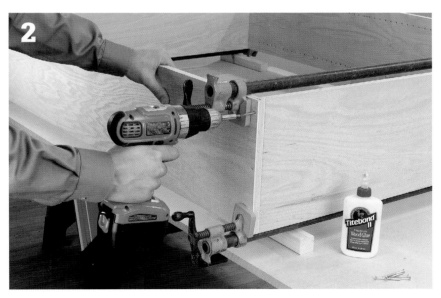

Clamp the bookcase top and bottom panels between the side panels. Bore a countersink and pilot hole through the side panel at each screw location. Attach the panels with 2" screws.

(continued)

Follow a similar assembly process to build the bench cabinet. Attach the bench bottom between the front and back panels and then attach the front, bottom, and back between the sides. Next, attach the lid rail between the sides (photo 3). The lid rail supports the bench back cap and the back edge of the lid.

ASSEMBLE THE FACE FRAMES

Cut the bookcase and bench frame parts. Pocket screws are used to assemble the face frames. A pocket screw is a washer-head screw that is driven into an angled counter-bore and pilot hole (called a pocket hole). A special angled jig and stepped drill bit are used to create the pocket hole. Pocket-hole jig kits include detailed instructions, making them very easy to use. If it's your first time using pocket screws, then practice fastening a few scrap pieces before working on the actual face frame pieces.

Bore two pocket holes in each end of each rail piece (photo 4). Place the front face frame rails and stiles face down on a work surface. Align the outside edges and clamp the face frame together. Next, drive a pocket screw into each pocket hole to secure the face frame parts (photo 5). Repeat this process for all three bookshelf face frames and the two bench face frames.

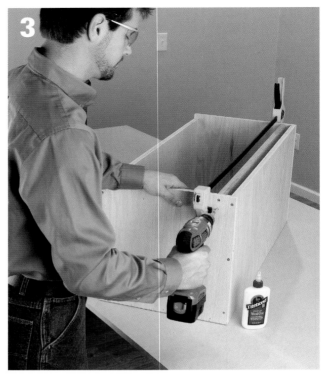

Position the top of the lid rail flush with the tops of the side panels and the back face of the lid rail 1" from the inside face of the back panel.

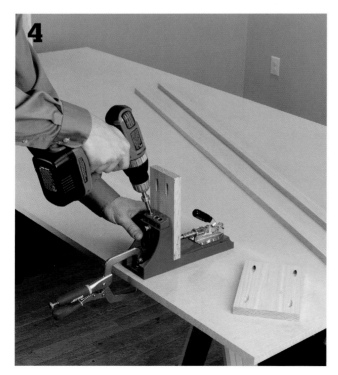

Clamp the pocket-hole guide in place on the rail. Use a stepped pocket-hole drill bit to bore the pocket holes on the back faces of the face frame parts.

Drive a 1¼"-long fine thread pocket-hole screw into each pocket hole. Drive the screw until it seats at the bottom of the hole and pulls the frame parts tight.

CUT THE DECORATIVE FACE FRAME EDGES

Stopped decorative edge profiles are cut on the inside edges of the face frames to add a decorative detail. A stopped cut or profile is a cut that does not run the entire length of the piece. In this case, a router and chamfer bit are used to cut a chamfer profile, but you could choose any other router bit profile, such as a cove or ogee, to suit your taste or match the existing moldings in your house.

The first step in cutting the stopped chamfers is to place the stop blocks inside the face frame. The stop blocks will stop the router's cutting progress exactly where the profile should end. The width of each stop block is 1½"—the distance from where the profile will stop to the corner of the face frame, plus the distance that the chamfer bit will cut past the bearing, in this case approximately ¼". The amount the bit cuts past the bearing varies depending on the depth of the cut. Cut two stop blocks from pieces of ¾"-thick scrap stock and clamp them into the corners at each end of the first cut (photo 6). It doesn't matter which rail or stile you cut first.

Install a 45-degree bottom bearing chamfer bit in your router. Set the router depth stop so the top of the bit bearing is ¼" below the bottom of the router base. You'll get the best results by making the cut in two passes. Raise the bit slightly to a depth of approximately ³⁄₁₆" for the first cut. Rout the chamfer profile into the inside edge of the face frame (photo 7). Then lower the bit to the ¼" depth stop setting and make a second pass. Repeat this process in the inside edge of all of the face frames. The bookcase back left stile and bookcase back bottom rail butt into the bench and do not meet other face frame parts to create corners. When cutting the stopped chamfers on these two parts you do not have a face frame corner to tuck the stop block into. You must position the stop block against the end of the part (the bookcase back left stile or the bookcase back bottom rail) that you are cutting.

ATTACH THE FACE FRAMES

Attach the face frames to the cabinets after all the stopped chamfers are cut. Attach the side face frames first. The edges of the side face frame are flush with the front and back edges of the shelf and bench cabinets (photo 8). Next, attach the front and back face frames. The face of the side face frames are aligned flush with the edges of the front and back face frames (photo 9). The face frames overhang the side of

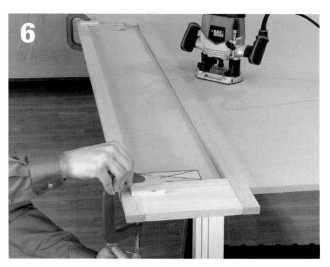

Make two ¾ × 2 × 6" stop blocks. Clamp one stop block in the inside corner at each end of the face frame piece that you will be routing.

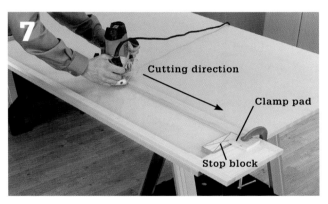

Push the router into the cut against the left stop block and then back into the face frame and cut from left to right along the face frame edge until the router contacts the right stop block. Lower the router depth to ¼" and make a second pass.

Attach the face frame sides to the cabinet sides with glue and brad nails. Align the sides of the face frame flush with the front and back edges of the cabinet.

(continued)

the bookcase and bench that will later be against the wall, allowing you to scribe or trim those edges to fit better against the wall.

Next attach the bench cap pieces. These pieces cover the top edges of the bench cabinet and frame the bench lid. Cut the cap pieces to size. Cut a ¾ × ¾" notch in the front corners of the bench front cap. Attach the cap pieces to the bench cabinet (photo 10).

MAKE THE SHELVES, BENCH LID & BOOKCASE TOP

The bookcase shelves are plywood panels with solid wood edging attached to the front edge for additional strength. Cut the panels to size on the table saw and rip the edge piece stock to width. Cut three edge pieces. Attach the edge pieces to the shelf panels with glue and 2" finish nails (photo 11).

The lid and top must withstand the most handling and use, so they are solid wood panels. You can use many combinations of board widths to create the panels. Make the panels slightly larger (roughly 1" in both dimensions) than the cutting list states. Double check to make sure your table saw blade is perpendicular to the saw table before ripping the pieces that will make the top and lid. If you have a jointer, then joint the edges to be sure the faces and edges are perpendicular.

Attach the front and back face frames with glue and 2" brads. The front edges of these face frames are flush with the face of the side face frame.

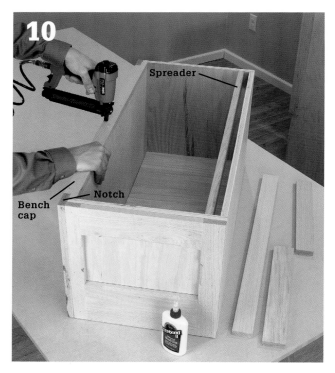

Attach the bench caps to the top of the bench assembly, using glue and brads.

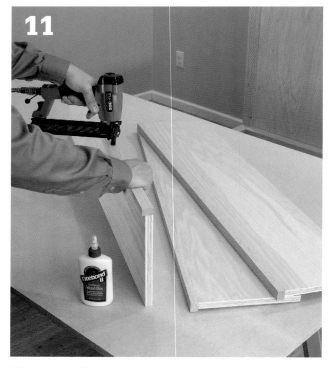

Attach a shelf edge to each shelf panel with glue and 2" brads.

Lay out the boards and clamp them without glue to be sure they fit together tightly. Then, spread a thin layer of glue onto the joining edges and clamp them together. Clamp narrow flat boards above and below the panels to keep them flat (photo 12).

Remove the panels from the clamps after the glue has cured. Scrape or sand off any excess glue and cut the panels to their final sizes. Cut the lid support cleats.

Apply finish to all of the components before the final assembly and installation. Sand the bench, bookcase, lid, finished top, and lid support cleats smooth. Apply wood stain (if you wish) and then a topcoat finish, such as polyurethane.

Mount the hinge on the lid and back cap piece. Position the lid so that when the lid is closed it rests on the lid rail. Next, attach the lid support cleats with glue and a couple brad nails to the left side panel. The back edge of the cleats is pressed against the lid rail and the top edge of the cleats is pressed against the bottom of the left cap. Install the lid support as directed in the instruction manual (photo 13). You can substitute another lid support that is designed to mount to the side of the cabinet or you can choose to not install a lid support.

Attach the finished top to the bookcase cabinet top. The finished top is attached through oversized pilot holes that are bored through the bookcase cabinet top. These oversized holes prevent the top from potentially splitting by allowing the screws to move slightly as the top expands and contracts with changes in humidity. Attach the finished top with pan head screws and washers (photo 14).

Attach coat hooks to the back middle rail.

INSTALL THE BENCH & BOOKCASE

Remove the base molding along the wall where the bench and bookcase will be installed. Move the bench and bookcase assemblies roughly into position and then attach the bench to the bookcase by driving 1" screws fitted with finish washers through the bookcase back and into the bench back.

Push the bench and bookcase into their installation location. Scribe, trim or sand the overhanging face frame edges to fit the wall better if necessary. Then attach the bench and bookcase to the wall. Bore countersink and pilot holes and drive 3" screws through the sides of the bench or bookcase into wall framing.

Finally, cut the old wall molding to fit the wall on either side of the bench and bookcase. If you have extra wall molding that matches, then cut it to fit around the bench and bookcase.

Apply a thin layer of glue to the mating edges of the lid boards and place them in clamps. Then sandwich the panel between pairs of boards positioned perpendicular to the glue seam. Clamp the cross boards (called "cauls") to help keep the panel flat.

Attach the hinge to the lid and bench back cap. Then, attach the lid support to the lid and support cleats.

Bore six ⅜"-dia. holes through the bookcase top. Attach the finish top to the bookcase cabinet top with No. 8 × 1¼" panhead screws and washers.

Recessed Cabinet

If you've got a recessed wall area that you're not sure how to use, then a built-in cabinet might be a perfect fit. For example, the set-back space created on one or both sides of a bumped-out fireplace is a perfect spot to install a built-in bookshelf or cabinet.

Building a recessed cabinet is very similar to building a freestanding cabinet. The key difference is that a recessed cabinet must fit perfectly between the side walls. The easiest way to make a cabinet that will fit is to make a basic interior cabinet case that's slightly smaller than the available space and then build a face frame and top cover that will cover the edges of the cabinet and fit snuggly against the walls. The secret to achieving a perfect fit is to make the face frame and top slightly oversized and then scribe them to fit against the walls.

You can build a recessed cabinet with or without doors. In the version seen here, glass panel doors were built, but you can also use solid, natural wood veneer or painted plywood panels to conceal the cabinet interior. It is important to purchase tempered glass when you are building glass panel doors. Tempered glass is treated with heat so that if it is broken, it will shatter into small pieces that are less likely to cause serious cuts. It's also stronger. You can't cut it yourself, so be sure to get the size correct when you order it cut-to-fit.

Building this cabinet requires intermediate woodworking skills and a few woodworking power tools, including a table saw, miter saw, and router table.

Tools & Materials ▸

Table saw
Miter saw
Drill/driver
Pocket hole jig kit
Finish or random-orbit sander
Eye and ear protection
Work gloves

Doors:
Router table
Rail and stile router bit set
$\frac{3}{8}$"-rad. rabbet bottom-bearing router bit

**Cabinet materials (to make one roughly
    4-ft.-wide × 4-ft.-tall × 12"-deep cabinet):**
(2) 2 × 4 × 8-ft. pine
(1) ¼ × 4 × 8 plain-sawn cherry veneer plywood

(1) ¾ × 4 × 8 plain-sawn cherry veneer plywood
(2) ¾ × 1½" × 8-ft. cherry
(2) ¾ × 2½" × 8-ft. cherry
(1) ¾ × 5 × 48" cherry
2" flat-head wood screws
2½" flat-head wood screws
1¼" fine thread washer-head (pocket) screws
18-ga. × 2" brad nails
(24) ¼"-dia. shelf pins

Doors (to make four roughly 11 × 46" doors):
(5) ¾ × 2" × 8-ft. solid cherry
(1) ¾ × 4 × 30 solid cherry
(4 pr.) non-mortise full-wrap hinges
(4) ⅛"-thick tempered glass panels
(4) magnetic door catches
18-ga. × ¾" brad nails

Cutting List

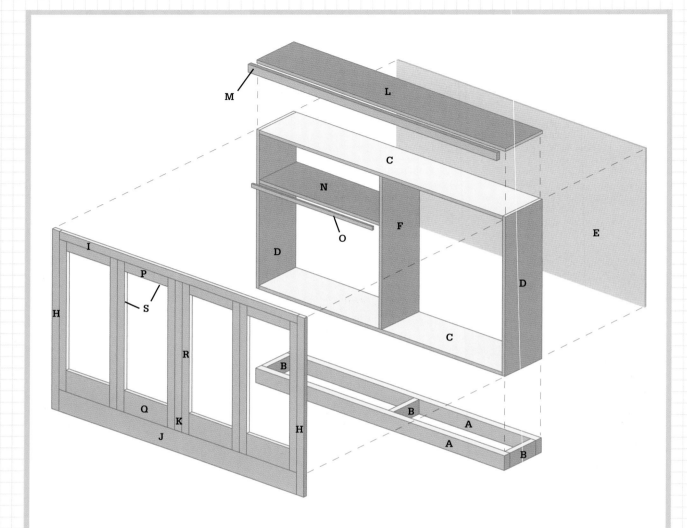

KEY	NO.	DESCRIPTION	DIMENSION
Cabinet			
A	2	Base rails	1½ × 3½ × 46"
B	3	Base cross pieces	1½ × 3½ × 8¼"
C	2	Cabinet top and bottom	¾ × 11 × 43½"
D	2	Cabinet sides	¾ × 11 × 48"
E	1	Cabinet back	¼ × 45 × 48"
F	1	Cabinet divider	¾ × 11 × 46½"
G	2	Back cleats	¾ × 2½ × 43½"
H	2	Face frame stiles	¾ × 2½ × 51½"
I	1	Face frame top rail	¾ × 2½ × 43"
J	1	Face frame bottom rail	¾ × 4¼ × 43"

KEY	NO.	DESCRIPTION	DIMENSION
K	1	Face frame center stile	¾ × 2¾ × 45¼"
L	1	Top	¾ × 11¾ × 48"
M	1	Top front edge	¾ × 1¼ × 48"
N	6	Shelf	¾ × 11 × 43¼"
O	6	Shelf edge	¾ × 1 × 43¼"
P	4	Top rail	¾ × 1⅝ × 6⅝"
Q	4	Bottom rail	¾ × 3⅝ × 6⅝"
R	8	Stiles	¾ × 2 × 44½"
S	16	Glass tack strips	¼ × ¼" × glass perimeter

How to Build a Recessed Cabinet

DETERMINE THE CABINET DIMENSIONS

Perhaps the trickiest aspect of building a cabinet that must fit between two walls is calculating the part dimensions so the finished cabinet will fit the space you have. The first step is to measure the width of the space. Walls are seldom plumb, so you must measure the width at several heights above the floor (photo 1). Record the smallest measurement (the narrowest width) and use that dimension to make adjustments to the cutting list (unless your space happens to be 48" wide—the width of the cabinet seen here.

Limit the shelf lengths to no more than 30" long—any span larger than that and they are likely to sag and break. Shorten shelf lengths in a wide cabinet by dividing the cabinet into multiple sections with vertical divider panels. If the space the cabinet is to be installed in is 32" or less, then you will not need a vertical divider. If the space is 32 to 60" wide, then you need at least one vertical divider in the center of the cabinet. Install additional vertical dividers if you plan to store heavy objects on the shelves.

MAKE THE BASE

Cut the base frame parts to length and assemble the base with 2½" wood screws. Center the base between the side walls and against the back wall. Level the base with shims and then secure it to the back wall (photo 2).

Measure the width of the space where the cabinet will be installed. Measure at several heights above the floor and at the front and back of the space. Record and use the smallest measurement.

Level the base with shims and then attach it to the back wall. Drive 3" drywall screws through the back base rail and into the wall studs. Trim off any exposed shims flush with the front edge of the base.

(continued)

MAKE THE CABINET FRAME

Cut the cabinet sides, dividers, top, and bottom to size. Bore the shelf-pin holes in the side panels. You can use a manufactured shelf pin jig or use a piece of pegboard as a template to align the holes. Then, cut the back cleats to length. Sand the faces of each part smooth with 150-grit sandpaper. Attach the sides to the top and bottom with 2" wood screws. Bore pilot holes before driving screws into plywood edges. Attach the back cleats to the sides and top with 2" wood screws. Next, cut a notch to fit around the back cleat in the top of each divider panel. Attach the dividers to the top and bottom with 2" screws (photo 3). Cut the back panel to size and attach the back panel to the cabinet frame with glue and brad nails or crown staples (photo 4).

Place the cabinet frame on the base. Center the cabinet on the base and align the front edge of the cabinet with the front edge of the base. Attach the cabinet to the base with 2" brad nails. Place shims behind the cabinet at each stud location to fill the gap between the cabinet and wall. Attach the cabinet to the back wall and side walls by driving a screw through the back cleat and side panels into the wall studs (photo 5).

Attach the divider panels to the top and bottom with 2" screws. Use a square to make sure the divider is perpendicular to the top and bottom. Bore a pilot hole and countersink hole for each screw. Drive the screws through the top and bottom.

Attach the back panel with glue and 1" brads or 1" narrow crown staples. Keep the cabinet sides, top, and bottom perpendicular as you attach the back panel.

Attach the cabinet to the wall. Bore a pilot and countersink hole through the back cleat and side panels at each stud location. Place scrap blocks or shims behind each screw hole to fill the gap between the wall and cabinet. Secure the cabinet with 3" drywall screws.

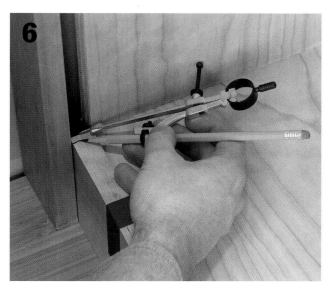

6

Temporarily attach the rails to the cabinet with tape. Then, scribe the stiles to follow the profile of the wall. Hold the stile perpendicular to the rails and against the side wall. Set a compass opening to match the distance that the stile overlaps the ends of the rails.

MAKE THE FACE FRAME & TOP

The face frame and top are made to fit exactly between the walls and will cover the gaps that were left between the cabinet and walls. Cut the face frame stiles and rails to size. Temporarily hold or attach the face frame rails in place against the cabinet frame. Then hold one of the stiles perpendicular to the rails and against the side wall. Scribe the wall profile on the outside edge of the stile (photo 6 and 7). Follow the same process to scribe the other stile. Trim the stiles along the scribe lines. Test the fit of the stiles and trim or sand as necessary to fit. The stiles should fit snugly between the walls and rails. Next, lay out the face frame parts on a flat surface and assemble the frame with pocket screws (photo 8). Sand the face frame smooth.

Attach the face frame to the cabinet frame with glue and a few 18 ga. × 1¼" brads. You only need a couple of brads in each piece to hold it securely while the glue cures.

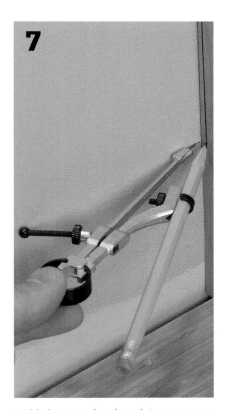

7

Hold the metal point of the compass against the wall and pull the compass down along the wall to trace the profile of the wall onto the face of the stile. The stile must remain perpendicular to the rails as you draw the scribe line.

8

Assemble the cabinet face frame with pocket screws. Clamp the parts to a large work surface to keep them perpendicular as they are connected.

(continued)

The top must fit against three walls. If the walls are perpendicular, then you can simply measure the width of the opening and cut the top panel. But, if the walls are not perfectly square to one another, the easiest way to make a top that fits is to create a template (photo 9). Transfer the template dimensions and cut the top panel.

Cut the top front edge piece the same length as the front edge of the top panel. Attach the top front edge to the top with glue. Clamp the front edge until the glue has cured. Remove the clamps, sand the top assembly and attach the top to the cabinet (photo 10).

Cut the shelf boards and shelf edge to size. Attach the shelf edge to the shelf board, aligning the top edges, with glue. Clean off excess glue and sand the shelves smooth.

Protect the surrounding wall surfaces with masking tape and drop cloths. Apply wood finish or paint to the cabinet and shelves. In this case dark brown oil-base gel stain was applied, followed by three coats of water-base polyurethane. After the finish is dry, attach base molding to match the existing base molding in the room.

BUILD THE DOORS

The first step in building doors is to determine the size of the doors. To prevent sagging, the maximum width of each door should be less than 24" If the cabinet opening is greater than 24" wide, then use two doors.

The bottom rail is wider than the top rail for two reasons. First, a wider bottom rail gives the door

Tape together pieces of paper or cardboard to make a template for the top. Leave a ⅛" space between the template and the walls. Then, trace the template on the top panel stock and cut out the top.

Attach the top to the cabinet with 1¼" screws. Drive the screws through the underside of the cabinet top panel and into the finished top. Use one screw in each corner and two screws evenly spaced near the front and back of the cabinet.

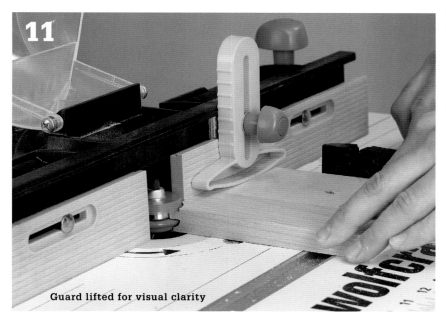

11

Guard lifted for visual clarity

This router bit set cuts a ⅜"–long stub tenon. The extra ¾" necessary for the two stub tenons must be added to the length of the rails. Rout the stub tenons on the ends of the rails. Set the router bit height so the top cutter will mill a ⅛"-deep rabbet above the stub tenon.

12

Rout the groove profile in the inside edges of the rails and stiles. Set the router bit height to align the groove with the stub tenon (inset). Make test cuts in a scrap piece to adjust the bit height for a perfect fit before cutting the actual parts.

good scale by adding a little more visual weight to the bottom of the door. Second, the wider dimension adds more gluing surface, creating a stronger frame to support the glass panel.

Measure the height and width of the face frame openings. Determine the door width and height by subtracting the width of the gaps that must be left around the edges of the doors and between doors (see page 188).

There are several ways to build frame and panel doors. The doors for this cabinet are made using a rail-and-stile (also referred to as a cope-and stick) router bit set. This set contains two router bits; one bit that cuts the stub tenon in the ends of the rails and another bit that cuts the panel groove and edge profile.

Cut the door parts to size. Then rout the stub tenon profile on both ends of the rails (photo 11). Next, rout the groove profile in the inside edges of the stiles and rails (photo 12). Make test cuts in a scrap piece to adjust the bit alignment.

(continued)

Assemble each door frame with glue (photo 13). Clamp the frames, checking them for square before the glue sets up. *Note: If you choose to install solid panels rather than glass panels, then install the panels when you assemble the frame.*

The back edge of the groove must be removed to create the rabbet that the glass fits against. Use a router and bottom-bearing rabbet bit to remove the back lip of the groove (photo 14). Use a chisel to clean up the corners of the rabbet that the router bit does not reach.

Hang the doors before you apply the finish and install the glass. These doors are mounted on full wrap-around, no-mortise hinges that offer the no-sag benefits of butt hinges and are easy to install. Attach the hinges to the cabinet and then mount the doors on the hinges (photo 15). Mount magnetic catches on the top rail to keep the doors closed.

After the doors are installed and operating correctly, remove the doors and hardware. Cut ¼ × ¼" tack strips to hold the glass panels in the door. Cut enough tack strips to cover the perimeter of all the glass. Sand and finish the doors and tack strips to match the cabinet.

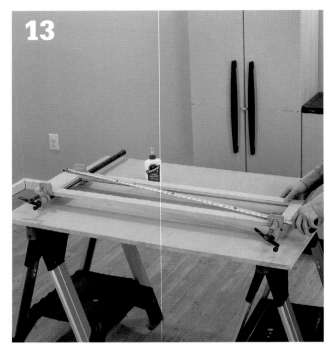

Assemble the door frame with glue. Measure diagonally across the corners to check the frame for square (or, just use a carpenter's square). If the diagonal measurements are equal, then the frame is square.

Use a bottom-bearing rabbet bit to remove the back lip of the groove. Set the bit depth so that the bearing rides on the front edge or "stick" profile of the door (inset).

Fasten the hinge to the door using the slotted screw holes first. These holes allow you to adjust the door position slightly. Drive screws in the fixed screw holes after the door is positioned correctly in the cabinet. Drill pilot holes for each screw to prevent stripping the screw head, breaking the screws or splitting the door stile.

Install the glass in the doors after the finish is dry. Place a sheet of glass in each door. Cut the tack strips to fit along each side of the glass. Bore $\frac{1}{32}$"-dia. pilot holes through the tack strips, spacing them 6" apart. Place the strips over the glass and drive a 18 ga. × ¾" brad nail into each pilot hole (photo 16). After the glass pieces are installed, reinstall the hardware and hang the doors.

Attach the tack strips to hold the glass in the doors. Use a brad push tool to drive the brads or gently tap the brads with a small hammer. Cover the glass with a piece of cardboard to protect it.

Door Dimensions ▶

To prevent sagging, the maximum width of each door should be less than 24". If the cabinet opening is greater than 24" wide, then use two doors.

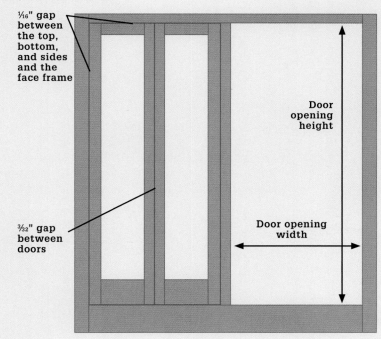

1/16" gap between the top, bottom, and sides and the face frame

3/32" gap between doors

Door opening height

Door opening width

Door overall dimensions:

Door width = face frame opening width – side gaps (1/16 sides and 3/32 between doors)

Door height = face frame opening height – top and bottom gaps (1/8 total)

Door part dimensions:

Door stile length = height of door

Door rail length = width of door – 2 (stile width) + 2 (tenon length)

Window Seat

One great way to add cozy charm to a room is to build a window seat. Not only do window seats make a room more inviting, they provide functional benefits as well, particularly when you surround them with built-in shelving. The window seat shown here has a base built from above-the-refrigerator cabinets.

This size provides just the right height (when placed on a 3" curb) to create a comfortable seat.

Above the cabinets and flanking each side is a site-made bookcase. A top shelf bridges the two cases and ties the whole thing together—while creating still more space for storage or display.

Tools, Materials & Cutting List

Eye and ear protection
Work gloves
Miter saw
Table saw
Circular saw
Drill/driver
Level
Stud finder
Hammer
Tape measure
Nail set
Pneumatic nailer/compressor
Router
Shooting board
Sander
Framing square
2) 15h × 24d × 36w
   stock cabinets
2) ¾" × 4 × 8 ft. pcs. MDF
   or plywood
Screws/nails
1) ¼" × 4 × 8 ft. birch plywood
Caulk
Primer
Paint

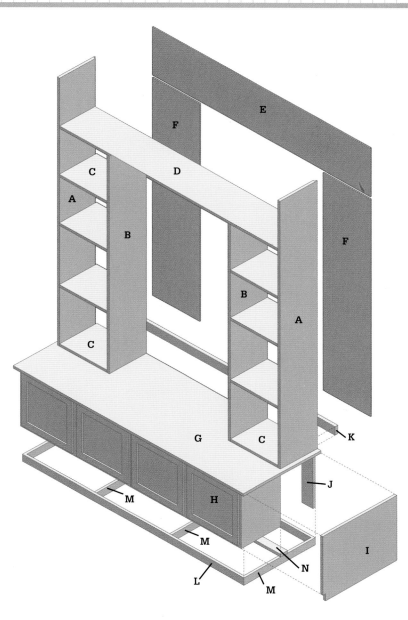

KEY	NO.	DESC.	SIZE	MATERIAL
A	2	Outer standard	¾ × 11½ × 77¼"	MDF
B	2	Inner standard	¾ × 11½ × 63¼"	MDF
C	8	Shelf	¾ × 16½ × 11¼"	MDF
D	1	Top shelf	¾ × 11¼ × 70½"	MDF
E	1	Top backer	¼ × 13¼ × 71⅜"	Plywood
F	2	Backers	¼ × 17½ × 63¼"	Plywood
G	1	Seatboard	¾ × 25 × 74"	MDF

KEY	NO.	DESC.	SIZE	MATERIAL
H	2	Cabinets	15 h × 36" w	Stock cabinets
I	2	End panel	¾ × 24 × 18"	MDF
J	4	Nailer	¾ × 2½ × 15"	Plywood
K	1	Ledger	¾ × 2½ × 72"	Plywood
L	2	Curb rim	¾ × 3 × 72"	MDF
M	4	Curb strut	¾ × 3 × 22½"	MDF
N	1	Cabinet nailer	¾ × 3 × 72"	MDF

How to Build a Window Seat

The key control point for laying this project out is the center of the window sill. Measure and mark it.

After striking a level line at cabinet height, measure from the floor in three locations to make sure the cabinets will fit.

Strike a plumb line on each edge of the cabinet run. Use a 4-foot level and strike the line from floor to ceiling.

LAY OUT THE PROJECT

This window seat is integrated with the existing window and trimwork. The key control point for laying out the base cabinets is locating the center of the window opening. It is also important that the cabinets sit level both left-to-right and front-to-back. Level cabinet tops make installing the upper cabinet cases much easier.

Before you begin building, relocate or remove any electrical outlets that'll be covered by the cabinet, according to your local electrical codes. For example, you can't just dead-end wires and leave them buried in a wall. They usually need to be capped and placed in a junction box with a removable faceplate that is accessible (which may mean making a cutout in the back of a cabinet panel).

Mark the center of the window opening on the sill (photo 1). Use a square and a level to transfer that mark down the wall to the cabinet height location. At the height of the cabinets mark a level line. Measure from the floor up to the level line in several locations to make sure the cabinets will fit all along their entire run (photo 2). If they don't fit, make the proper adjustments; that is, raise the line. Cabinets that don't come up to the line must be shimmed so they are level. Using an electronic stud finder, find and mark the wall stud locations beneath the window and on each side in the project area. *Note: You should find jack and king studs directly on either side of the window and a header above the window. Determine the overall span of the cabinets you choose. For the project shown here, the bank will be 6 ft. long, measuring from outside-edge to outside-edge. Use a level to mark the outside edges of the cabinet run on the wall. Mark plumb lines down to the floor and up to the ceiling (photo 3).*

INSTALL THE BASE CABINETS

With all the layout lines marked out, the next step is to install the cabinets that form the base of the window seat. This determines the control points for the rest of the project layout. Use a pull-saw and sharp chisel to remove base molding between the vertical layout lines (photo 4).

To elevate the cabinets that will be used for the seat to a more comfortable height, and to create a toe-kick space, build a short curb that matches the footprint of the seat. Since the curb will not be visible, you can use just about any shop scraps you may have to build it. The one shown here is made with MDF sheet stock that is rip-cut into 3"-wide strips. Then the curb is assembled into a ladder shape by attaching struts between the front and back curb members with glue and screws (photo 5). Once the ladder is built, set the cabinets on the curb so the cabinet fronts and sides align with the curb. Mark the location of the backs of the cabinets onto the top of the curb and then remove the cabinets. Attach a nailer to the curb just behind the line for the cabinet backs. Then, position the curb tight against the wall in the area where the base molding has been removed. Attach it to the sill plate of the wall with nails or screws.

To support the back edge of the seatboard, attach a ledger to the wall. The top of the ledger (we used a 2½"-wide strip of plywood) should be flush with the tops of the cabinets when they are installed on top of the curb. Attach the ledger with panel adhesive and nails or screws driven at stud locations (photo 6). Measure between the top of the curb and ledger and cut a few nailers to this length.

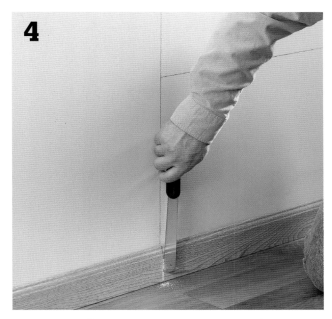

Because a pull-type saw requires almost zero clearance at the bottom of a cut (where it would hit the floor in this application), it's great for removing the base molding so the cabinet carcases fit tight to the wall.

Assemble the curb members into a ladder-like frame and secure the butt joints with glue and screws driven through pilot holes.

Attach a ledger for the back edge of the seatboard to the wall, using panel adhesive and screws driven at stud locations. Tack the ledger in place and then reinforce with wood screws driven at stud locations.

(continued)

7

Cut nailers to fit between the ledger and the curb and attach them to the wall at the ends of the project area.

8

For floors that are out of level, shim the cabinets up to the level line to keep them in a level plane.

9

After clamping the cabinet face-frames together, predrill and fasten them together with screws.

Attach them to the wall at the ends of the project, and add a couple near the center to help support the ledger (photo 7).

Set the cabinets in position on the curb, with the back edges against the nailer. Drive shims between the curb and the floor if necessary to level the cabinets (photo 8). Fasten the cabinets to the nailer strip. Predrill, countersink and fasten the face frames together with screws to form a "gang" of cabinets (photo 9). If you are using cabinets that have no face frames, screw the cabinet sides together as directed by the cabinet manufacturer. Cut off shims as necessary.

If the ends of your window seat are open (that is, they don't butt up against a wall), cut end panels to cover the ends of the cabinets and the open space behind them. Use ¾" plywood or hardboard. You may need to remove a sliver of the baseboard on each side so you can butt the panels up against the wall. Attach the panel to the cabinet ends and the curb with panel adhesive.

Cut, rout, and install the seat top. Cutting a 74" × 25" blank from MDF (medium-density fiberboard) works well. This will create a 1" overhang at the front and sides of the cabinets. Use a router

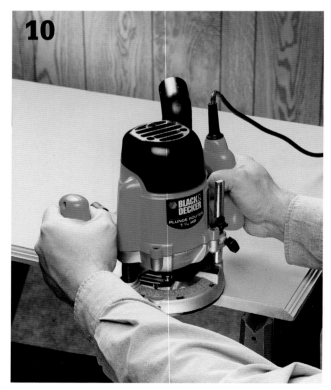

10

Before installing the seat top, rout a profile on the front and side edges. Don't rout the back.

and bit with a decorative profile (such as an ogee or a plain roundover) to smooth the hard edge of the MDF (photo 10). Profiling the edge reduces the chance that the edge will chip or crack. Position the seat top on top of the cabinets and the wall ledger and fasten it from the interior of the cabinets using predrilled coarse-threaded drywall screws. A bead of panel adhesive along the top edges of the cabinet and the ledger helps ensure a solid connection.

CUT THE CASE STOCK

The bookcase portion of the window seat can be assembled from sheet stock or solid 1× stock, such as 1 × 12 pine or poplar (pine is cheaper, poplar is stronger and takes paint better) or hardwood like maple, oak, or cherry for staining. Whatever material you choose, install a backer sheet of ¼" plywood that fits into rabbets in the backs of the case stock to help ensure square assembly and provide a strong connection point to the wall.

The actual width of 1 × 12 dimension lumber is 11¼", so if using sheet stock, rip all pieces to width. Any edges that face the interior of the room need to be sanded smooth to remove saw marks. Note that it's usually easier to dress the factory edge than the edge cut on-site. Running the pieces on a jointer or router table is a fast, accurate way to dress the edge. A belt sander or finish sander with fine grit paper works too, but be careful not to remove too much stock. Of course, you can also hand sand it.

Cut a ½" wide by ¼" deep rabbet (see drawing, page 81) on the backs of the standards (photo 11). You can do this with a table saw (either make multiple passes on the table saw to remove stock or use a stacked dado head cutter blade); using a router with a rabbeting bit; or on a jointer or router table. The remainder of the layout and sizing must be registered from the seat top to accommodate specific site conditions.

INSTALL THE TOP-SHELF BACKER

The remaining measurements for the backer and shelf dimensions are now determined by the distance between your window casing, vertical layout lines, and ceiling height. They must be site-measured for accuracy.

Lay out the top shelf backer (photo 12). It should fit between the ceiling and the top of the window casing—and between your vertical layout lines. To calculate the top shelf backer dimensions, measure between the vertical layout lines. Subtract ⅝". To calculate top shelf backer height, measure from the top of the window casing to the ceiling. Subtract ⅛".

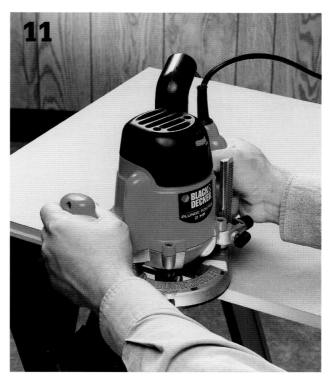

Clamp all work securely before milling the ½ × ¼ rabbet for the backers with a router, which will provide safe, accurate cuts. The remainder of the layout and sizing must be measured from the seat top to accommodate specific site conditions.

Use the layout lines to size the top shelf backer and the backers for the vertical shelf units.

(continued)

Marking layout lines all at once using a framing square is a good way to keep lines parallel from shelf-to-shelf. Make sure all bottoms are held flush during the marking procedure.

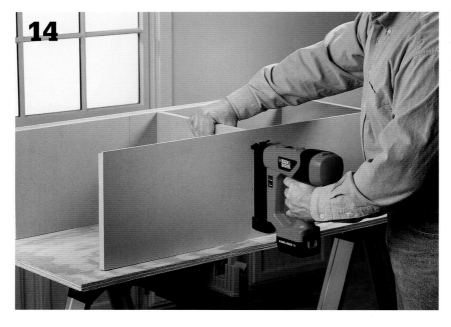

Install the shelves between the side standards. Glue the joints and clamp them. Tack them with finish nails. Drill countersink pilot holes and reinforce with three 2½" deck screws at each joint.

Install the top shelf backer tight to the ceiling by fastening to studs with finish nails or screws.

FABRICATE & ASSEMBLE THE BOOKCASES

The bookcases' outside edges run from the seat-top to the ceiling. The inside edges run from the seat-top to the top of the window casing. Measure and cut each vertical bookcase member to length. On a flat surface, lay all the bottoms of the bookcase members flush and mark out your shelves (photo 13). Use a framing square to mark them. Keep in mind there is a bottom

shelf that sits directly above the seat top. The top shelf is installed later.

Lay out and cut the backer stock. To calculate the width, measure the distance between the window casing and the vertical layout line, minus ⅝". To calculate the height, measure the distance from the seat top to the bottom edge of the top backer and subtract ⅛".

Assemble the cabinet sides and the backers. This is an ideal application for a pneumatic ¼" crown stapler, but it can also be done effectively by predrilling and

15

Hold the shelf assembly as tight as possible to the window trim, seat top and wall then fasten. Drive at least two or three screws to hold each unit, in addition to nails.

16

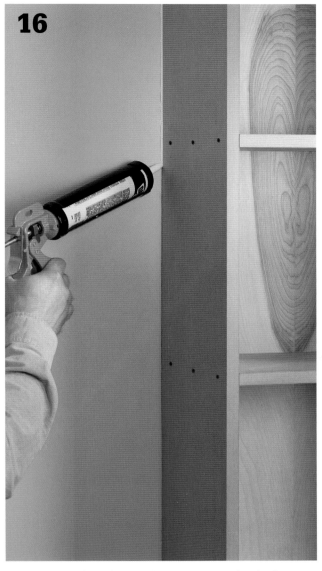

For paint grade units, caulk any gaps to make shadow lines disappear. You can caulk the gap on paint grade shelves too. Be extra diligent in wiping down the material after caulking.

screwing, or by using a pneumatic finish nailer. Use a framing square as a reference to be sure the cabinet carcases are as square as possible during assembly. Measure, cut, and install shelves at the layout lines (photo 14). Fasten through the cabinet carcass into the shelves. Predrill and countersink if using screws.

INSTALL THE BOOK CASES & TOP SHELF

Butt the left bookcase to the window trim and fasten it to a wall stud with a few screws or nails driven through the backer (photo 15). Make sure the case

sits as tightly to the wall, seat top, and window trim as possible. Expect to make some on-site corrections as necessary to accommodate out-of-plumb walls or other imperfections. Slight gaps can be caulked later. Repeat for the right-side bookcase and then measure, cut, and install the top shelf. If painting, caulk wherever necessary (photo 16). Fill exposed holes for nails and screws, then prime and paint or apply another finish of your choice. Make or buy a comfortable seat cushion. Finally, brew a cup of coffee, grab a good book, and get busy relaxing.

Wall Niche

A wall niche is kind of cubby hole carved into a stud wall, usually to house display shelving. These days, they are often seen in higher-end housing as prefashioned inserts with an arch shape and Greco-Roman styling, often with classical statuary within the niche sides. The niche shown here is a rather different animal. It is simply a wooden box that you slip into a hole in the wall and then trim out. As a quick and easy storage project, it is a perfect accompaniment to our Fast Country Diner project (see pages 84 to 93).

A niche creates a perfect spot to stash napkin holders, salt and pepper shakers, and other tableware so your table surface is clear for eating, relaxing or doing a bit of homework.

The steps, skills, and tools described here can be used to create wall niches of various sizes and in numerous locations. It is important to note, however, that these niches are intended for nonload-bearing walls. If the niche you wish to create would involve cutting framing members in a load-bearing wall, consider redesigning the project so you do not have to cut wall studs. Making structural alterations to a load-bearing wall should be done only by qualified professionals.

It's also important to be aware of any electrical wires or gas or water plumbing near your project area. Check to see if there are light switches or plugs above or below the niche opening before cutting and try to deduce where plumbing might be routed and located.

Safety notice: This project should be installed only in nonload-bearing walls. Do not cut wall studs in load-bearing walls unless you are working with a certified building engineer or licensed contractor.

Tools, Materials & Cutting List

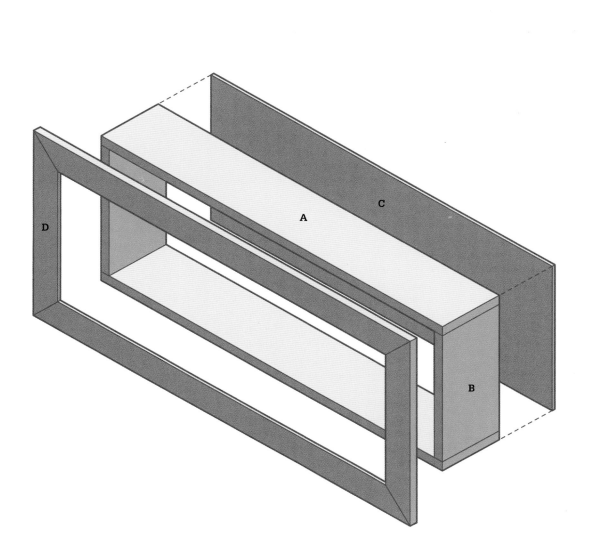

Eye and ear protection	Drywall finishing tools	
Work gloves	2-ft. level	
Drywall/plaster	Aviator snips	
cutting saw	1 × 6	
Reciprocating saw	Trim-head screws	
Cordless drill/driver	¼" birch plywood scrap	
Circular saw	1⅝" drywall screws	
Miter saw	Case molding	
Countersink	Paint	

KEY	NO.	DESC.	SIZE	MATERIAL
A	2	Top/bottom	¾ × 3⅝ × 25½"	Hardwood
B	2	Side	¾ × 3⅝ × 8"	Hardwood
C	1	Back	¼ × 9½ × 25½"	Plywood
D	4	Trim	½ × 2⅞" × miter to fit	Case molding

How to Build a Wall Niche

LAY OUT THE NICHE

Determine that the wall you're cutting into is not a load-bearing or exterior wall. Determine the opening's finished location and height and width. An 8" tall by 24" wide niche is just the right scale for the kitchen booth project we designed this niche to accompany (see page 84). Use a 2-ft. level and mark all four sides of the opening plumb and level at the finished location. These lines are the control points for all other measurements.

Measure ¾" out from each control point line (photo 1). Do this at two points on each line and connect the dots using a 2-ft. level.

MAKE THE CUTOUT

Check in the basement and adjoining walls for wiring and pipes. Open a preliminary hole with a razor knife to check if you're unsure. Use a drywall saw or reciprocating saw to cut along the cut line. Make the cut as shallow as you can in case there are hidden wires or pipes in the wall.

Remove the drywall, exposing the wall studs. More than likely, you're going to have a wall stud or two somewhere in the middle of the opening. Use a reciprocating saw to remove the studs. Or, you can use a circular saw to start the cut (photo 2), carefully aligning it with the edge of the drywall and using it to cut the stud. Then, finish the cut with a reciprocating

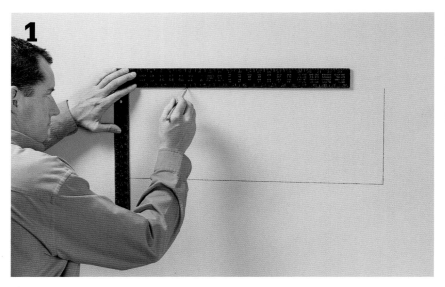

Start your layout by mapping out the niche's finished dimensions, then measure out from there for the rough opening where you will make your cuts. This is the cut line. With electrical power turned off, cut the opening in the wall covering. Use caution in case there are hidden wires or pipes in the area.

Cut as deeply into the wall studs as you can with a circular saw or trim saw.

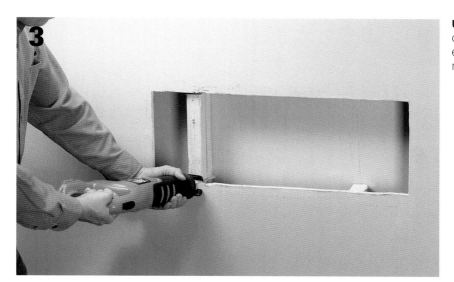

3

Use a reciprocating saw to finish the cut. This method is easier on the drywall—especially if the studs back up to another room—and provides a straighter cut.

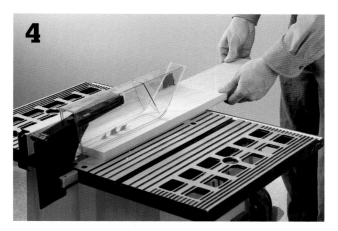

4

Rip-cut the niche frame boards to width. Cutting them so they stop just short of the opposite wallcovering when installed.

5

Assemble the niche box. Drill countersunk pilot holes for the screws.

saw (photo 3). Be careful not to cut through the drywall on the back side of the cut.

When removing studs, you may pull a fastener through from an adjoining room and have to repair that afterwards. Nails or screws may be penetrating from the other side of the wall into the stud. Carefully remove the stud section. It is likely that removing the stud section will cause the fastener to pull through the opposite side of the wall, so touch-up may be necessary. For most nonload-bearing walls the competed niche box should provide adequate support for the cut studs. But if you are cutting more than one stud, or if you simply want to be certain the niche box does not sag from downward pressure, make the opening larger and install a double 2 × 4 header over the niche box. This will require considerably more

patching of the wall covering, but you may appreciate it for your own peace of mind.

BUILD THE NICHE BOX

Measure the depth of your wall cavity and subtract ⅜" from the overall depth to give yourself a little bit of flexibility when installing the niche and to allow for the thickness (¼") of the backer material. This measurement yields the required width of the boards you'll use to make the niche box. Rip-cut 1 × 6 × 8 lumber to the required width, using a tablesaw or a circular saw with a straightedge guide (photo 4). Cut the frame parts to length.

Fasten top and bottom niche frame parts to the sides with drywall screws driven into countersunk pilot holes (photo 5). Cut the backer board to size and

(continued)

Use standard casing to trim out the niche like a picture frame. Preinstalling the trim means you can slip the niche box assembly into the opening. The trim guides how the box sets against the wall, similar to how a pre-hung door is installed.

Fasten the niche box up into the stud ends with finish nails.

attach it to the back edges of the frame with drywall screws or finish nails. Cut trim moldings (such as door casing or picture frame molding) to fit the niche box. For the most satisfying results, choose a molding style and approach that reflects the molding scheme already in the room. Fasten the trim to the niche box with finish nails and glue or panel adhesive (photo 6). Run a small bead of caulk/adhesive on the face of the niche box.

INSTALL THE NICHE BOX

The niche box is fastened through the interior walls of the box to the ends of the stud(s) you removed. It can also be fastened to blocks you install in the wall cavity on each side. Locate each stud and transfer its location to the interior of the box and mark it.

Test-fit the niche box to make sure it lays flat against drywall. When you have established that the fit is good, run a bead of caulk/adhesive on the backsides of the trim pieces.

Insert the niche box into the opening. Press firmly so the trim squeezes into the adhesive.

Predrill holes at stud locations and fasten with a pair of 6d finish nails driven through the frame boards and into the ends of the cut wall studs (photo 7).

Fill and sand fastener holes. Sand and caulk as necessary. Prime and paint or apply another finish of your choice.

Options for Making a Wall Niche ▸

One key to cutting in a wall niche is to understand that you must cut a larger hole in your wall than the finished dimensions of the wall niche. So first, you determine the niche's finished location and opening dimensions and mark them out on the wall. You then measure from those lines so that the niche box fits inside the wall. Although making the niche so it fits precisely within a stud bay has some built-in efficiencies, it is not necessary. As you'll see in this project, as long as you're building in a nonload-bearing wall you can locate your niche just about anywhere you choose. Three options for trimming out a wall niche are described here. The first is to frame a wood niche insert with picture-frame trim. The second is to use a drywall wrap created with blocking inside the wall cavity and finished with joint compound to blend with the surrounding wall. The third option simply involves installing a prefabricated product.

Build your niche completely out of wood, insert it into a hole cut in the wall and trim it with picture molding (as seen on previous pages).

Purchase a prefabricated wall niche from an architectural millwork supplier and install it in a properly sized wall opening.

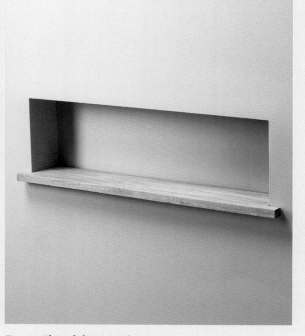

Frame the niche opening and install a wood shelf at the bottom, then trim out the opening with drywall using common taping and finishing techniques.

Formal Bookcase

Few furnishings add prestige to a space like a formal floor-to-ceiling bookcase. Typically built from clear hardwood, the classically-designed bookcase delivers a refined, Old World feel. The bookcase shown here is made from red oak plywood and red oak 1× stock and moldings finished with a high gloss urethane. What's also nice about this piece is that it incorporates the wall behind it to balance all that clear hardwood with a splash of color and depth. This is a fixed-shelf design that enables you to build shelves anywhere you like to match your needs. And, because the shelf bays are built in a modular fashion, you can design it to any dimensions you wish.

The formal bookcase shown here is 8 ft. long, 8 ft. high, and installed on a 12-ft. long wall. Because it's centered in the space, the moldings and sides return to the wall, creating niches on the left and right that are great for decoration. However, this bookcase can be built wall-to-wall if desired. It's a flexible design. Finally, the exact same style shelf can be built to take paint. Instead of using red oak, though, poplar is a great choice for a painted finish.

Tools, Materials & Cutting List

Miter saw
Table saw
Circular saw
Router
Drill/driver
Level
Stud finder
Pull saw
Flat bar
Step ladder or work platform
Air nailer
Combination square
Drywall or deck screws
Finish nails
Glue
Finishing materials
Eye and ear protection
Work gloves

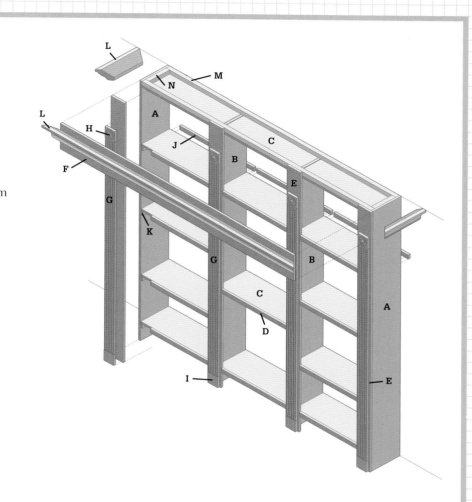

(3) 4 × 8 ft. sheets
   ¾" red oak plywood
(16) 1 × 2" × 8 ft. red oak
(4) 1 × 6" × 8 ft. red oak

(1) 1 × 10" × 8 ft. red oak
(4) ⅝ × 3⅜ × 84" oak molding
(4) Rosettes

(4) Plinth blocks
(11) lineal ft. red oak crown molding
(3) 2 × 2" × 8 ft. pine

KEY	NO.	DESC.	SIZE	MATERIAL
A	2	Upright (outer)	¾ × 11½ × 96"	Red oak plywood
B	2	Upright (inner)	¾ × 11½ × 94½"	Red oak plywood
C	14	Shelf	¾ × 11½ × 31	Red oak plywood
D	11	Shelf nosing	¾ × 1½ × 31"	Red oak 1 × 2
E	4	Upright backer	¾ × 5½ × 96"	Red oak 1 × 6
F	1	Fascia	¾ × 9½ × 96"	Red oak 1 × 10
G	4	Fluted molding	⅝ × 3⅜ × 78½	Red oak molding
H	4	Rosette	¾ × 4 × 4"	Red oak molding
I	4	Plinth block	¾ × 4 × 4"	Red oak molding

KEY	NO.	DESC.	SIZE	MATERIAL
J	11	Shelf cleat (wall)	¾ × 1½ × 31"	Red oak
K	22	Shelf cleat (side)	¾ × 1½ × 10¾"	Red oak
L	3	Crown molding	½ × 3³⁄₁₆" × cut to fit	Red oak
M	2	Ceiling cleat (long)	1½ × 1½ × 94½	2 × 2
N	2	Ceiling cleat (short)	1½ × 1½ × 8½"	2 × 2

How to Build a Formal Bookcase

Cut through the base molding at the edges of the project area and remove it so the bookcase can fit tightly up against the wall.

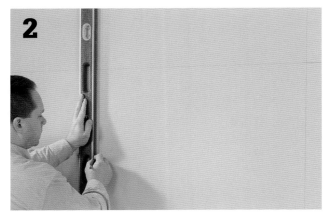

Carefully mark out the plumb lines for the outside edges of the uprights and continue the mark up onto the ceiling.

Use a spacer as a gauge for marking the position of the front edge of the 2 × 2 nailing frame that is attached to the ceiling.

LAY OUT THE PROJECT ON YOUR WALL

This bookcase is designed to be stick-built at your installation site. The best place to begin is by drawing layout lines on the wall. The most important lines mark the locations of the four uprights, which need to be vertical and parallel, and the shelf cleats, which must be horizontal and parallel. Start by locating the centerline for the bookcase installation and marking it on the baseboard and on the wall. Measure out 4-ft. on each side of the centerline and make marks for the outside edges of the bookcase. These lines represent the outer faces of the left and right uprights. Using a pull saw, cut and remove the baseboard between the left and right marks. Make your cuts as square as possible (photo 1).

Measure and make a mark at 15½ and 16¼" on each side of the centerline, dividing the project area into three equal bays and establishing locations of the ¾"-thick uprights.

Measuring up from the floor, mark horizontal shelf cleat locations on the walls at the back of each bay. The cleats should stop at the upright locations so the ¾"-thick uprights can fit snugly in between the cleat ends. In the drawing, there is one bottom shelf, set 6½" off the floor in all three bays. The left and right bays have shelves 24", 48", and 72" up from the floor. The center bay has a single center shelf set at 36" off the top of the bottom shelf ledger and a top shelf at 72" (see diagram, page 211). Using a 4-ft. level, mark horizontal reference lines for the shelf cleats in all three bays. Draw a small "X" below each line as a reminder of which side of the line to fasten the cleat. Then, use the 4-ft. level to extend the outlines for the uprights all the way up from the floor to the ceiling (photo 2). These sets of parallel lines should be ¾" apart and plumb.

At the ceiling, lay out the location for the 2 × 2 frame that creates nailing surfaces for the outer uprights and the 1 × 6 upright backers that are centered on the front edges of the uprights. The 2 × 2 frame should span from the inside faces of the outer uprights and extend 11½" out from the wall (photo 3).

Make a Marking Gauge ▸

Make an 11½" wide spacer to use as a marking gauge.

4

Attach the 2 × 2 nailing frame to the ceiling at the layout lines, making sure to catch a ceiling joist where possible and using appropriate anchors in spots where no joist is present.

5

Attach all of the shelf cleats to the wall, making sure to preserve an even ¾" gap between cleat ends to make room for the inner uprights.

If you're installing undercabinet lights such as puck lights, locate the center of each bay on the ceiling and mark them for lights. Get a qualified electrician to install the wiring, fixtures, and switches. If you're doing the work yourself, follow local building codes. Pull the wire through the drywall or plaster and pigtail (curl up) for fixture installation later.

INSTALL THE NAILING FRAME

For ease of installation, assemble the 2 × 2 nailing frame on the ground. Use 2½" pneumatic finish nails or drywall screws to join the 2 × 2 frame components. Test to make sure the assembly is square. Attach the frame to the ceiling by screwing up through the members at ceiling joist locations (use an electronic stud finder to identify these). Attach the frame to the wall's top plate at the wall/ceiling joint (photo 4). If the ceiling joists are parallel to the wall, you may need

to use toggle bolts or other wall anchors to secure the frame along the front edge.

ATTACH THE SHELF CLEATS TO THE WALL

While plenty of fasteners, including trim-head wood screws or 8d nails, may be dependably used to connect the 1 × 2 red oak shelf cleats to the walls at stud locations, a pneumatic or cordless finish nailer loaded with 2" nails is ideal for the task. It eliminates the need to pre-drill and countersink fasteners, as you would when driving screws or hand-nailing into hardwood. A pneumatic nailer also dispenses fasteners quickly and accurately, making it much easier when you're working alone. Cut and install the cleats at the layout lines. A few dabs of construction adhesive applied to the wall behind the cleats will add even more strength to the connection. Fasten the cleats so the upright returns can be installed around them (photo 5).

(continued)

INSTALL THE UPRIGHTS

Cut the outer uprights (11½" wide) to full room height in length. Rest the bottoms on the floor and nail the top ends to the ends of the 2 × 2 nailing frame (photo 6). Also drive 8d finish nails through the uprights and into the ends of the shelf cleats in the outer bays (drill pilot holes first).

Rout a roundover, bead, or chamfer onto each edge of the upright backer if desired (photo 7). Cut the inner uprights (11½" wide) to length. They should be 1½" shorter than the outer uprights because they butt up against the underside of the 2 × 2 nailing frame on the ceiling. Position the inner uprights between the ends of the shelf cleats that are attached to the wall in each bay. At the ceiling, use a framing square to make sure the inner uprights

are perpendicular to the wall and then position a 1 × 6 upright backer over the upright edge. Center the backer on the upright edge and nail it to the 2 × 2 nailing frame. Double-check that the upright is perpendicular to the wall by measuring the bays at the wall and at the front of the upright and making sure the measurements are the same. Then drill pilot holes and drive 8d finish nails (or pneumatic nails) through the backer and into the edge of the upright at 12" intervals (photo 8). Install both inner uprights.

INSTALL THE SHELVES

The shelves and shelf cleats help stabilize the structure, so install them next. Start by nailing a shelf to the 2 × 2 ceiling frame at the top of each bay (photo 9).

Nail the outer uprights to the ends of the nailing frame attached to the ceiling.

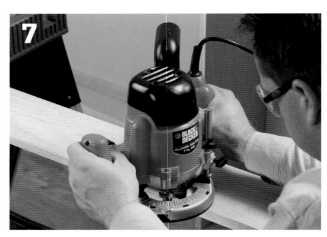

Routing a bead, round over, or chamfer adds nice detail and shadow lines to the upright backers.

Attach the upright backers to the front edges of the inner uprights with pneumatic or hand-driven finish nails.

Attach a shelf board at the top of each bay to conceal the framework attached to the ceiling.

Attach the shelf cleats to the uprights with 1¼" fasteners.

Edge the red oak shelves with 1 × 2 red oak nosing that's bonded to the shelves with glue and finish nails.

Conceal the gap between the top of the bookcase and ceiling with crown molding or sprung cove molding. Installing crown molding can get complicated. Consult a trim carpentry book if you are unsure how to work with crown molding.

Attach the plinth blocks, rosettes and fluted case moldings to compete the trimwork installation.

Attach the short shelf cleats to the sides of the uprights so each shelf is supported on three sides (photo 10). Use a level to make sure the cleats are level and attach them with 1¼" finish nails and adhesive.

Cut the remaining shelves to length and set them on the cleats. Cut the 1 × 2 shelf nosing and attach it to the front edges of the exposed shelves, making sure the shelves are flush with the top edge of the nosing (photo 11). Use 4d finish nails driven through pilot holes or pneumatic finish nails to attach the nosing.

ATTACH THE TRIM

Cut the 1 × 10 red oak fascia board the full width of the bookcase and nail it to the top so the ends are flush with the outer faces of the outer uprights. Make sure the fascia board is level before attaching it with nails driven into the tops of the upright backers. Once the fascia board is in place, cut, fit and attach the crown molding and molding return at the top (photo 12).

Install the plinth blocks at the bottom of each upright backer, resting on the floor and centered side to side. Then, attach the rosettes at the top of each upright backer, centered side to side. Measure from the bottom of the rosette to the top of the plinth block and cut fluted case molding to fit. Install with adhesive and nails (photo 13). Fill nail holes, sand, and apply finish. If the installation room has base shoe moldings, you may want to add them to your bookcase for a consistent look.

Understrairs Bookcase

If your home has a staircase with open space below, chances are you've wondered how to make the most of that oddly configured square footage. This bookcase project could be the answer. Behind the two pairs of gently rising birch-frame doors you'll find a bank of birch plywood shelves that are designed for use as a formal bookcase. Because the door panels are created with Plexiglas, the shelves are also quite suitable for display purposes.

While the bookcase cabinets must be custom-fit to your space, the basic design of the individual units is quite simple. Each cabinet is essentially a plywood box with an angled top. The boxes fit side by side in the understairs area, flush with the wall surfaces. The shelves in each unit incorporate birch 1 × 2 shelf edge to improve their appearance and stiffen the shelf boards.

A birch face frame is wrapped around the perimeter of the project, concealing the plywood edges. The hinged doors are also made of birch. The secret to building the face frames and the door frames is a clever woodworking technique known as the pocket screw joint made with angled screws driven into the back sides of the mating pieces.

Understairs storage units are often made with slide-out shelving or pull-out drawers. This strategy allows for efficient use of space since the pull-out units can be nearly as deep as the total stair width. The drawback is that the drawers or slide-out shelves can be a bit rickety, especially if you're not an experienced cabinetmaker. When designing your project, you can increase the storage space by deepening the shelves and using them as storage cubbies. If your staircase is bounded by another interior wall, you can add a bookcase on the other side, with the two bookcases sharing a divided panel or wall.

A rich formal bookcase inhabits the previously wasted space underneath a staircase. The books are protected by birch doors with Plexiglas panels that have a soft, contemporary design feeling.

Tools & Materials

Work gloves
Eye protection
Respirator
Stud finder
Level
Pencil
Utility knife or wallboard saw
Pry bar
Drill
Router (and rabbet bit)
Pilot bits
Chisel
Large pipe clamps
Framing square
Table saw
Pneumatic brad nailer
HVLP sprayer (optional)
Hammer
Nail set
2 × 4 lumber

Plywood stock (¼", ¾")
Wood glue
Brads
150- or 220-grit sandpaper
Desired finish
Pocket screws
6d finish nails
1¼" drywall screws
Coarse-thread drywall screws
Wood putty
Plexiglas
Glazier's points

Latches
Pulls
1 × 2 hardwood
Shims
Hinges

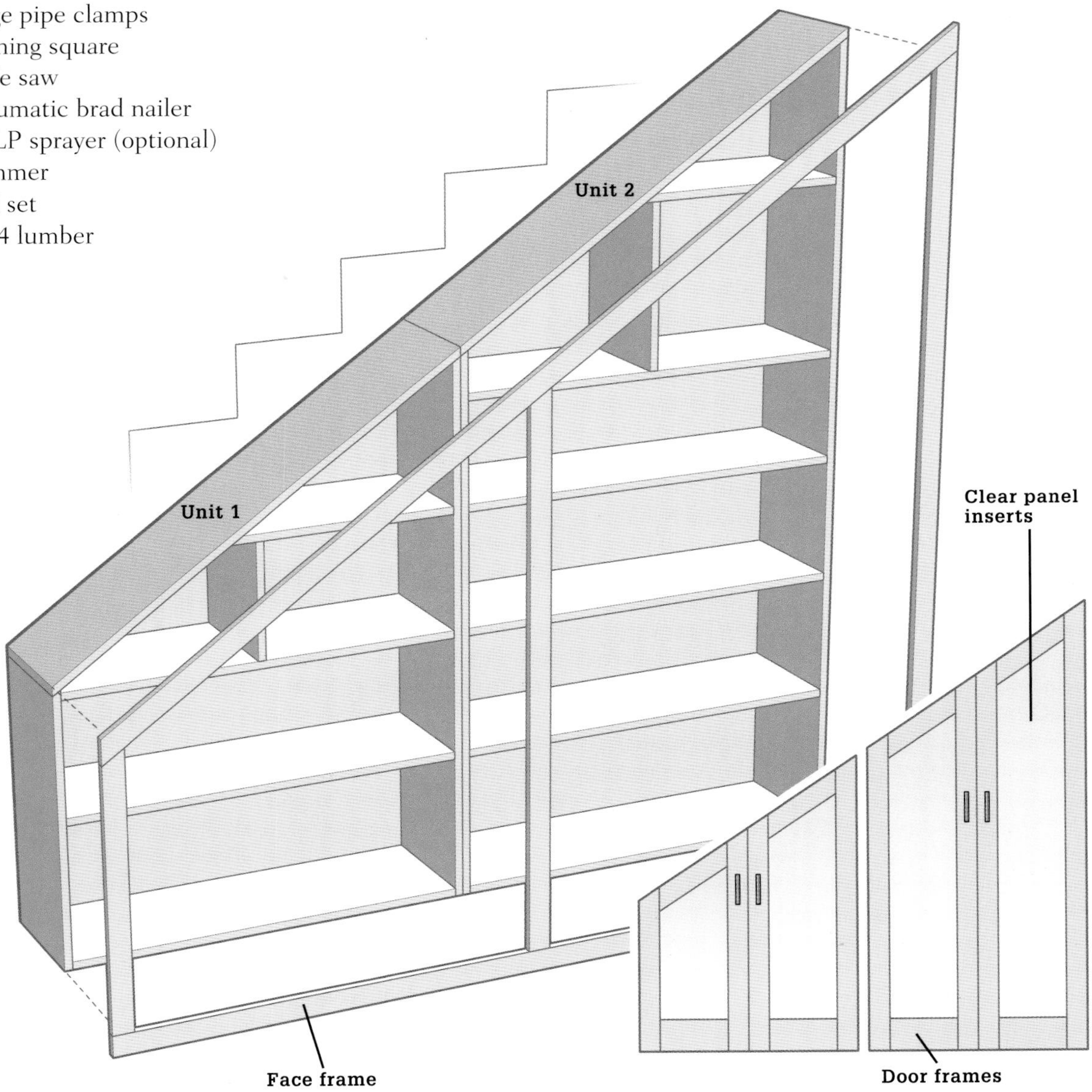

Unit 2

Unit 1

Clear panel inserts

Face frame

Door frames

How to Build the Understairs Bookcase

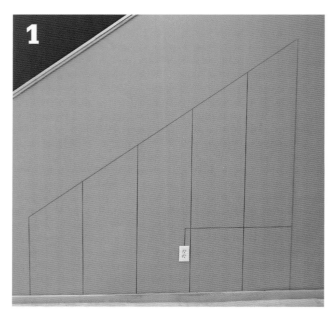

Lay out the planned project on the walls. Be sure to identify and label all stud locations as well as any wiring, plumbing or ductwork in the project area. Try to plan the opening in the wall so it will be bordered by existing studs, and with the wall covering cut up to the studs but not beyond.

Cut and remove the wall covering with electrical service. First shut off electricity at the main service panel. To minimize dust, use a utility knife or wallboard saw to cut the wall covering along the cutting lines. Pry off the wall covering, taking care not to damage surrounding wall surfaces.

Install 2 × 4 sleepers on the floor after you've thoroughly cleaned up the project area and disposed of all debris properly. Sleepers should butt against the wall's sole plate and run back in a perpendicular fashion slightly farther than the planned project depth. Install a sleeper at the end of the project area, beneath the midpoint, and at 16" intervals.

Rip plywood stock into strips for making the cabinet frame and shelves. We used ¾" birch-veneer plywood to match the birch that is used for the face frame and door frames. The cabinet frame pieces are ripped to 12" wide but the shelves should be only 11¼" wide to allow for the ¾"-thick shelf edge strips. Cut all parts to length.

5

Assemble the unit frames with wood glue and coarse-thread drywall screws driven through the outer faces and into the edges of the mating boards. Drill countersunk pilot holes for the screws. Work on a flat surface and check the joints with a framing square to make sure they are square. If you have large pipe clamps, use them to clamp the workpieces before driving the screws. Make both the Unit 1 and Unit 2 frames (tops, sides, and bottom panels).

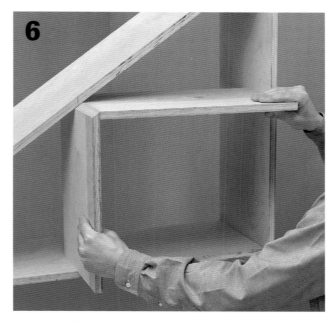

6

Install shelf boards in the cabinet frame. The shelves should be flush with the back edges of the frame, leaving a ¾" reveal in the front. Draw shelf layout lines on both faces of the frame pieces so you can center the screws. Install the full-width shelves first. Assemble the shorter shelves and their divider supports into L shapes, and then install them as a unit. Cut back panels from ¼" plywood and attach them with brads.

7

Attach hardwood shelf edge to the shelves and the divider support edges. The tops of the 1 × 2 edge boards should be flush with the top surfaces of the shelves. The vertical edging pieces should be flush with the outside edges of the dividers.

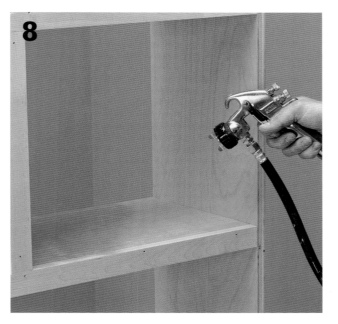

8

Apply a finish to the cabinet units. Sand all wood surfaces with 150- or 220-grit sand paper, wipe down with mineral spirits, and then apply two to three light coats of water-based polyurethane. We used an HVLP sprayer to apply the finish, but wipe-on polyurethane works just fine if you don't have spraying equipment.

(continued)

Install the first unit in the project opening. The front edges should be flush with the room-side surface of the wall. Check with a level and shim between the frames and sleepers as needed. Attach by driving 6d finish nails through the base panel and into the sleepers and also through the side panel and into the wall stud.

Install the second unit in the project opening, shimming as needed to make sure it is level and the top panel continues in alignment with the top of the first unit. Before securing the panels to the sleepers and stud, drive 1¼" drywall screws to join the units' side panels at each corner where they meet. Countersink the pilot holes and cover with tinted wood putty. Attach the other side panel to the wall stud and nail the bottom panel to the sleepers with 6d finish nails.

Make the face frame. It's possible to cut the pieces of the face frame and nail them individually to the cabinet units, but you'll get more professional-looking results with cleaner joints if you assemble the face frame, finish it, and then attach it to the cabinet as one piece. We used pocket screws to make the joints, but you can use dowels or biscuits instead. Apply a finish.

Attach the face frame to the cabinet frame edges with brads or pneumatic finish nails. Use plenty of nails, since the face frame will support the swinging door hinges. Set all nail heads and conceal with tinted wood putty.

Make the door frames. The frames will look best with the vertical stiles running full height and capturing the rails between them. As you work, lay each completed frame on a flat surface next to the previous one and make sure the line formed by the top rails follows the same angle as the top face frame rails. The joint options are the same for the door frames as for the face frames (we again used pocket screws). Make sure to leave at least 1" of clear stock on each corner so the router won't cut into any fasteners when cutting rabbets.

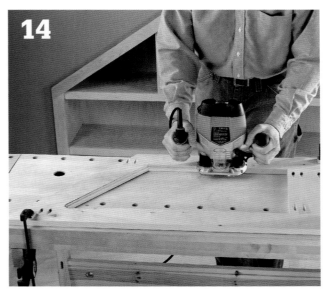

Cut rabbet recesses for the door panel inserts. Use a piloted rabbet bit and router. The rabbets should be ⅜" deep and ½" wide. Make the cuts in multiple passes of increasing depth—don't try to remove all the material in a single pass. Once all rabbets have been cut around the perimeter of each door frame back, square off the corners of the cuts with a sharp wood chisel. *Note: In most cases, to create clearance you will need to cut a ½" chamfer on the top inside edge of the two door frames where the hinges are on the side with the point.*

Install the door panels. You can use frosted glass (tempered is best), ¼" plywood, or Plexiglas. We used Plexiglas because of the risk of breakage. It is possible to cut both glass and Plexiglas to size yourself, but given the high cost of materials and relatively low cost of custom cutting, you'll be glad you chose to have the pieces cut to size at the store. Panels should be about ¼" smaller than the opening (including the rabbet widths) in each direction. Use glazier's points or tack strips (see page 195) to secure the panels.

Hang the doors and attach latches and pulls. Take great care when hanging the cabinet doors to make sure that the line created by the door tops is straight and parallel to the face frame, with a consistent reveal. Orient the cabinet door pairs so they close together in the center of each unit. Attach the door pulls roughly midway up each cabinet door. Add latches or catches so doors will stay closed. *Note: You may need to bevel the inside faces of the frames on the hinge side.*

Media Bar

Your snacks and beverages will always be close at hand during the big game when your flat-panel TV is mounted in this media cabinet. It combines the functionality of an entertainment center and the convenience of a mini kitchen. The base and upper cabinets provide storage for your home theater components, movies, games, and snacks. There's also a space between the base cabinets for a small refrigerator or beverage cooler. The counter serves as a perfect serving station or a place to keep a couple additional small appliances, such as a microwave or blender. And, the integrated matching wood wall conceals a structural frame that is easy to mount your TV to and provides a path for cables from the TV to your electronic components in the base cabinet.

This unit may look like a custom-built piece of furniture, but it's actually made from a combination of stock kitchen cabinets and matching cover panels. Building it only requires a few portable power tools and basic building skills.

Tools & Materials ▸

Table saw or circular saw and straightedge
Jigsaw
Drill/driver
Level
2"-dia. hole saw bit
Drill bits (⅛, ¼")
Caulk gun
(5) 2 × 4 × 8-ft.
(2) 1 × 4 × 8-ft.
Screws (1¼, 2, 2½")
Panel adhesive
(1) ½" × 4 × 8 finish-grade plywood
(3) 24" base cabinets
(2) 24" wall cabinets
(1) 25½" × 8 ft. countertop
Eye and ear protection
Work gloves

Cutting List

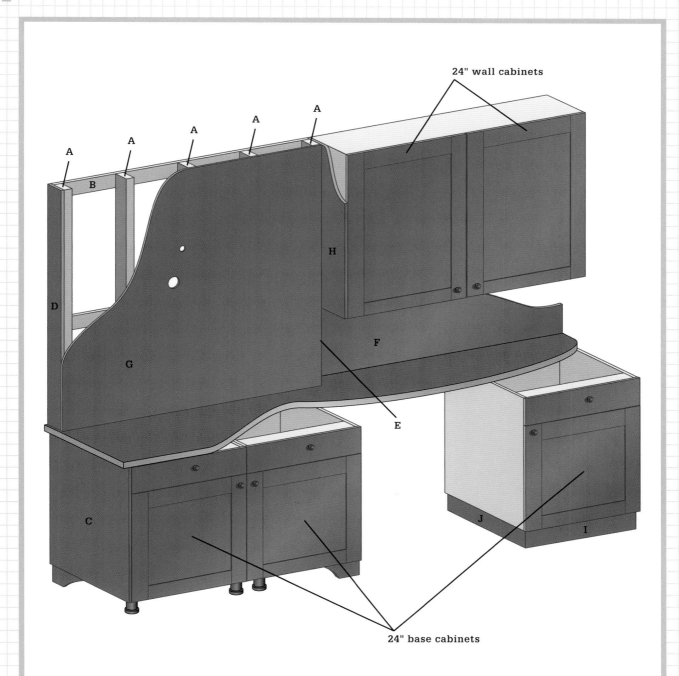

24" wall cabinets

24" base cabinets

KEY	NO.	DESCRIPTION	DIMENSION
A	5	Wall frame studs	1½ × 3½ × 60"
B	3	Wall frame cleats	¾ × 3½ × 47"
C	1	Base cabinet cover panel	½ × 24 × 30"
D	1	Left frame side cover panel	½ × 4¼ × 60"
E	1	Right frame side cover panel	½ × 4¼ × 20"

KEY	NO.	DESCRIPTION	DIMENSION
F	1	Back splash panels	½ × 20 × 48"
G	1	Wall frame front cover panels	½ × 48 × 60"
H	1	Wall cabinet side cover panel	½ × 8⅝ × 40"
I	1	Front toe kick	½ × 4½* × 24"
J	1 or 2	Side toe kick	½ × 4½* × 24"

How to Build a Media Bar

ROUTE THE WIRING

Install any necessary electrical outlets and home theater cables, such as speaker wire, before you install the cabinets. Install one outlet in the center of the base cabinet refrigerator space and another outlet behind one of the cabinets that will be below the television. You may also want to install one outlet below the wall cabinets (approximately 42" above the floor) that will serve appliances that may be used on the countertop. Install the outlet box above the countertop so that it extends ½" beyond the drywall and will be flush with the backsplash panel. If you are not familiar with the skills necessary to install the electrical devices, then hire a licensed electrical contractor to handle this work.

INSTALL THE CABINETS & COUNTERTOP

Locate and mark the wall stud locations. Follow the manufacturer instructions to assemble the wall and base cabinet frames if they are not preassembled. If the doors and drawers are not attached to the cabinets, then wait to install them after the cover panels are attached. Install the two wall cabinets. The method you use to attach the cabinets on the wall depends on the type of cabinet construction. In this case a metal bracket is attached to the wall and then the cabinet is fastened to the metal bracket (photo 1).

Cord and cable access holes must be cut in the back and top of the base cabinet that will be installed directly in front of the electrical outlet below the TV. Line up the base cabinets a few feet away from the wall, positioning them in the order that they will be installed. Measure the distance of the wall outlet from the end of the cabinets and from the floor and transfer those measurements to the back of the cabinet to mark the outlet location. Use a jigsaw to cut a 3"-wide × 5"-tall hole through the cabinet back panel exactly where the outlet will be located.

1

Attach the wall cabinet bracket to the wall as specified in the cabinet installation instructions. Then, fasten the cabinets to the bracket. Attach the cabinets to each other with fasteners provided by the cabinet manufacturer or by driving short screws through the cabinet sides.

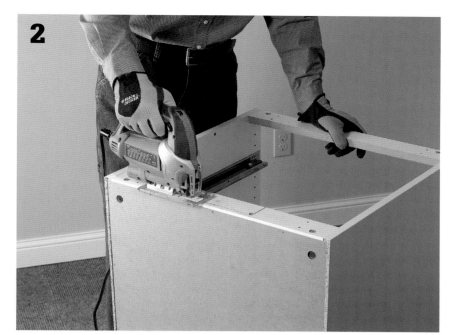

2

Cut access holes in the base cabinet.
Trace outlines for the access holes in the back panel and top spreader on the cabinet that will be installed in front of the wall outlet. Drill ⅜"-dia. saw blade starter holes at each corner of the outline. Use a jigsaw to cut the sides of the hole.

3

Cut the countertop access hole.
Attach masking tape to the countertop to help prevent chipping the surface when it is cut. Mark the access notch outline on the countertop. Cut the notch with a jigsaw.

Then cut a 2"-wide × 8"-long hole through the top spreader at the back of the cabinet (photo 2). Your cables could fit through a smaller hole in the top of the cabinet, but making a larger hole will make routing the cables much easier.

Slide the base cabinets against the wall. Adjust the legs or shim below the cabinets to level the tops of the cabinets. Attach the two adjacent cabinet sides together with the manufacturer-provided connector fasteners or with 1¼" screws. Then secure the cabinets to the wall studs with 2½" drywall screws.

Cut a notch in the back edge of the countertop that will align with the access hole you cut in the top cabinet spreader. Cut the notch in laminate or wood countertops with a jigsaw (photo 3). Natural stone countertop materials require a diamond abrasive blade and should be cut by a stone countertop fabricator. Attach the countertop to the cabinets (photo 4).

(continued)

Attach the countertop to the cabinets. Drive 1⅝" screws through the cabinet top and into the countertop. Be careful not to overdrive the screws and break through the top surface of the countertop.

Attach the wall frame to the room wall. Drive 2½" drywall screws through the wall frame cleats and into the room wall studs. Drive three screws into each stud.

INSTALL THE WALL FRAME & COVER PANELS

Build the wall frame. Cut the 2 × 4 wall frame posts and 1 × 4 cleats to length and assemble them with 2" wood screws. Then place the wall frame on the countertop and against the wall cabinet. Secure the wall frame to the room wall (photo 5).

Check to make sure all speaker cables or other component cables that are coming from other areas of the room are routed to the area behind the wall frame before concealing that wall with the cover panels. In this case, no additional speakers were installed so no additional speaker cables were routed to the media center. The cables that run between the TV, sound bar speaker and components in the cabinet are routed after the cabinet construction is complete.

Avoid driving fasteners through the face of the cover panels so that you don't have to fill in or conceal any fastener marks. Each panel is attached with screws and/or panel adhesive. Drive the screws through the inside face of the cabinet or

wall frame. Panel adhesive is a type of construction adhesive that has a high initial adhesion and is typically sold in a caulk tube (follow manufacturer application instructions).

Measure the width of the space below the wall cabinets and divide that measurement by two to determine the width of each backsplash panel. Cut the backsplash panels to size. Cut on the back, or apply a strip of masking tape over the cut line and use a plywood cutting blade with a high tooth count (80 tpi table saw blade and 60 tpi circular saw blade) to prevent the finished surface from chipping. If there is an outlet installed in the backsplash area, then cut openings in the panel to fit around the wall outlet. Attach the backsplash panels with panel adhesive.

Cut the two frame-side cover panels to size. Cut the cover panels with a table saw or circular saw and straightedge guide. Apply panel adhesive to the back face of each panel, clamp them to the wall frame and secure them with screws driven through the frame studs and into the side panel covers (photo 6).

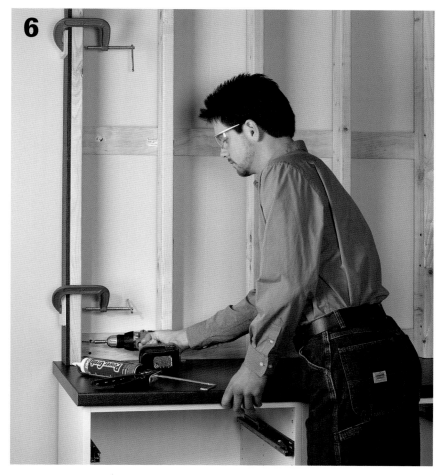

6

Attach the wall frame side cover panels to the wall frame with panel adhesive and 1⅝" screws. Clamp the panels in position while you drive the screws through the inside face of the wall frame posts. Drill a ⅛"-dia. pilot hole and countersink for each screw ⅛ to ¼" into the 2 × 4 so the screw goes into the plywood about ⅜".

(continued)

Cut the wall frame front panels to size. The cover panel stock features one finished edge. Install the wall frame front panels with the finished edges on the outside and the unfinished edges butt together at the middle seam. If you are using a cover panel stock that does not feature a finished edge, then you must cover the unfinished edge with heat-activated veneer edge tape or solid wood edging. Attach the panels to the frame with panel adhesive. No screws are used to secure the front panels.

Determine the required width of the wall cabinet side panel (photo 7). Cut the wall cabinet side cover panel to size. Clamp it to the wall cabinet side and attach it by driving 1" screws through the inside of the cabinet side. Then attach the base cabinet side panel (photo 8). Finally, attach the toe kick panels, doors and drawers.

Measure the distance from the face of the front panel to the front edge of the wall cabinet. Add the thickness of the door to determine the width of the wall cabinet side cover panel.

Attach the wall and base cabinet side panels. Clamp the panel to the cabinet side and drive 1" screws through the inside face of the cabinet side. Then install the toe kicks.

9

Use a 2" hole saw to bore an access hole through the wall frame front panel. This hole should be located directly above the notch in the countertop and close to the TV mounting bracket so that the TV will conceal it.

INSTALL THE COMPONENTS

Follow the manufacturer instructions to install the TV mounting bracket. Drive the mounting bracket anchor screws into the wall frame posts. Next, drill a 2"-dia. access hole through the front panel (photo 9). If you are installing a speaker above the TV, then drill a ¾"-dia. hole behind the speaker location to route the speaker cable.

Fish the component cables and speaker cable through the access holes and behind the front panels. Follow the manufacturer instructions to secure the TV to the mounting bracket and mount the speaker.

Club Bar

Owning your own in-house bar makes a statement about you. For some, it might say "I have arrived and this is my space!" While for others a bar might say "Welcome, friends, our home is your home." And for others, well, let's just say the possibilities are fairly wide-ranging. But whatever story your bar tells—be it one of quiet aperitifs before dining, casual afternoons watching the big game, or raucous evenings of wild revelry—building your bar yourself personalizes the tale and adds a feature to your home that will have a direct impact on how well you enjoy your home life.

The bar shown here is sleekly styled and smartly laid out for the efficient barkeeper. A small refrigerator gives you access to cold drinks and ice while convenient cabinets create excellent storage spots for party favors.

While this is a "dry bar" (no plumbing), the design could be modified in any number of ways to add running water if you wish. All you need to get the party started is a GFCI electrical outlet and the proper floor space.

This compact corner bar design features glossy black MDF aprons with decorative cherry appliqués forming a horizontal grid pattern on the aprons. A cherry plywood bartop sits atop a 2 × 6 L-shaped kneewall, harboring some practical amenities on the bartender side. A flip-up lift gate in the bartop on one end provides pass-through access and can even function as a wait station if you want to get really fancy in your hosting.

The key components—base cabinets, a laminate countertop, the fridge, and the wood for a sleek Asian-inspired style trim-out—set the stage for your next gathering. Let's party.

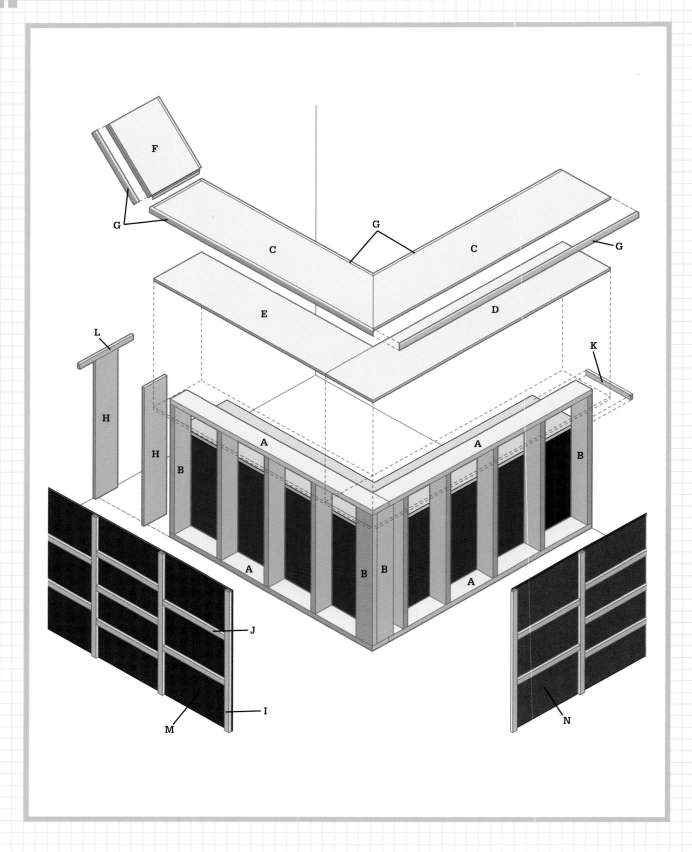

Tools, Materials & Cutting List

Eye and ear protection
Work gloves
Miter saw
Table saw
Circular saw
Drill/driver
Level
Stud finder
Pull saw
Flat bar
Pneumatic nailer/compressor
Combination square
(10) 2 × 6" × 8 ft. SPF

(1) ¾ × 4 × 8 particleboard
(1) ¾ × 4 × 8 cherry plywood
   for bartop
(2) 6 ft. strips ½ × 16"
   cementboard
20 sq. ft. 4 × 4 wall tile
Thinset and grout
¾" thick cherry—2 @ 8 × 42"
   (actual)
¾ × 1½" cherry
   approx 80 lineal ft.
(2) ½" × 4 × 8 ft. MDF
24" base cabinet

36" base cabinet—corner
   (12" wide doors)
Refrigerator (19w 22d 32-¾" h)
Postform countertop
   (mitered, 6 ft. each leg)
16d common nails
Panel adhesive
1½" drywall screws
Finish nails (4d, 6d)
Finishing materials
Glue
Piano hinge

KEY	NO.	DESC.	SIZE	MATERIAL
A	4	Sill/header	1½ × 5½ × 68"	2 × 6
B	11	Stud	1½ × 5½ × 38"	2 × 6
C	2	Bartop	¾ × 16½ × 80"	Cherry plywood
D	1	Bar substrate	¾ × 16½ × 80"	Particleboard
E	1	Bar substrate	¾ × 16½ × 65¼"	Particleboard
F	2	Lift gate	¾ × 16½ × 22¼"	Cherry plywood
G	-	Bartop trim	¾ × 1½" × cut to fit	Cherry
H	2	End cap	¾ × 7¾ × 41"	Cherry
I	7	Trim stiles	¾ × 1½ × 41"	Cherry
J	16	Trim rails	¾ × 1½ × cut to fit	Cherry
K	1	Countertop cleat	1½ × 1½ × 22"	2 × 2
L	1	Lift gate stop block	¾ × 1½ × 18"	Cherry
M	1	Apron	½ × 40½ × 68¾"	MDF
N	1	Apron	½ × 40½ × 73½"	MDF

How to Build a Club Bar

Anchor the sill plates for the kneewalls to the floor so they form a right angle at the corner where they meet.

Use panel adhesive and deck screws to attach the end kneewall stud to the back wall, attaching at a stud location. If there's no stud, open the wall and insert a horizontal nailer between the nearest studs.

BUILD THE KNEEWALLS

The bar top is supported by a pair of heavy-duty 2 × 6 kneewalls that are anchored to the wall and floor and meet in an L. This configuration presumes that you'll be installing the bar in the corner of the room. If that configuration doesn't work for your space, you can use similar building strategies, but redesign the project as a straight-line or a U-shape bar.

Cut the 2 × 6 sill plates to length (68"). Measure out from the corner the distance of the sill plates plus the pass-through opening width plus ¾" for the thickness of the end panel (92¾" here). Mark a reference line and lay a sill plate at this distance, perpendicular to the back project wall. Arrange the

second sill plate so the end overlaps the open end of the first sill plate and the two form a perfect 90-degree angle. Join the corners with screws or a metal connector to keep them from moving during installation, and then anchor the sill plates to the floor. Use 16d common nails or screws (shown in photo 1) and panel adhesive for a wood floor; use a powder-actuated nailer on a concrete floor.

Once the sills are in place, attach the end stud against the back wall. If you are lucky (or planned well) the stud will fall over a wall stud. If the new kneewall falls over a stud bay in the room wall, you'll need to remove some wallcovering and install a nailing cleat between the closest wall studs so you

3

Toe-nail the corner studs to the sill plates. Use a level to make sure the studs are vertical.

4

Complete the framing for the L-shaped kneewall section. For extra strength, drive a few 3" deck screws through the studs where they meet at the corner.

have a very sturdy surface to anchor the end of the wall (photo 2).

Next, make the stud wall corner. Use 16d common nails to toe-nail the studs to the sill plates (photo 3). Install a stud at the free end of the return, then fill in with evenly spaced intermediate studs spaced no more than 16" apart. Cut cap plates the same size as the sill plates and install them with three 16d common nails driven through the tops of the caps and into the end of each wall stud (photo 4). Check each stud with a level before nailing.

MAKE THE APRONS AND TRIM

The decorative front aprons for this bar are made from ½"-thick MDF (medium-density fiberboard) panels that have a glossy black finish and are trimmed with strips of cherry arranged in a staggered ladder pattern. If you're feeling ambitious, apply a genuine black lacquer finish. Or, you can come close to the black lacquer look with a quality satin or gloss jet black enamel paint. Either way, for the smoothest possible finish, cut and prepare the panels and spray on the black lacquer finish with an HVLP sprayer.

(continued)

Rip two sheets of ½" MDF to 40½" wide and then trim them to length to make the bar front panels. Sand the edges to remove any saw marks. Then, apply primer to all faces and edges. When the primer dries, spray black lacquer or paint onto the front face and edges (photo 5). If you do not have access to a good sprayer, use a paint roller with a short-nap sleeve.

After installation, the black aprons will be decorated with a grid made from strips of cherry. You can use dimensional 1 × 2 cherry for this, but you'll save a lot of money and get better edges if you purchase random width cherry, then plane and joint it to thickness and rip it to width (photo 6). For the project shown here, you'll need at least 40 lineal feet of stock for the apron trim, plus another 40 ft. for the bar countertop edging.

Sand the edges of the cherry trim to remove saw marks and smooth the surfaces. Apply a clear protective wood finish, such as wipe-on polyurethane varnish, to half the stock for use as apron trim (photo 7). The other half of the stock will be used for edging the countertop. You'll need to cut an edge profile in this stock and attach it to the countertop before finishing it.

INSTALL THE KNEEWALL COVERINGS

The front faces of the L-shaped kneewall are covered with the aprons and apron trim. The back sides (the bartender view) can be covered with just about anything you wish. We used a cement board backer and some wall tile for a nice looking wall covering that's durable and easy to clean. It's easier to install these wallcoverings before the bartop has been installed.

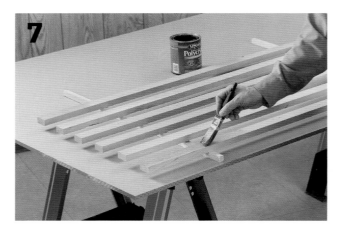

For the smoothest possible finish, spray the front apron panels with an HVLP sprayer. Apply the paint or lacquer over primer, in thin coats.

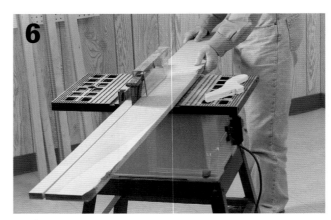

Prepare at least 80 lineal feet of ¾ × 1½" hardwood stock to trim out the aprons and edges of the bartop.

For efficiency, apply a protective finish to the cherry apron trim stock. Dab some finish on the cut ends after you cut each trim piece to length.

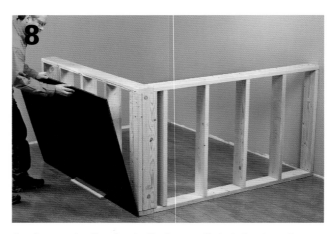

Apply panel adhesive to the kneewall studs to strengthen the bond with the black aprons. Slip a ¼-thick spacer beneath each apron to create a gap between the panel and the floor.

Nail the apron panels to the wall studs at 8" to 12" intervals.

Attach cement board strips to the edges of the kneewall framing members as a backer for the backsplash area.

Install the inside wallcovering before you cap the wall.

You don't need to create full toe-kick recesses at the bottoms of the apron panels, although you certainly can if you wish. But it is a good idea to install the MDF aprons so they are not in contact with the floor, especially if your installation is going into a basement or any other area that may be subject to moisture problems. The easiest way to do this is simply to cut a piece of ¼"-thick sheet stock scrap and slip it up against the sill plate. Then, test the fit of the apron panels. Trim if needed, then apply beads of panel adhesive to the front edges of the wall frame members (photo 8) and attach the aprons with a pneumatic nailer and 2½" finish nails (photo 9). You can hand-nail them at wall stud locations with 6d finish nails if you prefer. Cover nail heads with wood putty.

Depending on what type of cabinets you're installing, it likely is not necessary to finish the inside faces of the kneewalls lower than the countertop height. For installing wall tile, we cut 16"-wide strips of ½"-thick cement board and attached them to the wall studs flush with the top of the cap plate (photo 10). Make sure that seams fall over studs.

Install the wall tile (photo 11). We used inexpensive 4 × 4" ceramic wall tile set into a layer of thinset adhesive that's troweled onto the cement board. Whichever wall covering you use, it should extend down past the top of the countertop (in this case, the top of the preformed backsplash), and the edges should be covered by the end panel you'll be installing at the free end of the kneewall.

(continued)

Bond the particleboard subbase directly to the top plates of the kneewalls, taking care to achieve even overhangs of 6" in front and 4" on the bartender side of the walls.

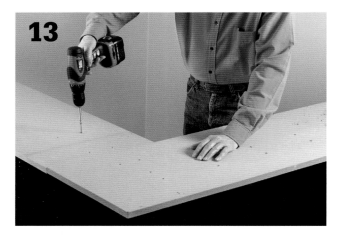

Drive plenty of 2" deck screws to secure the subbase to the walls. The screw heads must be sunk beneath the wood surface.

Make 45-degree miter cuts in the bartop top layer using a circular saw and cutting guide.

INSTALL THE BARTOP

The bartop installed here is made of a particleboard subbase that's thoroughly bonded and screwed to the top plates of the kneewall. A cherry plywood top layer then is attached to the narrow particleboard subbase. The subbase is laid out with a butt joint at the corner for ease and for strength, but for a more refined appearance the plywood top is mitered at the corner. When ¾"-thick cherry edging is added on all sides, the bartop grows to a finished width of 18" (a normal countertop, such as the bartender's countertop on the cabinets below, is 25" wide).

Rip the particleboard to 16½" wide and then crosscut it to length (one piece is longer so they can be butted together). Attach the strips to the top plates of the kneewalls using panel adhesive and countersunk deck screws (photo 12). Make sure to align the subbase strips carefully. They should overhang the kneewalls by roughly 6" in front and 4" in back.

Once you have both subbase parts arranged perfectly, drive 2" deck screws through the subbase and into the bar wall (photo 13). Be very generous here. If you can't get the screw heads to seat beneath the surface of the subbase, drill counter-sunk pilot holes.

Cut the cherry plywood sheet into 16½" wide strips, then cut mating miter joints at the ends (photo 14). Take care here: most hardwood plywood has one side that is much nicer, so be sure the cuts are made so the correct faces will be facing up when the bartop is installed. A circular saw with a sharp panel-cutting blade and a straightedge guide may be used to make these cuts.

Attach the top layer of cherry plywood to the subbase with panel adhesive and 1¼" wallboard screws driven up through the subbase and into the underside of the plywood layer (photo 15). Make sure the mitered corner fits together correctly before applying any adhesive or cutting the plywood strips to length *Tip: Wait until the plywood layer is attached to the subbase to cut the strip on the free end to length. That way, you can cut it and the subbase at the same time and ensure that they are exactly flush.*

Check to make sure the edges of the glued-up bartop are smooth and flat, and sand with a belt sander if they are out of alignment or there is a lot of glue squeeze-out (use fine grit sandpaper to help prevent any splintering of the veneer layer). Mount a ½" roundover bit in a router or router table and cut roundover profiles along one edge of the 1 × 2 stock you dressed to use for bartop edging. Attach the edging strips to the countertop with glue and 4d finish nails driven into pilot holes (photo 16). Make sure the tops of the edging boards are flush with or slightly higher than the plywood surface. If necessary, sand the edging until it is flush after you remove the clamps. At the open countertop end, extend the edging ¾" past the end of the glued-up layers.

Cut a piece of 1 × 2 edging to fit between the ends of the edging on the open end of the countertop and attach it with glue and finish nails (photo 17). Sand all wood surfaces. Apply multiple coats of very durable, glossy polyurethane varnish to achieve a protective built-up finish. Also paint the underside of the bartop black where it is visible. Build the lift

gate section of the countertop as well and finish it the same way, except make it from two layers of cherry plywood and apply a clear finish to both faces.

INSTALL TRIM & HARDWARE

Rip-cut a strip of cherry that's slightly wider than the distance from the tiled wall surface to ¾" past the apron fronts (about 8") and then cut it to fit between the floor and the underside of the bartop, which should overhang the end wall stud by ¾" or slightly more (photo 18). Cut another identical strip. Attach one strip to the end of the kneewall and attach the other to the wall on the opposite side of the pass-through so the two strips are perfectly aligned.

Laminate the top layer of cherry plywood to the subbase with panel adhesives and 1¼" screws driven up through the subbase.

Cut a roundover profile in one edge of the cherry edging stock and then cut the parts to length and attach them to the edges of the bartop with nails and glue.

Square-cut a piece of 1 × 2 edging to fit exactly between the ends of the roundover edging, and nail and glue it into place.

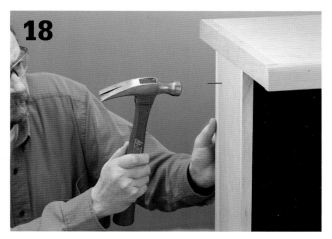

Nail the cherry end panel to the wall end to conceal the stud wall and the edges of the wallcoverings and trim.

(continued)

19

Attach a 1 × 2 stop block for the lift gate to the wall directly above the wall-mounted end panel.

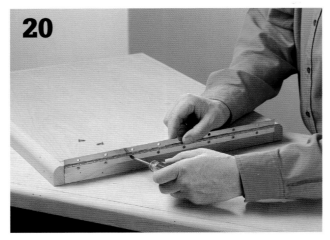

20

Attach the piano hinge to the lift gate section of the countertop first, then attach the other leaf to the countertop.

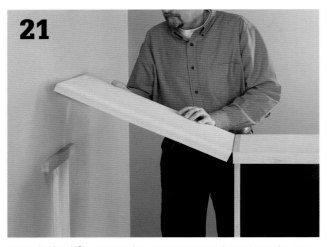

21

Attach the lift gate to the countertop and test to make sure it operates smoothly and correctly.

Cut a strip of 1 × 2 cherry to 18" long and attach it to the wall, centered over the 8"-wide end panel (photo 19). This strip will function as the stop for the lift gate section of countertop. For consistency, roundover the top edges of the 1 × 2 so it looks like a section of countertop.

Attach a piano hinge to the square-cut mating edge of the lift gate countertop section (photo 20). The barrel of the piano hinge should be oriented upward relative to the bartop surface. Attach the other leaf of the piano hinge to the edge of the main countertop and test to see if it opens and closes easily and is level when open (photo 21).

Cut the cherry trim pieces to size to make the ladder grids that decorate the aprons. Install the strips, following the patterns shown in photo 22. Make sure the ends of the strips are tucked flush against the inside face of the cherry end panel.

INSTALL THE CABINETS

You can appoint the bartender's area of the Club Bar just about any way you wish because the bartop and wall are freestanding, independent structures. We chose to install a couple of base cabinets, a dorm-size refrigerator and an economical, low-maintenance postform countertop. Start by placing the corner cabinet in the corner. Place the 24" cabinet to the right of the corner cabinet. Flush up the face frames (if they have them; the ones seen here are frameless) and clamp the cabinets together with bar clamps. Predrill, countersink, and screw the face frames or cabinets sides together.

22

Add the decorative cherry strips in a ladder grid pattern, using an air nailer. Start with the vertical strips, then cut the horizontals to fit.

Attach a countertop to the base cabinets to create an easy-to-clean work surface for the bartender.

Slide in a refrigerator, keg-o-rator or any appliance you choose.

Install a countertop for the bartender (photo 23). We chose an inexpensive postform countertop with a precut mitered corner. If you've left one end of the bar open for a refrigerator, install a wall cleat to support the countertop above the refrigerator. Plug in and slide in your refrigerator (photo 24) and add a couple of strands of holiday lights or any other décor you fancy.

PARTY TIME

Invite friends and family to gather 'round. As they say in Latin: *Res Ipso Loquitor:* "The Thing Speaks For Itself." Or, as one of your friends might say: "It's beer-thirty."

Trimwork Shelves

Here's a neat trick: Build a shelf that stores, displays, and elevates your favorite collectibles and knickknacks so they're well within sight but safely out of the way. Building these built-up projects is a fun mix of rough and finish carpentry. We show you how to make two variations here: one is a mass of stepped-back MDF strips that has real presence when painted. The other is a more refined three-part assembly similar to cornice molding that is made with pine and pine moldings and can be painted or left natural. The feature both shelves share is a broad, flat surface that performs as a handy display shelf.

If you're building the crown-molding version of this project, one skill you may wish to brush up on ahead of time is cutting and coping crown molding. Working with crown molding requires some mental gymnastics, but once you learn the routine you'll be glad you did.

You can hang your new shelves at just about any height, although they naturally look more comfortable higher up on the wall. At least try and position them at or slightly above eye level. Locating the shelves so the bottom edge rests on top of a door head casing is one good strategy.

In this project we detail two basic interpretations of the shelving strategy. Both are essentially built-up box beams, although one uses crown molding as the featured trim while the other is based on stepped-back strips of stock. There are also different variations on how the shelf can be installed. For example, you can wrap the entire room with it, simply span from one wall to another, or place it on three walls only, etc. Not only is this built-in totally homemade, but the design is flexible to suit different needs and tastes.

And by choosing trim types and styles that already are present in your home you can enhance the built-in look.

The two styles of trimwork shelves seen here are constructed with simple butt joints for ease of building. If you have the woodworking equipment and skills, consider using dado joints instead of butt joints where it makes sense. With dado joints, the wood parts can expand and contract (as they are prone to) without creating separation gaps.

Tools, Materials & Cutting Lists

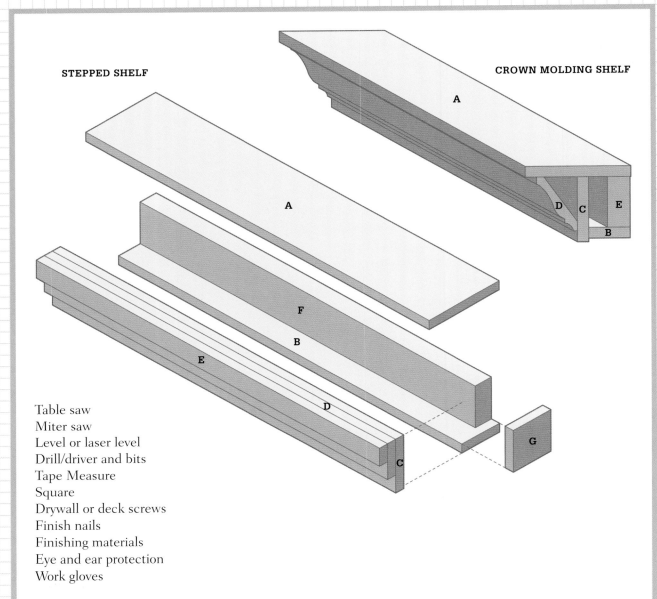

STEPPED SHELF

CROWN MOLDING SHELF

Table saw
Miter saw
Level or laser level
Drill/driver and bits
Tape Measure
Square
Drywall or deck screws
Finish nails
Finishing materials
Eye and ear protection
Work gloves

Crown Version

KEY	DESC.	NO.	SIZE	MATERIAL
A	Shelf top	1	¾ × 7¼" × length	Pine or oak
B	Shelf bottom	1	¾ × 2¾" × length	Pine or oak
C	Shelf front	1	¾ × 4½" × length	Pine or oak
D	Crown	1*	¾ × 4¼" × length	Crown molding
E	Ledger	1	1½ × 3½" × length	2 × 4
F	Filler (opt.)	1 or 2	¾ × 2¾ × 3½"	Pine or oak

* Make mitered return if end of shelf is open

Stepped Version

KEY	DESC.	NO.	SIZE	MATERIAL
A	Shelf top	1	¾ × 6½" × length	MDF
B	Shelf bottom	1	¾ × 3½" × length	MDF
C	Shelf front	1	¾ × 4½" × length	MDF
D	Shelf front	1	¾ × 3" × length	MDF
E	Shelf front	1	¾ × 1½" × length	MDF
F	Ledger	1	1½ × 3½" × length	2 × 4
G	End filler (opt.)	1 or 2	¾ × 3½ × 3½"	MDF

How to Build Trimwork Wall Shelves

MARK LAYOUT LINES AND INSTALL LEDGER

While you can use a spirit level to create level lines at the specified height across the wall, use a laser level instead if you have access to one (photo 1). There are many types of laser levels on the market and each is operated differently from the others, but all will do a fine job of accurately projecting a line around the room quickly so you can mark it on the wall. Some, such as a rotating laser level, allow you to use the light beam cast by the laser level as the reference, so you don't need to make marks on the walls.

If you plan to install your shelving flush with the tops of your door or window casing and you find that they are not level but are close to level (say, within ¼"),
use the highest opening as the control point for your layout and fill the gap that'll be created over the other windows with caulk.

Select a straight 2 × 4 and cut it to length. Use an electronic stud finder to locate wall studs in the installation area, and mark the wall studs just below the level line. Choose high-quality, 3½"-long screws for attaching the ledger: either use hex-head deck screws or square drive multipurpose cabinet screws. Apply panel adhesive to the back of the ledger and position it so the bottom edge falls just above the level line and the ends are in the correct spot. Drive a pair of screws through the ledger and into the wall studs at each stud location (photo 2). These screws don't normally require a pilot hole.

How to Build a Crown Molding Shelf

Use a laser level to create a level reference line for the shelf ledger installation. Mark the location of the bottom edge of the ledger, making sure to allow room for the bottom panel above the door trim and for the full height of the finished project.

Attach the ledger to the wall studs with 3½" screws and panel adhesive. Double-check to make sure the ledger is level after you drive the first screw.

(continued)

3

Attach the bottom strip to the ledger board with panel adhesive and wood screws driven into counterbored pilot holes. Use finish nails if you're leaving the wood natural.

4

Attach the shelf to the top of the ledger, making sure the ends are flush with the ends of the bottom strip.

BUILD A CROWN-MOLDING SHELF

Install molding pieces from the bottom and work your way up. If you're wrapping a room, do "laps" with each layer of trim. Rip wood for the bottom panel to width (2¾" as seen here) and cut it to length. Finish sand all wood parts to 150 grit before installing the parts. On the bottom strip, drill a counterbored pilot hole every 12", located in a line ¾" in from the back edge of the strip. Attach the bottom strip to the ledger with panel adhesive and 2¾" flathead wood screws (photo 3).

Next, crosscut the top panel to length and then attach it to the top of the ledger with panel adhesive and 6d finish nails (photo 4). The ends should be flush with the bottom strip ends, and the top panel should be butted cleanly against the wall.

Measure the distance from the front face of the ledger to the front edge of the bottom strip and cut a few spacers to this length from scrap. Attach the spacers to the face of the ledger at several spots along the length of the ledger (photo 5). These spacers will ensure that the front panel is vertical when it is positioned against the spacers.

Rip and crosscut the front panel to width and length, press it against the spacers so the top edge is flush against the underside of the top panel and all ends are aligned. Install the front panel by driving 6d finish nails through the front panel and into the edge of the bottom strip. You also may nail at the spacer locations if you wish. Also drive nails through the top panel and into the top edge of the front panel (photo 6). Set the nail heads with a nail set.

5

Attach wood spacers to the front face of the ledger to align the front panel when it is pressed against the spacers.

6

Attach the front panel by nailing it to the bottom strip first, and then driving finish nails through the top panel.

7

Finally, nail the crown molding in place at 12" intervals.

Cut the crown molding to length. If your shelf has one or more open ends or occupies more than one wall, make a crown molding return or mitered or coped corners. Fit the molding between the bottom of the top panel and the top of the bottom strip, making sure the flat ends of the molding are flush against the surfaces. Drill pilot holes and drive nails at 12" intervals through the molding and into the top and bottom strips (photo 7).

Cover nail and screw heads with wood putty and then sand and finish the shelf, matching the other room trim if possible.

How to Build a Stepped Shelf

This variation of the trimwork wall shelf idea uses face-glued strips of MDF to create a stepped-down waterfall effect. While you can certainly build the whole project piece-by-piece, you'll be able to do faster, more accurate work if you can preassemble the three stepped-down strips on your worksurface. If you are adding a return on the shelf, as we do here, preassemble the strips for the long wall only, then cut each strip for the mating section to length and butt them up against their counterpart on the first section of shelving.

Lay out and install the ledger or ledgers as shown for the previous crown molding project. Make a simple butt joint in the corner (photo 1). If the return shelf is short, you can strengthen the ledger by driving a couple of screws through the long ledger and into the end of the return ledger.

Attach the top and bottom strips as shown in photos 3 and 4 of the crown shelf molding project. Then rip stock for the three step strips to width (1½", 3" and 4½"). Cut the strips slightly too long and then glue them together on your worksurface, making sure the tops are flush. Drive some 2" wallboard screws through the back face of the tall strip and into the two shorter strips to draw them together (photo 2).

After the glue-up dries, cut the glue-up assembly to final length. Trim both ends to make sure the ends are aligned. Then, attach some spacers to the front face of the ledger and attach the three-strip glue-up by driving screws through the assembly and into the front edge of the bottom panel (photo 3). Also drive screws through the top panel and into the tops of the glued-up strips.

Attach the 2 × 4 ledgers to the wall at your installation lines using 3½" screws and panel adhesive.

On a flat work surface, join the three stepped strips together to create strong joints and simplify assembly of the shelf.

Attach the stepped strips to the top and bottom strips mounted on the ledger.

Cut each stepped strip individually to butt up against the mating strip in the corner and fasten with wallboard screws.

Caulk gaps and fill nail and screw holes before sanding and painting your shelf project.

Attach the top and bottom strip for the return shelf. Make the top long enough to overhang the end of the return, if visible, by 1". Butt the ends of the top and bottom strips up against the top and bottom strips already mounted on the wall. Then, measure for each of the three stepped strips, measuring from the mating edge of its counterpart on the wall to the end of the return (each successive strip will be approximately 1½" longer working from top to bottom). Install the

tall strip first, and then attach the shorter ones in succession using glue and screws (photo 4).

If the return has an exposed end, measure the opening between the ledger and the shelf front and cut a filler piece to fit (in this project, the piece was 3½" wide and 3½" tall. Glue and nail the filler into the opening. Then cover nail and screw heads with wood filler, caulk any gaps (photo 5), and then sand, prime and paint the project.

Conversions

Metric Conversions

TO CONVERT:	TO:	MULTIPLY BY:
Inches	Millimeters	25.4
Inches	Centimeters	2.54
Feet	Meters	0.305
Yards	Meters	0.914
Square inches	Square centimeters	6.45
Square feet	Square meters	0.093
Square yards	Square meters	0.836
Ounces	Milliliters	30.0
Pints (U.S.)	Liters	0.473 (Imp. 0.568)
Quarts (U.S.)	Liters	0.946 (Imp. 1.136)
Gallons (U.S.)	Liters	3.785 (Imp. 4.546)
Ounces	Grams	28.4
Pounds	Kilograms	0.454

TO CONVERT:	TO:	MULTIPLY BY:
Millimeters	Inches	0.039
Centimeters	Inches	0.394
Meters	Feet	3.28
Meters	Yards	1.09
Square centimeters	Square inches	0.155
Square meters	Square feet	10.8
Square meters	Square yards	1.2
Milliliters	Ounces	.033
Liters	Pints (U.S.)	2.114 (Imp. 1.76)
Liters	Quarts (U.S.)	1.057 (Imp. 0.88)
Liters	Gallons (U.S.)	0.264 (Imp. 0.22)
Grams	Ounces	0.035
Kilograms	Pounds	2.2

Converting Temperatures

Convert degrees Fahrenheit (F) to degrees Celsius (C) by following this simple formula: Subtract 32 from the Fahrenheit temperature reading. Then, multiply that number by $5/9$. For example, 77°F - 32 = 45. 45 × $5/9$ = 25°C.

To convert degrees Celsius to degrees Fahrenheit, multiply the Celsius temperature reading by $9/5$. Then, add 32. For example, 25°C × $9/5$ = 45. 45 + 32 = 77°F.

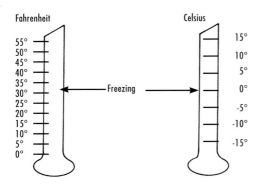

Metric Plywood Panels

Metric plywood panels are commonly available in two sizes: 1,200 mm × 2,400 mm and 1,220 mm × 2,400 mm, which is roughly equivalent to a 4 × 8-ft. sheet. Standard and Select sheathing panels come in standard thicknesses, while Sanded grade panels are available in special thicknesses.

STANDARD SHEATHING GRADE		SANDED GRADE	
7.5 mm	(5/16 in.)	6 mm	(4/17 in.)
9.5 mm	(3/8 in.)	8 mm	(5/16 in.)
12.5 mm	(1/2 in.)	11 mm	(7/16 in.)
15.5 mm	(5/8 in.)	14 mm	(9/16 in.)
18.5 mm	(3/4 in.)	17 mm	(2/3 in.)
20.5 mm	(13/16 in.)	19 mm	(3/4 in.)
22.5 mm	(7/8 in.)	21 mm	(13/16 in.)
25.5 mm	(1 in.)	24 mm	(15/16 in.)

Lumber Dimensions

NOMINAL - U.S.	ACTUAL - U.S. (in inches)	METRIC
1 × 2	3/4 × 1½	19 × 38 mm
1 × 3	3/4 × 2½	19 × 64 mm
1 × 4	3/4 × 3½	19 × 89 mm
1 × 5	3/4 × 4½	19 × 114 mm
1 × 6	3/4 × 5½	19 × 140 mm
1 × 7	3/4 × 6¼	19 × 159 mm
1 × 8	3/4 × 7¼	19 × 184 mm
1 × 10	3/4 × 9¼	19 × 235 mm
1 × 12	3/4 × 11¼	19 × 286 mm
1¼ × 4	1 × 3½	25 × 89 mm
1¼ × 6	1 × 5½	25 × 140 mm
1¼ × 8	1 × 7¼	25 × 184 mm
1¼ × 10	1 × 9¼	25 × 235 mm
1¼ × 12	1 × 11¼	25 × 286 mm
1½ × 4	1¼ × 3½	32 × 89 mm
1½ × 6	1¼ × 5½	32 × 140 mm
1½ × 8	1¼ × 7¼	32 × 184 mm
1½ × 10	1¼ × 9¼	32 × 235 mm
1½ × 12	1¼ × 11¼	32 × 286 mm
2 × 4	1½ × 3½	38 × 89 mm
2 × 6	1½ × 5½	38 × 140 mm
2 × 8	1½ × 7¼	38 × 184 mm
2 × 10	1½ × 9¼	38 × 235 mm
2 × 12	1½ × 11¼	38 × 286 mm
3 × 6	2½ × 5½	64 × 140 mm
4 × 4	3½ × 3½	89 × 89 mm
4 × 6	3½ × 5½	89 × 140 mm

Liquid Measurement Equivalents

1 Pint	= 16 Fluid Ounces	= 2 Cups
1 Quart	= 32 Fluid Ounces	= 2 Pints
1 Gallon	= 128 Fluid Ounces	= 4 Quarts

Drill Bit Guide

Twist Bit	Self-piloting	Spade Bit	Adjustable Counterbore	Hole Saw
		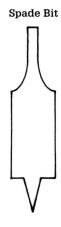	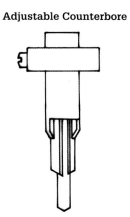	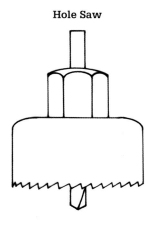

Counterbore, Shank & Pilot Hole Diameters

Screw Size	Counterbore Diameter for Screw Head	Clearance Hole for Screw Shank	Pilot Hole Diameter	
			Hard Wood	Soft Wood
#1	.146 9/64	5/64	3/64	1/32
#2	1/4	3/32	3/64	1/32
#3	1/4	7/64	1/16	3/64
#4	1/4	1/8	1/16	3/64
#5	1/4	9/64	5/64	1/16
#6	5/16	5/32	3/32	5/64
#7	5/16	5/32	3/32	5/64
#8	3/8	11/64	1/8	3/32
#9	3/8	11/64	1/8	3/32
#10	3/8	3/16	1/8	7/64
#11	1/2	3/16	5/32	9/64
#12	1/2	7/32	9/64	1/8

Abrasive Paper Grits - (Aluminum Oxide)

Very Coarse	Coarse	Medium	Fine	Very Fine
12 - 36	40 - 60	80 - 120	150 - 180	220 - 600

Resources

American Institute of Architects
800-242-3837
www.aia.org

American Society of Interior Designers
20002-546-3480
www.asid.org

Black & Decker
Portable power tools & more
800-544-6986
www.blackanddecker.com

Construction Materials Recycling Association
630-548-4510
www.cdrecycling.org

Energy & Environmental Building Association
952-881-1098
www.eeba.com

National Kitchen & Bath Association (NKBA)
800-843-6522
www.nkba.org

Red Wing Shoes Co.
Work shoes and boots shown throughout book
800-733-9464
www.redwingshoes.com

Rockler Woodworking and Hardware
Woodworking aids and accessories
Pages 51, 66 and 178
800-279-4441
www.rockler.com

Credits

Photolibrary: Karyn Millet, p. 8 top; **Julien McRoberts,** p. 9 top right; **Douglas Gibb,** p. 10 top; **Huntley Hedworth,** p. 11 top right; **Kate Gadsby,** p. 12 top right; **Dan Duchars,** p. 13 top; **Ewa Stock,** p. 13 bottom; **Peter Margonelli,** p. 15 top left; **Chris Gascoigne,** p. 16 top right; **Simon McBride,** p. 17 bottom left; **Auda & Coudayre,** p. 17 bottom right.

Dreamstime, p. 9 top left; p. 15 bottom.

Shutterstock, p. 10 bottom left; p. 11 bottom.

Johnny Bouchier/Getty Images, p. 11 top left.

Paul Ryan-Goff/Red Cover/Alamy, p. 12 top left.

Index